Peacebuilding in Practice

Peacebuilding in Practice

Local Experience in Two Bosnian Towns

Adam Moore

Cornell University Press
Ithaca and London

First published 2013 by Cornell University Press

Printed in the United States of America

Library of Congress Cataloging-in-Publication Data

Moore, Adam, 1976– author.
    Peacebuilding in practice : local experience in two Bosnian towns / Adam Moore.
        pages cm
    Includes bibliographical references and index.
    ISBN 978-0-8014-5199-7 (cloth : alk. paper)
    1. Peace-building—Bosnia and Hercegovina—Brčko. 2. Peace-building—Bosnia and Hercegovina—Mostar. 3. International agencies—Bosnia and Hercegovina—Brčko. 4. International agencies—Bosnia and Hercegovina—Mostar. 5. Brčko (Bosnia and Hercegovina)—Ethnic relations. 6. Mostar (Bosnia and Hercegovina)—Ethnic relations. I. Title.
    DR1785.B7M66   2013
    949.74203—dc23   2013008334

Cornell University Press strives to use environmentally responsible suppliers and materials to the fullest extent possible in the publishing of its books. Such materials include vegetable-based, low-VOC inks and acid-free papers that are recycled, totally chlorine-free, or partly composed of nonwood fibers. For further information, visit our website at www.cornellpress.cornell.edu.

Cloth printing   10 9 8 7 6 5 4 3 2 1

Contents

Maps

ACKNOWLEDGMENTS

One accumulates many debts over nearly a decade of research. I am particularly grateful for the generous support of people I met during fieldwork in Bosnia. Asim Mujkić at the University of Sarajevo has been a great mentor and friend throughout the project. This book would not have been possible without the invaluable assistance over the years of Djanan Bakamović, Ljiljana Četić, Dragan Dunjić and Goran Karanović. There is insufficient space to mention all the friends who made my time in Mostar and Brčko a wonderful experience, but a special mention is necessary for Čato and Ado at the Iron Horse in Brčko.

Several local and international officials and academics in Bosnia were especially gracious with their time, hospitality, and information (including access to archival materials). I would like to thank in particular Jasmin Adilović, Peter Appleby, Mark Bowen, Amela Bozić, Edin Čelebić, Robert "Bill" Farrand, Susan Johnson, Ivan Krndelj, Osman Osmanović, Roberts Owen, Matthew Parish, Nikola Ristić, Adin Sadić, and Gerhard Sontheim.

Bill, Susan, Roberts, and Matthew also provided detailed comments on an earlier version of chapter 7, as did Gerhard on chapters 4 and 6.

This project has also benefited greatly from conversations with friends, colleagues, and mentors at various stages in the process, including Fedja Burić, Katie Hampton, Peter Locke, Paul Nadasdy, and Scott Straus. Special thanks goes to Bob Kaiser, my graduate advisor at the University of Wisconsin, Madison, who, over the years, has taught me more than I can recount here. Séverine Autesserre provided very helpful feedback on chapters 6, 7, and the conclusion, as did Lieba Faier with the introductory and concluding chapters. Gail Kligman, John Agnew, and Reece Jones read a full draft of the manuscript. I would like to thank them and the two anonymous reviewers for their insightful comments. My editor, Roger Haydon, has been a joy to work with, as have all the other staff at Cornell University Press. Matt Zebrowski, our cartographer here at UCLA, did yeoman's work in transforming my rudimentary maps into finished versions that are much more informative and aesthetically pleasing.

Funding for this research was provided by the Council for European Studies; International Research and Exchanges Board (IREX); the United States Institute of Peace; the University of Wisconsin, Madison, Geography Department; and both the International Institute and Geography Department at UCLA. I am grateful for the generous financial support offered by all of these institutions.

Finally, I would like to recognize my parents, my wife, Lori, and my daughter, Danica: without your love and support none of this would have been possible. This book is dedicated to Danica, *moja mala princeza*.

Abbreviations

ARBiH	Army of the Republic of Bosnia and Herzegovina
BCS	Bosnian/Croatian/Serbian
BiH	Bosnia and Herzegovina
BLRC	Brčko Law Review Commission
CoM	Council of Ministers
EU	European Union
DMT	District Management Team
DPA	Dayton Peace Agreement
EUAM	European Union Administration of Mostar
EUFOR	European Union Force
EUPM	European Union Police Mission
HDZ	Croatian Democratic Union
HOS	Croatian Defense Forces
HSP	Croatian Party of Rights
HSS	Croatian Peasant Party
HVIDRa	Association of Croatian Military Invalids of the Homeland War

HVO	Croatian Defense Council
ICTY	International Criminal Tribunal for the former Yugoslavia
IDP	Internally Displaced Person
IEBL	Inter-Entity Boundary Line
IETA	Inter-Entity Transfer Agreement
IPTF	International Police Task Force
ITA	Indirect Taxation Authority
JNA	Yugoslav People's Army
KM	Convertible Mark
MIU	Mostar Implementation Unit
MND-S	Multi-National Division South
NATO	North Atlantic Treaty Organization
NDH	Independent State of Croatia
NHI	New Croatian Initiative
OSCE	Organization for Security and Co-operation in Europe
OHR	Office of the High Representative
PDHR	Principal Deputy High Representative
PIC	Peace Implementation Council
RS	Republika Srpska
SBiH	Party for Bosnia and Herzegovina
SDA	Party of Democratic Action
SDP	Social Democratic Party of Bosnia and Herzegovina
SDS	Serbian Democratic Party
SFOR	Stabilization Force
SK-SDP	League of Communists-Social Democratic Party
SNSD	Alliance of Independent Social Democrats
TO	Territorial Defense
UN	United Nations
UNCITRAL	United Nations Commission on International Trade Law
UNDP	United Nations Development Programme
UNHCR	United Nations High Commissioner for Refugees
UNMIBH	United Nations Mission in Bosnia and Herzegovina
UNPROFOR	United Nations Protection Force
USAID	United States Agency for International Development
VRS	Bosnian Serb Army
WEU	Western European Union
ZoS	Zone of Separation

Peacebuilding in Practice

INTRODUCTION

My first visit to Brčko came as a shock. The southern parts of the town made
it look as if the world had come to an end. Snow covered the ruins, which
stretched as far as the eye could see. But what made the greatest impression
was not what could be seen, but what the ear could not hear. There was
absolute silence. Life always involves sounds—a dog, a child, traffic on a
distant road. But here there was nothing, just silence and ruins.
There was nothing left at all.

CARL BILDT, BOSNIA'S FIRST HIGH REPRESENTATIVE

In November 2007 I was conducting fieldwork in the city of Mostar in
the Herzegovina region of southeastern Bosnia when the town was rocked
by two days of violent clashes between Croat and Bosniak youth.[1] It began
on a Saturday night when up to two hundred youths brawled along the
former wartime frontline in the center of the city, the Bulevar Narodne
Revolucije (Boulevard of the National Revolution).[2] Three people were
hospitalized—one with a severe knife wound to the neck—and a dozen
arrested.

The following day was the Derby, the annual game between Zrinjski
and Velež, the Croat- and Bosniak-supported football teams in the city,
respectively. The match was held in a stadium in West Mostar, the Croat-
dominated side of the city. At previous Derby matches fights between Zrin-
ski and Velež fans had broken out during and after the game, so several
hundred police were already scheduled to be on duty at the stadium and in
the streets of Mostar. As a further precaution Velež supporters were to be
bussed to and from the stadium. I came across these preparations the next

morning in the city's Old Town in East Mostar while walking to a café to meet friends for coffee. Dozens of police wearing riot gear were searching the belongings of Velež supporters as they boarded a line of buses. Two police vans idled in front and behind, ready to escort the procession to the stadium a mere kilometer away. Meanwhile hundreds of police wielding shields and batons lined the procession route in West Mostar.

Despite these precautions another incident erupted as dozens of youths emerged from cafes along the route and pelted the passing convoy with rocks and bottles while shouting "Zrinjski!" and "This is Croatia!" When riot police intervened with tear gas and armored vehicles to prevent them from physically reaching the buses filled with Velež supporters, the rioters turned their fury toward the authorities, erecting impromptu blockades in the streets and stoning police vehicles and officers from a distance. Scattered confrontations between rioters and police in the streets continued into the evening as shops were trashed, several more people hospitalized, and dozens arrested.

In the days and weeks following this violence, tension in Mostar was palpable. Heightened ethnic tensions were accompanied by a "thickening of place." That is, the violence reinforced not only a categorical, but also a spatial "boundary activation," whereby the wartime frontline (the boulevard) and respective social spaces (East and West Mostar) underwent a renewed process of ethnic polarization.[3] In the immediate aftermath of the clashes the act of crossing to the "other side" to shop or meet friends, or living on the "wrong" side of town, once again became potentially fraught with dangerous consequences and weighed heavily on many residents' minds.[4]

This was not the only instance of violent conflict in the city in recent years. Following a World Cup game between Brazil and Croatia the previous summer hundreds of Bosniak and Croat youth clashed along the boulevard, leading to the hospitalization of twenty people, including one with gunshot wounds.[5] Since 2007 several similar incidents have also occurred, most, but not all, connected to football matches either in the city, or international competitions such as the 2012 Euro Cup.[6] Nor were these clashes the only form of violence in Mostar during my fieldwork. For example, in October 2006 unknown assailants fired a rocket at a newly rebuilt mosque in West Mostar just before worshipers were set to arrive for a predawn Ramadan meal.[7] Indeed, Mostar is often cited as emblematic of the failure of international peacebuilding efforts to overcome deep divisions that continue to stymie the postwar peace process in Bosnia.

However it is not the case that all of Bosnia has been plagued by such troubles. Perhaps the most marked contrast to Mostar is the Brčko District in the northeast corner of the country. Like Mostar, Brčko is one of the few remaining ethnically heterogeneous municipalities in Bosnia. Following the war, international and local observers identified both towns as trouble spots with high levels of ethnic tension and potential

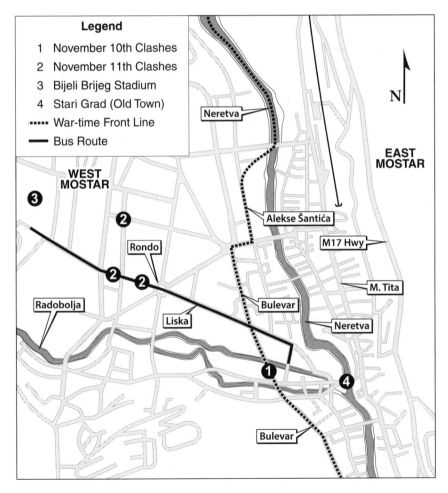

Figure 1. 2007 violence in Mostar

for renewed conflict. Consequently both places have been singled out for intensive and lengthy international peacebuilding intervention in the postwar period. Despite these similarities the trajectories of Brčko and Mostar over the past seventeen years could not be more different. While Mostar remains mired in distrust and division, with a barely functioning municipal government, Brčko has become something of a model of what postwar Bosnia could have been. Thousands of Bosniak and Croat families driven from their homes during the war have returned to downtown Brčko and its outlying suburbs, and thousands of ethnic Serbs driven out of Croatia, and Bosniak and Croat-controlled areas in Bosnia, during the wars in the 1900s have also been successfully resettled in the Brčko area. Moreover, the District's multiethnic institutions operate relatively well compared to other municipalities in Bosnia and are broadly supported by residents of all backgrounds. Brčko also boasts the only integrated school system in the country, which has operated relatively smoothly since its establishment in 2001.

The basic question that this book seeks to answer is: *What accounts for the striking divergence in the peacebuilding process in these two Bosnian towns since the end of the war?*

Argument in Brief

Postwar peacebuilding is a complex phenomenon, the dynamics of which are irreducible to simple causal explanations. I argue that a conjunction of four factors accounts for the contrasting peacebuilding outcomes in Mostar and Brčko: the design of local political institutions, local and regional legacies from the war, sequencing of political and economic reforms, and the practice and organization of international peacebuilding efforts in the two towns.

First, the integrative political framework established in Brčko has been more effective in mitigating conflict than the ethno-territorial consociational institutions adopted in Mostar. Second, for various reasons the legitimacy of each of the three main nationalist parties in Bosnia was weakened in the eyes of a significant portion of the population in Brčko due to specific wartime events and the contradictory aims of local elites and their parties' national leadership in the immediate postwar period. Mostar, in contrast, became a bastion of the Croat nationalist party HDZ and its mafia allies, both of which were strongly supported by the Croatian government during and after the war. Consequently, Croat nationalists were in a better position to play a spoiler role against early peacebuilding efforts in Mostar than were opponents of reform in Brčko. Third, decisions by international officials to delay elections and privatization in Brčko until after the District's new institutions took root benefited more moderate local elites and provided a sounder basis for inclusive economic development. Conversely, in Mostar early elections and the rapid privatization of public firms and property further empowered wartime nationalist leaders and solidified the economic and social division of the city along ethnic lines. Fourth, the peace process has been profoundly influenced by peacebuilding practices and institutions. In particular, the unique Office of the High Representative (OHR) supervisory regime established in Brčko created a relatively high degree of political independence, cohesion of international peacebuilding efforts, and effective international-local cooperation. In contrast, international officials operating in Mostar struggled to coordinate policy across different organizations, were constantly undercut by distant superiors in Sarajevo and Brussels, and failed to develop productive working relations with local elites.

Finally, this analysis rejects the argument that progress in Brčko was a product of the degree of international resources—both aid and personnel—expended in the area. This capacity explanation is often cited by international officials in Bosnia and was also forwarded by Michael Doyle and Nicholas Sambanis in their influential analysis of international peacekeeping missions, which includes a short analysis of the Brčko District.[8] However a brief comparison of Brčko and Mostar is sufficient to illustrate the weakness of this argument. To begin, Brčko has not received a disproportionate amount of aid relative other areas in Bosnia. At the end of his mandate in 2006 former High Representative Paddy Ashdown estimated that Bosnia had received $16 billion in aid since the end of the war. He calculated Brčko's share to be only $70 million while Mostar had received an estimated $300–$400 million.[9] Indeed, by 1996 the European Union had already invested 144 million European Currency Units

(ECU, roughly $110 million at 1996 exchange rates) on infrastructure and housing reconstruction projects in Mostar—equivalent to 2,400 ECU per person—which is more than the entire amount of postwar aid Brčko has received.[10]

Doyle and Sambanis also highlighted the significance of a robust military and civilian presence—Stabilization Force (SFOR) military peace-keepers, UN International Police Task Force (IPTF) monitors, and expert consultants in administrative reforms—in Brčko. Again, a comparison with Mostar casts doubt on this being a decisive factor. Throughout the entirety of SFOR's mission in Bosnia a substantially greater number of military peacekeepers were stationed in Mostar than Brčko, due to the former's site as the headquarters of SFOR's Multi-National Division South (MND-S). International civilian-led peacebuilding in Mostar has also been similar in intensity to that in Brčko—and for a much greater period of time. At the height of operations from 1994 to 1996 the EU-run administrative and police missions in Mostar (the European Union Administration of Mostar [EUAM] and the Western European Union police task force [WEU], respectively) were staffed with more than 70 civilian experts, over 180 European police officers and roughly 300 local staff.[11] A comparable civilian peacebuilding presence was not established in Brčko until late 1997. In short, international capacity may be a necessary condition of successful peacebuilding, but it is far from sufficient.[12]

There are two points that require further clarification here. First, none of the four factors I identify are sufficient on their own to account for the outcomes in Brčko and Mostar. Nor can they be properly understood if treated simply as variables, the causal effects of which may be parsed and analyzed independently. Rather their impacts are inter-related. In other words, it is the spatially and temporally contingent configuration of these factors that explains the divergence in the peace-building process in these two cities since the end of the war. For example, while I argue that the integrative institutional reforms underpinning the Brčko District have proven to be superior to the ethno-territorial consociational framework implemented in Mostar and the rest of Bosnia, their successful implementation was also dependent on the development of strong international-local relations and the relatively weak standing of nationalist actors in the Brčko area following the war. Likewise, it is a mistake to view Croat nationalists' ability to spoil peacebuilding reforms in Mostar as a simple outgrowth of their influence at the end of the war. Rather, their ability to maintain political power was tied to postwar developments such as rapid political and economic liberalization, the introduction of consociational political institutions, and the lack of independent authority afforded international officials working in the city.

The explanation put forward here, then, is: (1) contextual in that it treats time and space as "thick," or "drenched with causes that inhere in sequence, accumulation, contingency, and proximity,"[13] and (2) conjunctural in that it places emphasis on a particular combination of causes and events.[14] In the sociologist Andrew Abbott's words, "things happen because of constellations of factors, not because of a few fundamental effects acting independently."[15] To be clear, I am not claiming that this constellation of factors represents the only configuration that explains peacebuilding outcomes elsewhere in Bosnia or beyond. Ultimately each case is shaped by its own specific conditions and processes. This having been said, as I argue in the conclusion, more general insights can be gleaned from a grounded analysis of localized peacebuilding—a key concept that I outline in greater detail in the next section of this chapter—in these two cities, especially regarding international-local relations and the ways in which they are shaped by peacebuilding practices and institutions.

The second point concerns the evaluation of peacebuilding interventions, specifically, what constitutes success, failure, or significant progress? For instance, is the establishment of a "negative" peace—that is, the absence of violence—enough, or should success be claimed only when progress is made toward "positive" peace outcomes that deal with the "root causes" of conflict?[16] More minimalist definitions of success, which broadly correspond with the former view, include the fulfillment of peacekeeping mandates or implementation of peace agreements,[17] a self-enforcing cease-fire after peacekeepers have left,[18] the length of time without recurrence of war,[19] or the absence of large-scale violence and progress toward basic democratic governance;[20] more ambitious standards like the creation of legitimate, effective, and sustainable state institutions (statebuilding);[21] reconciliation;[22] justice;[23] or the attainment of conditions compatible with "human security"[24] lean toward the latter. Not only is there no agreed-upon standard concerning peacebuilding success and failure, local and international perceptions often differ greatly on whether interventions have been successful or not.[25]

As one can see these are complex issues, and they have been extensively debated in recent years.[26] This is not the place to go into detail concerning the nuances of these debates. However it is necessary to clarify the approach adopted in this book. To begin, I do not think it is helpful to assess peacebuilding outcomes in Brčko and Mostar according to a dichotomous categorization of success and failure. As Séverine Autessere observes, "The relationship between war and peace is that of a continuum, not a dichotomy."[27] Indeed in many cases societies continue to be plagued by intermittent and small-scale violence, social polarization, and ineffective governance following civil war, an ambiguous situation aptly characterized by Roger MacGinty as "no war, no peace."[28] Bosnia is no different in this regard. More analytically useful, then, is to focus on the degree of progress toward peacebuilding goals.

I focus on three critical areas when assessing progress in Brčko and Mostar. The first is the level of ethnically charged conflict in the two cities. As described above, such conflict—in particular violent clashes among youth along the former wartime frontline—continues to plague Mostar on a periodic basis. Brčko, in contrast, has experienced no significant violence in recent years.[29] Consequently, people living there have a greater sense of security. As one District Assembly councilor observed during a recent conversation: "The way I see the Brčko District at the moment is that it seems to be the most acceptable method to protect all three ethnicities. . . . Any representative of any ethnicity can feel safe and secure living under this system. I do not think that I, my family, or anyone else has to fear for their safety and that is the biggest thing."[30]

The second area is the quality and perceived legitimacy of local institutions. Here the contrast is perhaps most stark as the District's multiethnic institutions—especially the police, judicial system, and schools—function at a relatively high level compared to other municipalities in the country. They are also broadly supported by residents of all three ethnic communities. In contrast, Mostar's institutional framework is plagued by political obstructionism and dysfunctionality; the government, police, and courts are not trusted by residents; and informal administrative parallelism is rampant, despite the formal political unification of the city in 2004.

The third area of focus is the level of reintegration in the two cities. This includes returns of people who were ethnically cleansed from their homes—as well as the incorporation of those originally from other areas of the country or region who decided to stay—and the more difficult to measure degree of social integration. Reintegration and the unmaking of the ethno-territorial order of space created by ethnic cleansing during the war has been a central goal of peacebuilding intervention in Bosnia, a priority that is reflected in Annex 7 of the Dayton Peace Agreement (DPA), which guarantees people the right of return.[31] For years returns in Mostar lagged behind the rest of the country. Indeed, as I discuss in chapter 4, it was one of the few municipalities in the country in which the violent expulsion of families from their homes continued into the postwar period. While some progress was made in subsequent years, especially among Bosniaks who have reclaimed apartments in West Mostar, return rates remained modest, with fewer than fifteen thousand returns by the middle of 2004 according to UNHCR estimates (by which time the return process had slowed considerably throughout the country and the bulk of returns had taken place).[32] Relatively few Bosnian Serbs, in particular, have returned to the city.

Moreover, at the social level Mostar remains a profoundly divided city, with separate concert theaters, schools, universities, football teams, bus companies, restaurants, and coffee shops. Even the famous Stari Most (Old Bridge), the rebuilding of which was hailed as a seminal moment in the city's reunification by international officials in 2004, is a point of contention.[33] Few Croats from Mostar attend or participate in the annual bridge jumping contest, and West Mostar is littered with graffiti that portrays the bridge with superimposed Ustaše symbols from the fascist Independent State of Croatia (NDH) in WWII—in particular the letter "U" with a cross in the middle—or derisive comments such as *jebo vas novi stari most* ("fuck your new old bridge"). Mostar, in sum, resembles two separate cities living uneasily side by side. As a group of university students in Mostar put it to me a few weeks after the violent events recounted above: "The wall is invisible, but yet sensible. . . . We say the 'other side.' Well, what is the other side? If there is another side you have to cross through or over something to get there. . . . The wall is there, I think it will be there forever."

Here again the progress achieved in Brčko to date has been greater. To begin, the returns process been more successful: out of forty thousand people who were driven from their homes in the Brčko area during the war, approximately 65 percent (about twenty-six thousand) returned.[34] Moreover, more than twenty thousand displaced Serbs who elected to remain in the District have also been accommodated.[35] This is a frequently overlooked and hard-fought accomplishment, especially the social integration of this previously marginalized population, where progress has only occurred in recent years.[36] Social integration in general is also further along in Brčko than Mostar. The District boasts the only integrated school system in the county, and shared social spaces—such as the various cafes and bars along the Brka River and Trg Mladih (Youths' Square), the central square downtown that has hosted numerous well-attended concerts and book fairs—are beginning to re-emerge.

One should avoid painting an overly rosy picture on this front, however. The majority of restaurants and coffee shops remain rather segregated, as are the rural villages in the District.[37] And most residents choose to socialize primarily within their own communities. Additionally the majority of residents with whom I have talked in Brčko over the years characterize their daily interactions with people from other ethnic backgrounds as peaceful but superficial. More than once this was explained to me through the metaphor of public "masks" that are adopted to avoid contentious topics or situations. There is, in short, still a long way to go in terms of trust, reconciliation, and what is referred to in Bosnia as *komšiluk* (neighborliness). That said, I think it is not helpful to assess peacebuilding in Brčko according to positive peace standards of interethnic relations that often fail to obtain even in countries that have not recently experienced mass violence.[38] I would wager, for example, that many bars, churches, and neighborhoods in the District are no more socially or residentially segregated than those in Los Angeles, the city where I now live.[39] Moreover, interethnic conflict and a lack trust in the equity of public institutions are also well-documented features of the greater Los Angeles area.[40] Perhaps, then, rather than evaluating postwar peacebuilding efforts in Brčko—and Bosnia—according to standards such as the fulsome embrace of cultural pluralism following a war that occurred only a generation ago, a more practical goal is the peaceful resumption of coexistence.

A final point to consider when evaluating the relative success of peacebuilding efforts in Brčko is sustainability. Here the picture is more equivocal. Corruption remains high and could pose a threat to the fiscal sustainability of the District, especially given the public services such as health care and education that are self-financed, a situation that is unique among municipalities in the country. More ominously, politicians in Bosnia's two substate entities—the Republika Srpska (RS) and the Bosniak-Croat majority Federation—have never fully reconciled themselves to the continued political independence of the District. This is especially the case with the RS. As I detail in chapter 7, until recently the OHR Brčko office played the role of patron protecting the District's interests against the entities. Now that active supervision has ended it remains to be seen whether political independence can be sustained, and what effects the specter of entity interference and instability in the rest of the country may have on political and social relations in Brčko.

Research Design and Methods

Studies of postwar peacebuilding generally follow either a cross-country comparative or single-country case study approach. The former tend to be medium-n qualitative comparisons, large-n quantitative studies, or some combination of the two, which draw primarily on secondary source material; the latter in-depth case studies, with the relevant unit of analysis defined as either the country as a whole or a specific region or place within a country. This project is unique in providing an in-depth, subnational, comparative analysis of two distinct peacebuilding missions in Bosnia since the end of the war.

The subnational comparative method I have pursued has several advantages over cross-national analyses of peacebuilding, two of which are useful to highlight here.[41] First, in contrast to cross-country studies, which tend to focus on national level actors and data, this research is grounded in detailed fieldwork and primary source material that offers a nuanced understanding of the ways in which the intersection of local, national, and regional factors shapes peacebuilding processes. Second, this book is also distinct from most within-country analyses in that it is explicitly structured as a paired analysis of two similar, medium-size cities in a single country with clear variation in the degree of peacebuilding progress—which allows us to better understand the spatially and temporally uneven processes of peacebuilding within states following war.[42]

To date these localized dynamics of postwar peacebuilding remain inadequately addressed and poorly understood. I use the term *localized*— rather than *local*—advisedly. One reason for this is that it avoids reifying the local level as the only relevant scale of analysis.[43] Indeed, as this research makes clear, the peace process in Mostar and Brčko has also been profoundly shaped by national, regional, and international political dynamics. A related point is that like intrastate wars, international peacebuilding intervention inevitably destabilizes preexisting social and political networks, thus heightening the influence that fluid relationships between and among domestic and international actors have on peace and conflict. Peacebuilding interventions, in turn, are always mediated by evolving social and political conditions in the locations where they take place, and the responses of communities that inhabit these places.[44] They become, in effect, more or less localized. This applies to both missions themselves, and those who are charged with implementing them, who adapt mandates and activities depending on local conditions more commonly than is assumed by both critics and proponents of peacebuilding intervention.[45] The concept of localization, then, serves both as an orienting apparatus, directing attention toward the need for disaggregated and geographically sensitive analyses of peacebuilding processes, as well as a means of describing how these processes unfold as projects are reworked, resisted, or unevenly implemented on the ground due to a variety of actors and place-specific conditions. The point is not simply that localization matters, but to better understand how, when, and why this is the case.

There are three further advantages to conducting a comparative analysis in Bosnia in general and Mostar and Brčko in particular. To begin, Bosnia is one of the longest running and most complex peacebuilding projects undertaken to date, consequently there is a greater diversity and quantity of data from international organizations to draw on than is typical in postwar contexts. Second, Bosnia's domestic media—especially its newspapers—were especially vibrant prior to and during the war and remain so today, hence there is also a wealth of accessible domestic media accounts, which provide a greater level of contextual detail than is usual for countries that have experienced violent conflict. Finally, Mostar and Brčko are excellent sites for comparative inquiry: both are similar in population (roughly 111,000 in Mostar and 100,000 in the Brčko District);[46]

both were ethnically heterogeneous towns before the war and remain so today; both experienced extensive ethnic violence during the conflict; both were widely identified—by international and local observers—as potential postwar flashpoints with high levels of ethnic tension and political conflict; and distinctive peacebuilding missions were established in both towns due to their contested status in Bosnia. This last point is especially important as it offers unique opportunities for a detailed study of the impact that specific peacebuilding practices and institutions have on international-local relations and peace outcomes.[47]

Another distinctive aspect of this study is the use of multiple methods in generating data for analysis. This research is based on eighteen months of fieldwork spanning eight years (2004–12) during which time I utilized three methodological approaches: formal interviews, archival research, and ethnography. Though the three methods in themselves present an incomplete picture, this triangulation strategy has enabled me to construct a comprehensive account of the dynamics of peacebuilding in Mostar and Brčko since the end of the war.

First, I conducted more than 120 unstructured interviews. The majority of these interviews were with one of two social categories. The first consisted of politicians and civil servants (e.g., teachers, police officers, judges, and administrative officials) who are either currently active in politics or governance in Brčko or Mostar, or who played important roles in the prewar, wartime, or immediate postwar period. The second group was international officials who have worked in Brčko, Mostar, or organizational headquarters in Sarajevo since the end of the war, primarily— but not exclusively—those working for OHR and the Organization for Security and Co-operation in Europe (OSCE). In addition to meeting with local and international officials I also conducted several interviews with residents and NGOs in the two cities.[48] I used an interpreter while formally interviewing local officials and residents, for two reasons: first, although my BCS (Bosnian/Croatian/Serbian) proficiency was enough for everyday interactions, I did not feel it was sufficient for formal interviews. Second, utilizing an assistant allowed for the comparison of notes and impressions following the interviews, which proved especially useful for identifying narrative gaps, silences and evasions, and picking up on subtle nonverbal and culturally specific signals. As Lee Ann Fujii notes, attention to "metadata" such as this is crucial for developing a fuller understanding of political and social conditions in communities that have experienced large-scale violence.[49]

Second, as a supplement to the interviews, I conducted extensive primary source archival research. The bulk of this took place at the archives of OHR Brčko, where I spent more than two months reviewing thousands of pages of unpublished documents. These archives, which had not previously been accessible to scholars, provide a wealth of information about the processes through which peacebuilding policies have been negotiated and implemented by local and international officials in Brčko, as well as the contentious relationship between internationals working in Brčko and the rest of Bosnia. Beyond the OHR Brčko archives I also consulted materials provided by the OSCE and OHR offices in Mostar, the MediaCentar's comprehensive wartime and postwar Bosnian media archive in Sarajevo, the International Criminal Tribunal for the former Yugoslavia's (ICTY) online archives of war crime trials, and both the East and West Mostar municipal archives. Due to the extensive use of primary source material this book utilizes a hybrid approach to citation practices. All primary sources—whether publically available or not—are cited in full in the endnotes. Secondary sources, in contrast, are indicated according to an author-date format with full citations found in the reference section at the end of the book.

Finally, in addition to interviews and archival research this project is also grounded in ethnographic methods. Indeed, the majority of my time in Brčko and Mostar consisted of informal conversations with, and observations of, people going about their "daily paths and projects."[50] This included both observation of the interactions of residents and local and international officials in the two cities in a variety of social contexts, and informal discussions with them about their experience and interpretation of postwar politics and social relations. Ethnographic observations were particularly useful for identifying and rectifying oversights in my initial research focus. For example, going into the field I gave little thought to potential differences in international-local relations in Brčko and Mostar, assuming that these dynamics would be similar, or that whatever disparities existed would be relatively unimportant compared to wartime legacies, political institutions, and the sequencing of peacebuilding reforms. While legacies, institutions, and sequencing do indeed matter (as

I discuss in chapters 3, 4, and 5), I came to realize that my initial focus was overly narrow and insufficient for explaining the different postwar trajectories in the two towns.

The "aha" moment came eight months into research during a conversation with two local employees of international organizations (OHR and EUFOR) in Mostar. My first six months of research in Brčko had gone swimmingly, with nearly every request for an interview with local officials accepted and promptly arranged. In contrast, my first two months in Mostar had been a grind; I was having difficulty making contact with city officials, or getting them to agree to talk with me. Voicing these frustrations, I asked the two Mostar residents if they had any advice. They replied that my experience was not unusual, as their organizations too had difficulty in arranging meetings. In fact often the procedure involved sending written requests to local officials with whom they wished to meet, and then waiting days for a reply. The contrast with Brčko was striking. While conducting interview and archival research at the OHR Brčko office I had observed dense interactions between local and international officials, either of which could—and frequently did—merely pick up the phone and arrange a meeting within a day's time. At this point it became clear that I had been overlooking a critical factor in postwar peacebuilding in the two cities: the presence of close and productive local-international relations in Brčko, and their near complete absence in Mostar.

Plan of the Book

The four factors I highlight in my comparison of Mostar and Brčko are also central themes or points of debate among contemporary peacebuilding practitioners and scholars. In the next chapter I outline the pertinent theoretical literatures and briefly discuss the relevance of these research findings. The war in Bosnia was a complicated affair characterized by shifting and locally contingent alliances. Chapter 2 offers background for readers who are not Bosnia specialists by providing a brief narrative of events in Bosnia as a whole, and Brčko and Mostar in particular, from the collapse of Yugoslavia to the end of the war. It also describes the country's intricate postwar political institutions and provides an overview of the complex and evolving international peacebuilding mission in Bosnia from the end of the war to present.

Chapters 3 through 6 provide a comparative analysis of peacebuilding in Mostar and Brčko, with each focusing on one of the four critical factors—political institutions, wartime legacies, sequencing, and peacebuilding practices and institutions. In Chapter 7 I trace the emergence—and recent decline—of a patron-client relationship between Brčko's supervisory regime and local political and economic elites following the establishment of the District in 2000. This relationship was a key factor in the development of close and productive local-international relations and thus is critical for understanding the degree of peacebuilding progress achieved in Brčko. The concluding chapter discusses more general theoretical and policy-relevant insights that can be extracted from this analysis of localized peacebuilding efforts in Mostar and Brčko, especially regarding the promise and limitations of subnational peacebuilding missions and how these are shaped by the spatiality of peacebuilding practices and institutions.

1

THE STUDY OF PEACEBUILDING

Over the past twenty years the study of peacebuilding has exploded, fueled in part by a surge in multilateral peacebuilding missions around the world. While much progress has been made in understanding peacebuilding processes there is "still no reliable formula for transforming a fragile ceasefire into a stable and lasting peace."[1] If anything, in fact, there is a greater appreciation for just how little we still know about the transition from war to peace. This analysis of localized peacebuilding in Brčko and Mostar does not purport to offer a general template for achieving stable and lasting peace, but it does aim to inform certain key topics of interest in contemporary peacebuilding research. In this chapter I situate this project more fully by outlining the relevant theoretical literatures and briefly discussing how my findings relate to current debates.

Institutions

One of the most contentious debates in the peacebuilding literature concerns the design of political institutions to mitigate conflict. Despite years of research the question of which configurations of political institutions are most appropriate for ethnically plural states in the aftermath of war remains unresolved. Broadly framed, the debate revolves around two competing models: consociational, or what are sometimes called power-sharing compacts, and centripetal, or integrative, arrangements.[2]

Consociational theorists prescribe a political architecture based on two broad principles: (1) proportional sharing of power, representation, and resources along ethnic lines, and (2) ethnic autonomy.[3] Several institutional measures are recommended in order to achieve the first goal, foremost being a proportional representation electoral system, governing coalitions consisting of elite representatives from all major ethnic factions, mutual group vetoes on major political issues, and allocation of financial resources and civil service positions in proportion to ethnic membership in the country.[4] The second goal, ethnic autonomy, can be facilitated through either ethno-territorial political arrangements—most frequently, though not exclusively, this means ethno-federalism—nonterritorial measures, or some combination of both approaches. Examples of nonterritorial forms of ethnic autonomy include separate educational systems, independent cultural affairs councils, ethnically based courts with jurisdiction over family or religious laws, and language rights policies such as separate broadcast networks for different ethno-linguistic communities.

In practice, consociationalists tend to prefer a combination of power sharing and ethno-territorial autonomy, though in some situations where ethnic communities are more intermixed, corporate forms of autonomy may be a preferable option.[5] As Arend Lijphart, the scholar most responsible for developing the consociational model, succinctly puts it, "Good fences make good neighbors."[6] Smaller ethno-federal units are considered preferable to the extent that they enable a more precise division of ethnic groups into autonomous territorial spheres, limit the incentives for secession, or prevent one region from dominating state politics.[7] However the proper size of federal structures, consociational advocates maintain, is best determined with reference to the territorial concentration of ethnic groups in a given state rather than any theoretical prescription. If they are already relatively geographically isolated, then few regions are necessary.[8]

In contrast to the consociational approach, centripetal advocates call for institutional arrangements that promote ethnic interaction and cross-ethnic political coalitions in order to blunt the sharp edges of ethnic antagonism and solidarity. It is possible to distinguish between "weak" and "strong" centripetalist prescriptions. The former generally has a limited focus on electoral systems that create incentives for the formation of multiethnic parties or moderate ethnic parties that seek cross-ethnic votes and coalition partners.[9] Thus while consociationalists view proportional representation as the most desirable solution for divided states, centripetalists prefer electoral arrangements that promote "aggregative majoritarianism."[10] In practice this means that the latter favor preferential systems such as the alternative vote, which requires voters to rank-order their candidate preferences and encourages "vote pooling." Stronger centripetal prescriptions, perhaps more accurately called integrative approaches, go beyond a narrow emphasis on electoral systems and aim for political solutions that "deliberately promote social integration across group lines."[11]

Centripetalists are generally suspicious of ethno-federal solutions, especially those based on relatively few large and ethnically homogenous provinces, arguing that such arrangements can allow a single ethnic group to leverage control of a region into outsized power at the state level, as happened in the first Nigerian Republic.[12] Ethno-federalism, they maintain, also does little to promote cross-cutting cleavages or disperse political conflict down to the subnational level. Indeed, as the Nigerian case demonstrates, it tends to heighten conflict as ethnic majorities with secure domination over large federal regions fight even more intensely for control of the levers of state power. Consequently, if the goal is to create homogenous substate spaces centripetalists prefer that federalism be organized around a large number of small regions, a solution that is more likely to facilitate the emergence of intraethnic political differences and promote the diffusion of bargaining points that allow regional and other cross-cutting cleavages to emerge.[13]

An alternative to ethno-territorial solutions that is favored by some centripetalists involves the creation of ethnically heterogeneous political units. Ethnically mixed regions can serve as important sites of political socialization as interethnic bargaining and cooperation at these lower levels of government may create norms of interaction that moderate interethnic political relations at the state level.[14] Heterogeneous federalism is most practical when ethnic communities are relatively dispersed across state territory. But it is also possible to design federal systems that maximize heterogeneity—rather than maximize homogeneity as is typically the case—in states with varying degrees of territorially concentrated ethnic settlement patterns.

At root the debate between the two camps revolves around differing assumptions along two axes: ethnic identity and interaction. Supporters of centripetalism see identity as relatively malleable and are more optimistic that properly designed institutions can modify social relations in divided societies. This leads them to criticize consociationalists' reliance on ethnic parties, the explicit ethnic distribution of government resources and jobs, and the corporate or territorial division of society along ethnic lines. They contend that these policies entrench ethnicity and foreclose the possibility that alternative forms of collective identity and association can emerge as politically salient. The result is that consociational policies tend to harden and reproduce rather than ameliorate ethnic antagonisms. Furthermore, consociational policies force individuals to choose a recognized group identity in order to enjoy certain political and social benefits, thus violating the rights of certain groups and individuals.[15]

Advocates of integrative approaches also point out that ethnic interaction in divided societies is, short of partition, inevitable. Therefore the relevant question is, what types of interaction, and what types of institutional frameworks that govern interaction, lead to a reduction of ethnic conflict? Centripetalists find fault with consociationalism's reliance on elite-led interaction and accommodation. At a theoretical level, they argue that Lijphart's conceptualization of consociational democracy is tautological: "Consociational democracy is defined by a deeply divided society and by elite cooperation; in other words, both the problem and its solution are part of the definition."[16] They also claim that the assumption that ethnic elites in divided societies tend to be more moderate and likely to seek accommodation than the masses is empirically dubious. Instead, research on ethnic violence suggests that elites often play a central role in fomenting conflict for political advantage, as was the case in the wars across former Yugoslavia in the 1990s.[17] Centripetalists also maintain that elites have little incentive to compromise in consociational democracies. As Horowitz argues: "The mere need to form a coalition will not produce compromise. The incentive to compromise, and not merely coalesce, is the key to accommodation."[18] Others go further, suggesting that the structural logic of consociationalism promotes elite-initiated conflict by pushing elites to pursue antagonistic politics in the interethnic parliamentary arena in order to protect themselves from ethnic outbidding by rivals in the intraethnic electoral sphere.[19]

Consociational partisans have ready responses to these criticisms. First, they note that ethnic identities are already salient in divided societies. Any viable political compromise has to take this fact into account. Moreover, they argue that identity is less fluid than centripetal advocates assume. This is not to say that consociationalists are ethnic primordialists. Most subscribe to a constructivist view of identity that is now the orthodox scholarly position. But they tend to believe that ethnic identities and relations are relatively "sticky" and difficult to alter, especially after violent conflict. To think otherwise—to believe that it is possible to design political institutions that are capable of transforming or dissolving these collective identities—is misplaced optimism.[20]

Supporters of consociational arrangements also rebut the charges that consociations necessarily reify ethnic identity and violate the rights of unrecognized groups and individuals. Two prominent consociational scholars in particular, John McGarry and Brendan O'Leary, have replied to these criticisms by developing the argument that consociations come in two types: "corporate" and "liberal." The former privileges collective groups according to ascriptive criteria such as ethnicity or religion. An example of this was Cyprus's 1960 constitution, under which citizens had to register with either the Greek or Turkish Cypriot electoral rolls. McGarry and O'Leary concede that this form of consociation, based on the assumption of fixed ethnic or religious identities, forecloses opportunities for political movements that are not associated with privileged identity categories. However they maintain that most consociational scholars are proponents of liberal consociations in which citizens are free to vote for whatever political option they wish. In such liberal consociations political identities and associations that emerge as salient through elections are "self-determined" rather than "pre-determined."[21]

Finally, consociationalists contend that direct interaction, especially in sensitive areas such as political competition and cultural reproduction, almost inevitably exacerbates tensions, thereby reproducing ethnic conflict. Hence centripetalists' call to design institutions that promote the integration of antagonistic communities is a futile, utopian goal that rests on wooly thinking about ethnic relations. In contrast consociational politics is based on hard-headed political "realism." It is rooted in, as O'Leary puts it, "a politics of shared accommodation, of shared fears, but not one in which an imagined or imaginary unity can or should be presented. At most, consociation is a politics with a shared vision of catastrophe."[22] This leads consociationalists to conclude that the best possible approach for divided societies is to manage conflict by limiting interaction, with the hope that this may lead to a gradual lessening of ethnic division over time.

Mostar and Brčko offer an interesting, if imperfect, test of the relative merits of consociational and integrative approaches to institutional design. Interesting because given the different assumptions concerning ethnic identity and interaction there is a surprising lack of research that explores the effects of these two political arrangements in local communities, the scale at which everyday interactions and identity practices take place and are mediated by political institutions. Imperfect because while the political framework in Mostar has closely followed ethno-territorial consociational prescriptions, the Brčko District is more of a hybrid in which the pursuit of broad social and territorial integration is balanced in part by the sharing of power, representation, and resources through consociational measures such as proportional elections. Nonetheless, as I argue in chapter 3, it is clear that the integrative approach pursued in Brčko has proven to be more successful to date in mitigating conflict and creating an effective multiethnic government. Conversely Mostar's political institutions have, as predicted by critics, bolstered the position of the most obstructionist nationalists and hardened ethnic divisions in the city—both spatially and socially.

Wartime Legacies

Perhaps one of the most important, but least understood, elements of postwar peacebuilding is the ways in which wartime social processes shape postwar peace outcomes. It is well known that countries that have experienced civil war are more likely to experience further outbreaks of violence. In general the political economy literature that explores this "conflict trap" phenomenon—which tends toward cross-country analysis relying on national-level data—has focused on negative legacies of war such as economic hardship, the destruction of social capital, and weak governing institutions.[23] While these variables undoubtedly influence the recurrence of violence, cross-country comparative research does little to open up the black box of wartime social processes that alter institutional structures and reconfigure local and regional social and political networks.[24]

At the other end of the spectrum is a rich literature of case studies highlighting the various social and political legacies of civil war such as a sharpening and polarization of ethnic identities,[25] the militarization of society,[26] the rise of authoritarian governments,[27] the spread of strategies of secrecy and concealment,[28] new forms of political mobilization,[29] the growth of criminal shadow economies and political networks,[30] and dynamics displacement and reintegration,[31] to highlight just a few examples. One insight from these in-depth studies is that it is a mistake to assume that legacies of war are necessarily negative. For instance, recent micro-level research in Sierra Leone and Uganda suggests that those who have experienced wartime violence in the former are more likely to vote and join political or community groups,[32] while former abducted child soldiers in the latter are also more likely to vote and be politically active.[33] Moreover, creative strategies to maintain normality in the face of violence may strengthen peacebuilding movements following war, especially if political mobilization produces new democratic alliances.[34]

While this latter literature has greatly enriched our understanding of important social and political legacies of war it has seldom directed attention toward subnational differences in wartime processes and the effect such variations have on postwar peacebuilding.[35] As Elizabeth Wood has recently observed:

> Under what conditions does each process occur with particular force? Under what conditions do these processes have enduring, important consequences? To what extent do answers depend on who wins the war? To what extent do they depend on the intensity of conflict, or its duration? Is it possible to distinguish the legacies of distinct processes of war? The challenge

will be to develop research designs that allow the untangling of the consequences of distinct processes, a challenge that may be best addressed by
research strategies that take advantage of subnational variation.[36]

Wood is one of a number of scholars who in recent years have turned
to microlevel analysis in order to better understand spatial and temporal
variations in violence in intrastate wars.[37] One of the key insights to come
out of these works is that "top down" accounts which rely on "master
cleavage'" narratives often obscure rather than illuminate the dynamics of violence. This is because violent conflict is jointly produced by the
interaction of local actors and national elites.[38] Microlevel social antagonisms such as conflicts over land; economic disparities; political rivalries;
and personal, family, or clan feuds are utilized and manipulated by national leaders in pursuit of their own political goals, while local actors
appropriate and rearticulate master cleavages and pursue alliances with
distant elites for their own benefit. As Stathis Kalyvas puts it, "It is the
convergence of local motives and supralocal imperatives that endows
civil wars with their particular and often puzzling character, straddling
the divide between the political and the private, the collective and the
individual."[39]

Like violence, political mobilization in intrastate wars is also a complex process shaped by the intersection of local conditions and actors, and
broader political projects. In "ethnic" civil wars, fear and violence tends to
polarize ethnic identities and group antagonisms.[40] Consequently the position of nationalist parties is often strengthened while political alternatives
are marginalized.[41] One consequence of the war in Bosnia, for instance,
was that the three main nationalist parties representing their respective
ethnic communities in the country—SDA (Bosniaks), SDS (Serbs), and
HDZ (Croats)—eventually fused together both politically and militarily
most of the different factions within each community. A common refrain
I heard while talking to people in both cities was that it was more accurate
to characterize SDA, SDS, and HDZ during the wartime period as "national movements." By this they meant that they felt they had to join, or at
least nominally ally, with the parties in order to defend themselves. This
was especially the case for those living in towns such as Mostar and Brčko,
which were sites of violent conflict. Nonetheless treating ethnic groups
as unitary actors and ethnic identity as fixed[42] can blind us to important

countervailing currents such as identity shifts and ethnic defections, which are not uncommon in civil wars.[43]

More important for this story, ethnic or nationalist master narratives conceal important intragroup tensions that may not rise to the level of open conflict. What Kalyvas calls the "disjunction between center and periphery" often results in wartime alliances of convenience or necessity.[44] During moments of political fluidity in the postwar period these alliances can come under heightened risk of unraveling as the selective benefits decrease and the contradictory aims of national and local elites come into sharper relief. This is exactly the dynamic that unfolded in Brčko following the war as the wartime actions of each of the three main nationalist parties—as well as their immediate postwar policies—ran against important local interests and reduced their legitimacy among a significant portion of the population in each of the three communities. Consequently international officials found more fertile conditions to cultivate alliances with local moderates— or at least more pragmatic nationalists—who were willing to work with them to implement peacebuilding reforms.

A similar dynamic took place within the Bosniak community in Mostar, where there was widespread suspicion that SDA's central leadership in Sarajevo sold out their position to Croats in exchange for other political favors during the war. Consequently prominent local leaders who emerged during the wartime period owed a great deal of their legitimacy to the perception that they resisted the abandonment of Mostar by politicians in Sarajevo. In the initial postwar period they also exhibited political independence and willingness to work with international officials to recreate a unified city. Unfortunately, the opposite process unfolded within the Croat community in Mostar as HDZ and its mafia allies were in an unchallenged position of authority by the end of the war. Moreover, as elites from the surrounding region of Herzegovina took control of leadership positions in both the Croatian and Bosnian branches of HDZ, the interests of Croats in West Mostar increasingly became defined as one of the most important issues for the broader Croat community in former Yugoslavia. The result of this alignment of local, national, and regional interests was that Croat nationalists were relatively united in their opposition to peacebuilding reforms such as returns and the administrative unification of Mostar and were in a stronger position to play a spoiler role against peacebuilding efforts in Mostar than were opponents of reform in Brčko.

Sequencing

A third prominent theme in the peacebuilding literature concerns the proper sequencing of political, economic and institutional reforms. Early peacebuilding missions in the 1990s were guided by the belief that rapid political and economic liberalization was a key element in transforming war-torn states into stable societies.[45] Influenced by research that suggested that democracies—in particular market-based democracies—are less likely to engage in wars or experience intrastate violence,[46] international peacebuilders set about remaking states in their own image.

This near missionary belief in the transformative powers of liberal market democracy[47] is perhaps best reflected in *An Agenda for Democratization*, an ambitious policy statement published by then UN Secretary General Boutros Boutros-Ghali:

> Because democratic Governments are freely chosen by their citizens and held accountable through periodic and genuine elections and other mechanisms, they are more likely to promote and respect the rule of law, respect individual and minority rights, cope effectively with social conflict, absorb migrant populations and respond to the needs of marginalized groups. They are therefore less likely to abuse their power against the peoples of their own State territories. Democracy within States thus fosters the evolution of the social contract upon which lasting peace can be built. In this way, a culture of democracy is fundamentally a culture of peace. . . . In today's world, freedom of thought, the impetus to creativity and the will to involvement are all critical to economic, social and cultural progress, and they are best fostered and protected within democratic systems. In this sense, the economic act of privatization can be as well a political act, enabling greater human creativity and participation.[48]

In the political sphere support for liberal market democracies meant that peacebuilders emphasized the importance of democratization and endeavored to organize elections shortly after the termination of wars. Economically this led to the promotion of market-oriented reforms aimed at reducing government involvement in the economy.

Though still widespread in practice, peacebuilding liberalization has come under increasing criticism in the past decade. Jack Snyder has argued that democratic transitions in ethnically divided states tend to lead to nationalism and war.[49] While Snyder's argument applies primarily to democratization and interstate war, subsequent research indicates that democratizing states are also more likely to experience civil war,[50] and that early elections following conflict often spark renewed fighting or the ratification of militarized factions,[51] though the conditions or mechanisms that exacerbate or mitigate the potential for electoral violence remain underexplored.[52] Economic liberalization has also come under greater scrutiny, with critics contending that it has fueled instability and violence in a number of developing countries across the globe.[53] Two of the more robust factors increasing the risk of civil war are low per capita income and low economic growth rates;[54] therefore market-based states are more likely to be peaceful in the long run. However several studies suggest that the move away from state-controlled economies may increase instability in the interim period.[55] In sum, though market democracies are more stable and peaceful than authoritarian governments with state-dominated economies, the process of transitioning toward the former is fraught with danger.

Realization of the potentially destabilizing effects of political and economic transitions has led to a rethinking of the prescription for rapid liberalization in states that have experienced violent conflict. In the past decade a number of critics have argued that the prioritization or sequencing of reforms should be reversed: that is, the process of building institutional capacity—statebuilding—should take precedence over democratization and privatization efforts.[56] The best-known and most-systematic expression of this thesis is Roland Paris's call for "Institutionalization Before Liberalization" (IBL). The framework of IBL, outlined in Paris's 2004 book *At War's End*, is worth citing in detail here:

> I have described several institutional elements that peacebuilders should seek to construct before they launch comprehensive political and economic liberalization programs in countries that are just emerging from civil wars. These elements include a constitutional court to resolve disputes surrounding elections and to uphold the articles of the constitution against challenges; a reliable police force to maintain domestic order and enforce the rulings of the constitutional court and any other court legally constituted under the constitution; a procedure for regulating hate speech in the media; a system for overseeing the conduct of political parties and civil-society organizations; a legal framework capable of regulating the market economy;

and a redistributive mechanism to protect the welfare of the most vulnerable sectors of the population. The common denominator across all of these recommendations is that institutionalization should precede liberalization to a significant degree in order to limit the destabilizing effects of the liberalization process itself.[57]

This sequencing argument is not without its critics. One concern is that international peacebuilders may lack the legitimacy to continue to administer postwar states for the period of time it may take to build effective institutions.[58] Another is that delaying elections may make it more difficult to attract international aid necessary to rebuild state institutions in the aftermath of conflict.[59] A more forceful critique is that unelected international officials often implement reforms through authoritarian means in order to overcome the resistance of domestic elites, thus undermining the goal of liberal statebuilding.[60] A related concern is that internationally led institution building may undermine "local ownership" of the peacebuilding process and ultimately weaken the very state institutions that are meant to be strengthened.[61]

As I outline in chapter 5 this research provides strong support for Roland Paris's IBL argument. In Mostar early elections in the spring of 1996 (the first postwar elections held in Bosnia, in fact) were marred by violent attacks against moderate candidates and did not produce a functioning municipal government. And the elections were quickly followed by renewed ethnic violence in the year that followed. Likewise, the quick privatization of public firms and property further entrenched the city's wartime nationalist leaders who ended up controlling the most valuable entities. In turn these ethnically controlled firms refused to rehire workers who lost their positions during the war, thus solidifying the economic and social division of Mostar along ethnic lines.

In contrast, decisions by multiple Brčko supervisors to delay elections and privatization until after the District was formed in 2000 and its new institutions had taken root provided a sounder basis for inclusive economic development and promoted the prospects of more moderate local elites. It also facilitated more thorough and durable institutional reforms. Relative to the rest of the country, Brčko's institutions are held in high regard by District residents. This is especially true of those responsible for upholding the "rule of law"—the police and courts—which are the most professional and independent in the country. Despite the vast authority wielded by international peacebuilders in Brčko, the supervisory regime has also generally received broad support from District residents, and participation by local elites in the reform process has been greater than elsewhere in Bosnia. In chapters 6 and 7 I explain how international peacebuilders in Brčko were able to maintain legitimacy throughout this long period of political and administrative intervention.

Peacebuilding Practices and Institutions

The transition from violence to stable peace is an incredibly difficult and complex process involving social, political, and economic transformations. As such there are no simple solutions, no checklist of rules for peacebuilding practitioners to follow which will ensure success. Moreover there are a number of tensions and contradictions inherent to international peacebuilding interventions. This is especially the case with the more intensive missions of the past two decades, which aim not just to aid peace negotiations or enforce a cease-fire, but to assist in statebuilding—the rebuilding of governmental institutions (preferably democratic)—in the aftermath of war. Long-term internationally assisted peacebuilding risks alienating local populations who may come to resent it as intrusive and unresponsive to domestic concerns. On the other hand short-term missions that promote rapid political and economic liberalization over institution building may increase instability, empower spoilers who do not seek peace, and further marginalize social groups who suffered during the war.

Recognition of these tensions has led to increased scrutiny of the dilemmas of postwar peacebuilding in recent years. In an influential 2008 edited volume devoted to the topic Roland Paris and Timothy Sisk noted that "fundamental and unresolved tensions in the idea of externally-assisted statebuilding have given rise to a recurring series of policy problems facing peacebuilding actors in the field. Directly acknowledging and confronting these problems is crucial to the future success of the international community's peacebuilding efforts."[62] They identify five broad contradictions: (1) outside intervention is used to foster self-government, (2) international control is required to establish local ownership, (3) universal values are promoted as a remedy for local problems, (4) statebuilding requires both a clean break with the past and a reaffirmation of history, and (5) short-term imperatives often conflict with longer-term objectives. These inherent contradictions in turn are the source of concrete policy dilemmas confronting peacebuilders, such as the footprint and duration of international operations, the proper balance of international and local ownership in peacebuilding reforms, and problems of policy coordination and coherence.[63] As Paris and Sisk observe, at best these dilemmas can only be managed, not resolved. Consequently the question of how to best navigate the various tensions inherent in peacebuilding interventions should be a central issue for scholars and practitioners alike.[64] Put another way, how peacebuilding is done (practices) is as fundamental a concern as what is to be done (policies).

One persistent critique of how peacebuilding is done concerns the prevalence of "top-down" models in which international officials lacking in-depth knowledge of local conditions devise and implement general policy templates with little input from domestic actors. Critics contrast this with "bottom-up" peacebuilding, which prioritizes the voice, needs, and participation of local communities in the peacebuilding process.[65] In practice, of course, this is a difficult distinction to maintain as peacebuilding missions contain both bottom-up and top-down elements. Moreover, the two approaches are irreducibly interdependent.[66]

While critiques of top-down practices are frequently couched in broader critiques of the "liberal" peacebuilding model,[67] it is perhaps more accurate to consider this as a shortcoming of institutional centralism rather than liberalism.[68] Lise Howard, for example, has found that UN peacekeeping operations in which field missions are given substantial autonomy—thus allowing personnel on the ground greater ability to adjust to the postwar environment they encounter—are more likely to succeed than missions dependent on directives from UN headquarters, which are often the product of higher-level political disputes and may bear little relevance to local conditions.[69] Likewise Séverine Autesserre's empirically rich case study of the Congo traces peacebuilding failure in that country to international peacebuilders' reluctance to address local rivalries over land, resources, and power in addition to their focus on regional and national issues.[70] Peacebuilding inevitably involves encounters between international officials and local populations. Thus, in addition to knowledge of, and concern for, conditions on the ground, peacebuilders also need to cultivate productive relationships with local actors, whose support and perceptions of legitimacy are necessary conditions for any successful peacebuilding mission.[71]

As chapter 6 details, in Mostar peacebuilding practices and the institutions that shaped them, militated against the establishment of an effective localized presence. As elsewhere in Bosnia the various military and civilian international organizations in Mostar lacked sufficient coordination of policy creation and execution in the city and surrounding region, a problem exacerbated by shifting and poorly aligned areas of responsibility dictated by disparate organizational priorities. Additionally internationals in Mostar suffered from a lack of independence from distant superiors, and a lack of political and social embeddedness, which was exacerbated by rapid turnover of staff. These two factors not only hampered their ability to create productive working relationships with local officials, they also frequently resulted in policy decisions—such as early elections and privatization—that reflected distant political priorities rather than local needs and conditions.

In Brčko, in contrast, the broad supervisory powers concentrated decision-making authority and policy formulation responsibilities in the hands of the OHR supervisory regime responsible for peacebuilding in the area. This decentralized, place-based hierarchy, along with strong relations with U.S. SFOR forces, gave supervisors significant influence over other Brčko-based international staff, improving the coordination of policy activities in the District and providing the political independence necessary to resist policy suggestions that ran counter to local interests and conditions. It also imparted greater legitimacy on peacebuilding efforts in the District due to the relative independence of the OHR Brčko office from outside interference, and the development of dense daily interactions between deeply embedded international officials and their local counterparts, which heightened the sense of constructive participation in the reform process among the latter.

In chapter 7 I expand on my argument about the importance of international-local relations and the effect that peacebuilding practices and institutions have on them by detailing the emergence of a patron-client relationship between Brčko's supervisory regime and local political and economic elites following the establishment of the District in 2000. As I noted in the introduction, this relationship was a key factor in the development of close and productive local-international relations, and thus is critical for understanding the degree of peacebuilding progress achieved in Brčko. In effect OHR Brčko used its influence and authority to provide protection for the District in the latter's battles against the Federation and RS and their frequent allies in the headquarters of international organizations in Sarajevo, while District authorities reciprocated by supporting—or at the least not actively opposing—the various peacebuilding reforms that have been pushed by the supervisors and other international officials in Brčko.

2

THE COLLAPSE OF YUGOSLAVIA
AND THE BALKAN WARS

Spring 2012 marked the twentieth anniversary of the beginning of the war in Bosnia, which was the longest and bloodiest conflict in Europe since World War II. In total nearly 100,000 people were killed during the conflict, almost half of them civilians, and more than 2 million were driven from their homes.[1] The war also introduced to the world the phrase "ethnic cleansing" to describe the murderous campaigns to carve out ethnically homogenous territories from Bosnia's formerly mixed spaces. The most notorious instance of this was the slaughter of eight thousand Bosniak men and boys by the Bosnian Serb army (VRS) at Srebrenica in July 1995. After three and a half years of fighting the warring parties signed the Dayton Peace Agreement in November 1995. The DPA established a complex consociational state in Bosnia. It also made provisions for extensive postwar peacebuilding activities by a variety of international actors. The international presence continues to this day, albeit in a much more limited fashion, making it one of the longest running and most intensive cases of postwar peacebuilding intervention to date. Indeed, Bosnia represents a pivotal transition from international peacekeeping interventions with limited mandates and timetables which proliferated at the end of the Cold War—e.g., Angola, Namibia, El Salvador, Mozambique—to more robust and open-ended peacebuilding and statebuilding projects in the past decade such as Kosovo, East Timor, Afghanistan, and Iraq.[2]

To date the record in Bosnia is decidedly mixed. On one hand the country remains at peace, thousands of displaced families and individuals have reclaimed their prewar homes—though fewer have returned to live in them—and multiple parties compete in elections that are generally regarded as free and fair. On the other hand, postwar economic growth has been desultory, corruption is endemic, and Bosnian politics is still dominated by nationalist parties that continue to pursue divisive policies aimed at maintaining control over what they perceive as their respective ethnic territories. Additionally, as noted in the introduction, tensions remain high and small-scale, ethnically charged violence is not uncommon. Conditions in the country have also declined precipitously in recent years. Following general elections in October 2010 squabbling political elites took more than fourteen months to agree on a new governing coalition. Moreover, the global economic crisis hit Bosnia especially hard, exacerbating already high unemployment figures and causing budget deficits to balloon. Political and economic stagnation has also been accompanied by mounting nationalist rhetoric, with politicians—especially in the RS—now openly challenging the state structures established at Dayton.[3]

The war and postwar period in Bosnia can be quite confusing. Even those who study the region often have trouble keeping track of the various places, actors, political alliances, and institutional arrangements. In this chapter I provide (1) a brief narrative of Bosnia and the broader region from the collapse of Yugoslavia to the end of the war, as well as a short sketch of events in Brčko and Mostar, and (2) a description of Bosnia's current political system as well as the various international organizations and actors who have been involved in postwar peacebuilding efforts. The purpose here is not to plumb the causes of the disintegration of Yugoslavia and subsequent war in Bosnia, or provide a detailed analysis of peacebuilding activities throughout the country, all of which have already been discussed elsewhere.[4] Rather, the aim is to provide sufficient background for readers with an interest in postwar peacebuilding in Bosnia who are not area specialists.

The Collapse of Yugoslavia

The outbreak of armed conflict in Yugoslavia was a surprise to most outsiders. Prior to this the country was known around the world for more positive reasons such as playing successful host to the 1984 Winter Olympics; it's long and beautiful Adriatic coastline, which attracted several hundred thousand European vacationers each summer; and being one of the driving forces behind the nonaligned movement, a group of countries that sought out a third way between the capitalist West and the Soviet-led Communist bloc during the Cold War. The nonaligned movement was the brainchild of Josip Broz "Tito," the country's iconic communist leader from the end of World War II until his death in 1980. Tito's deft diplomatic maneuvering produced significant foreign aid, loans, and investment from the West, contributing to one of the highest standards of living in Eastern Europe. Yugoslavs also generally enjoyed greater political openness than their communist brethren, including the freedom to travel and work abroad. In the decades before the war, in fact, hundreds of thousands of Yugoslavs found temporary or permanent work in Western Europe. These *gastarbajteri* (guest workers) usually maintained close ties to the communities they came from, sending back remittances and investing in property or businesses, which further benefited the Yugoslav economy.[5]

Though relatively prosperous as a whole, Yugoslavia's economic development was highly variable across the country's six federal republics. Croatia and Slovenia were the two wealthiest, with a standard of living comparable to Portugal, Spain, and Greece. Less-developed republics like Bosnia, Montenegro, and Macedonia were much less well off, with Serbia falling in between the two poles. Bosnia's GNP per capita, for example, was one-third that of Slovenia in 1988.[6] These economic disparities contributed to growing political tensions between the two wealthiest republics and the rest of the country in the decade following Tito's death. During this period Yugoslavia also suffered from economic stagnation, spiraling inflation, a balance of payments crisis, and rising unemployment.[7]

Even before the end of Tito's rule it was clear that the Yugoslav model of decentralized labor self-management combined with openness to foreign trade was in need of significant reform, but there was little consensus among political elites on how to proceed during the 1980s. Serbia and the

poorer republics argued for increased state involvement in directing economic development, which by necessity involved greater political centralization—and not coincidentally would strengthen Serbia's power vis-à-vis
the other republics. In contrast, Slovenia's leaders advocated economic liberalization and more autonomy for the constituent republics to set their
own political and economic policies.[8] As Yugoslavia's republics—with
the exception of Bosnia—were organized along ethnic lines with a titular
nation constituting a majority in each, these economic and policy differences gradually took on more nationalist hues. This was especially the case
after Slobodan Milošević took over as president of Serbia in 1989.

Figure 2. Former Yugoslavia

Milošević came to power by successfully exploiting ethnic Serbs' griev-ances concerning Kosovo and their broader position in Yugoslavia follow-ing constitutional reforms in 1974. The 1974 constitution shifted power from the central state to the six federal republics and two autonomous provinces (Kosovo and Vojvodina), which received most powers granted to the republics.[9] These reforms rankled many Serbs in Yugoslavia who considered the two provinces to be integral territories of Serbia. Further-more, decentralization had the effect of decreasing Serb political power in the country as a significant number of ethnic Serbs lived in Croatia and Bosnia. Following Tito's death these grievances were increasingly articu-lated in the public sphere, most notoriously through a 1986 memorandum written by prominent intellectuals at the Serbian Academy of Sciences and Arts (SANU).

This memorandum was widely denounced by Yugoslav officials, including Milošević—at the time a rising member of the Communist Party in Serbia due to the support of his political mentor, Ivan Stam-bolić, the president of Serbia—who condemned it as "nothing else but the darkest nationalism."[10] Yet within a year Milošević had changed course and adopted the causes forwarded by the SANU document, in particular that of the Kosovar Serbs who feared the loss of political control over the province due to the growing assertiveness of the dis-gruntled Kosovar Albanian majority. Following a trip to the province in April 1987, during which he famously denounced ethnic Albanian police who had beaten Serb protesters, Milošević and his supporters began plotting an intraparty coup against Stambolić, which ultimately resulted in the latter's resignation as president that December.[11]

The ascension of Milošević prompted officials in Croatia and Slovenia to redouble their efforts to gain further autonomy within the Yugo-slav confederation, especially following "antibureaucratic" revolutions in Montenegro, Vojvodina, and Kosovo in 1988, which resulted in the re-placement of republican and provincial leadership with a new cadre of officials politically aligned with Milošević.[12] With these new allies Milošević controlled four of the eight votes in the collective State Presidency, which allowed him to block any reforms that would lead to further decentraliza-tion.[13] Ironically, the institutional changes introduced by the 1974 constitu-tion to limit Serbian influence in Yugoslavia were now the basis of outsized political power.

Elections in the six republics in 1990 further exacerbated the divide between the two richest republics on one side, and Milošević and central state institutions—particularly the Yugoslav National Army (JNA)—on the other.[14] In the former, Milan Kučan (Slovenia) and Franjo Tudjman (Croatia) swept to power. Both were strong proponents of greater republican autonomy and even independence. Shortly after the elections the JNA moved to confiscate weapons from Territorial Defense (TO) forces in these two republics. It also began covertly training, and funneling weapons to, separatist Serb groups in Knin, a city located in the Krajina region in Croatia.[15] In response the newly elected leaderships in Slovenia and Croatia moved to procure arms from neighboring Hungary and establish military formations under their own control, despite orders against these moves by the JNA.

By the beginning of 1991 it was clear that Yugoslavia was in the midst of an existential crisis that was leading the country down the path toward civil war. Several armed skirmishes between Croatian police and Serb separatists in the republic erupted that spring, leaving dozens dead. Meanwhile vicious nationalist media campaigns in Serbia and Croatia were sowing fear, hatred, and suspicion of ethnic "others."[16] That March JNA general Veljko Kadijević, who was also the Yugoslav minister of defense, demanded that the State Presidency declare a state of emergency, which would allow the JNA to take control of the country—a move angrily rejected by the four-member anti-Milošević bloc. Viewing the Yugoslav compact as irretrievably broken, Slovenia and Croatia declared independence in June.

The fight for independence in Slovenia was brief, with Slovenian forces gaining control of most of the country after ten days of sporadic clashes with the JNA. In July a conference was convened at the Slovenian resort town of Brioni, at which Yugoslavia agreed to remove the JNA by fall in exchange for a three-month moratorium on further moves toward independence. Unlike Slovenia, Croatia had a significant minority Serb population, concentrated primarily in Slavonia and Krajina, much of which was already in open rebellion against the government.[17] In July the JNA invaded Slavonia in support of the rebels, setting off a war between Croat and Serb forces that would last until 1995.[18]

Social Polarization and the War(s) in Bosnia

Despite the bloody conflict in neighboring Croatia, the outbreak of war in Bosnia in 1992 came as a shock to many living there. The country's president, Alija Izetbegović, had optimistically declared the previous month in an interview with Radio Sarajevo that "there will be no war in Bosnia, [neither] local, nor imported."[19] In hindsight it seems difficult to believe that so many were taken by surprise by the violence. Since the elections in November 1990 there had been a steady process of social polarization and the division of Bosnia along ethno-territorial lines.

The elections greatly boosted the standing of the three newly formed nationalist parties in Bosnia—the Serbian Democratic Party (SDS), the Croatian Democratic Union (HDZ), and the Party of Democratic Action (SDA)—which together captured 202 out of 240 seats in the two Bosnian parliamentary chambers, far outpacing the reformist League of Communists-Social Democratic Party (SKBiH-SDP), which finished a distant fourth.[20] Despite their mutually exclusive ethnic agendas the SDS, HDZ, and SDA formed an uneasy political coalition to share power in Bosnia following the elections. SDA was given the role of president of the collective Presidency (Izetbegović), while SDS received the position of parliamentary speaker and HDZ that of prime minister. This tripartite coalition was also extended down to the local level. Consequently SKBiH-SDP ended up governing only two *opštine* (a unit of local government similar to a municipality or county) in the country (Tuzla and Vareš), even though the party received a plurality of votes in several locations, including Brčko.[21] Ostensibly the nationalist coalition provided a workable power-sharing solution for Bosnia's complex ethnic and political geographies. In practice, however, it amounted to little more than a restructuring of the existing patronage system along ethno-nationalist lines. And from the beginning effective governance was inhibited by a lack of trust and cooperation among the three parties.

The most destabilizing development in Bosnia in the year following the elections, though, was the push to reorganize the country along ethno-territorial administrative lines. According to Mirko Pejanović—the head of the non-nationalist Democratic Socialist Alliance party (DSS), and later one of the ethnic Serb members of Bosnia's wartime Presidency—even before the elections Radovan Karadžić, the president of SDS, was "obsessed with the idea of forming Serb municipalities."[22] In the fall of 1991 SDS announced the formation of several Serb Autonomous Oblasts (SAOs), or regions, claiming about half the territory in Bosnia.[23] Then on November 9 it organized a referendum asking ethnic Serbs whether they wished to remain in a rump Yugoslavia. Shortly thereafter HDZ announced the creation of the "Croatian communities of Posavina and Herceg-Bosna."[24] In all, nearly three-quarters of the country was claimed by either Serb or Croat nationalists by the end of the year.[25]

As noted above, Bosnia was different from the other Yugoslav republics in that it was not the imagined homeland of a titular national community, but rather the shared home of three "constituent peoples"—Croats, Serbs, and Muslims—none of which constituted a majority of the population.[26] Indeed, Bosnia was a complex patchwork of more or less mixed communities. In one quarter of the 109 *opštine* in the country there was no ethnic majority, while in another 54 municipalities 25–50 percent of the population claimed a different identity than the majority population. Only in 26 *opštine* did the majority community constitute more than 75 percent of the total population (see figure 3). Even these statistics and the accompanying map underplay the significance of shared spaces in Bosnia: nearly one-third of the country's 4.3 million citizens lived in a nonmajority *opštine*, while only one-eighth of the population came from predominantly monoethnic municipalities. Thus, despite the claims of Serb and Croat nationalists who promoted brightly colored maps suggesting homogenized ethnic spaces, the division of Bosnia along ethno-territorial lines could not be achieved without the violent unmixing of peoples. If the maps did not conform to lived reality, then the facts on the ground would have to be made to conform to these cartographic fantasies. As Gerard Toal and Carl Dahlman trenchantly observe, "Coloring space was a prelude to cleansing space."[27]

It was not only nationalist politicians who championed the creation of ethnically homogenous territories. Religious elites also played an important part.[28] The Franciscan Order in Herzegovina—which had also been closely linked with the WWII NDH regime—played a key role in espousing a militant nationalist vision of a Greater Croatia encompassing much of Bosnia, both within the country and among the Croat diaspora abroad.[29] The Serbian Orthodox Church also aggressively promoted nationalist narratives, in particular those evoking historical—and possible future—"genocide" against Serbs by their "Ustaše" and "Turk" enemies, and supported the creation of a separate national state unifying all Serbs in Yugoslavia. In 1991 the church's newly elected patriarch, Pavle, justified his support for Serb separatists in Croatia by stating, "It is time to comprehend that the victims of genocide cannot live together with their former but perhaps also their future executioners."[30]

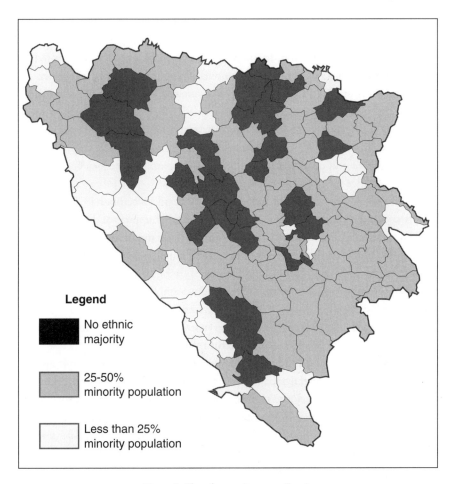

Figure 3. Shared spaces in prewar Bosnia

By the beginning of 1992 Bosnia's formal institutions had effectively ceased to function. The previous fall SDS established a separate Assembly of Serb People. In January the assembly proclaimed an autonomous Serb Republic of Bosnia and Herzegovina—later renamed the Republika Srpska. Many firms also ceased paying taxes to the state, as the monies were now funneled off to the nationalist parties and their nascent ethno-political structures.[31] And all three sides were frantically working to establish ethnic military formations and arm themselves.[32] In this SDS was greatly aided by Milošević and the JNA, which was training local volunteers and redeploying weapons and Bosnian Serb personnel to the country. These forces would become the nucleus of the VRS later that spring. Yet even as the country was disintegrating, Izetbegović—with the support of the United States and European Community—moved forward with a planned referendum on Bosnian independence. SDS organized a boycott of the referendum and stated that in the event that Bosnia declared independence from Yugoslavia, Serbs would secede from the state. Despite these threats the referendum took place on February 29 and March 1, with more than 99 percent of the participating voters choosing independence. The next day barricades went up around Sarajevo.

The war in Bosnia lasted from March 1992 till December 1995. Properly speaking, what took place was not one war, but a series of distinct conflicts, as one can identify at different points in time and in different regions of the country an array of combinations of alliance and opposition. For instance, in 1993 Fikret Abdić, a former SDA official who had won the most votes for president in the 1990 elections, established the Autonomous Province of Western Bosnia in the northwestern town of Velika Kladuša.[33] Allied with the RS, Abdić's Muslim forces waged a vicious war against the Fifth Corps of the Bosnian army (ARBiH) from 1993 to 1995.[34]

In addition to a number of such *mali ratovi* (little wars) there was also a great degree of spatial and temporal variation in violence and ethnic cleansing during the war.[35] The largest number of people killed was in the Sarajevo area, followed by Srebrenica. In general, the geographical distribution of deaths followed patterns of ethnic cleansing by Bosnian Serb forces, with the greatest concentration occurring in towns located along the Drina River (the Podrinje region) in eastern Bosnia, and a number of ethnically mixed *opštine*—for example, Brčko, Doboj, and Prijedor—in northern Bosnia (see figure 4).[36] The bloodiest period was the first year, when an estimated 44 percent of the deaths occurred.[37] That the bulk of deadly violence occurred where and when it did follows from the ethnoterritorial logic of the nationalist projects envisioned by political and religious leaders in Yugoslavia—and Bosnia in particular—which were not "only a matter of imagining allegedly "primordial" communities, but rather of making existing heterogeneous ones unimaginable . . . the point has been to implement an essentialist definition of the nation and its state in regions where the intermingled population formed living disproof of its validity: the brutal negation of social reality in order to reconstruct it."[38]

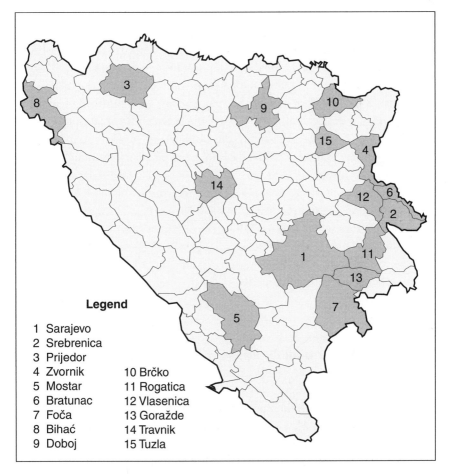

Figure 4. Municipalities with the largest number of deaths during the war

By the end of the first year of the war the VRS controlled roughly 70 percent of the territory in Bosnia, prompting Karadžić to declare that the RS had achieved its territorial objectives.[39] While the VRS transitioned toward a more defensive position, a new war between Croat and Bosniak forces broke out. Though formally allies, tensions between the two communities had steadily risen following the replacement of Stjepan Kljuić with Mate Boban in early 1992 as head of the HDZ in Bosnia. Kljuić, whose power base was in Central Bosnia and Sarajevo, supported the vision of a multiethnic and indivisible Bosnia, while Boban, who was from West Herzegovina, advocated the creation of Herceg-Bosna, an independent Croat state with Mostar as its capital.[40] Strongly supported by Croatian president Franjo Tudjman, who advocated the partition of Bosnia between Croats and Serbs, Boban purged the HDZ of its moderate ranks and directed the Bosnian Croat Army (HVO) to establish control over Croat majority parts of Bosnia in the latter half of the year, setting off a number of small skirmishes with Bosniak forces. Tensions between Bosniaks and Croats were further exacerbated by the publication of the Vance-Owen peace plan in January 1993. The Vance-Owen plan envisioned Bosnia as a decentralized state with ten provinces, a decision that fueled militarized attempts to create "facts on the ground" which would justify competing ethno-territorial maps.[41] In April 1993 an all-out war erupted following a major HVO offensive in Central Bosnia. This conflict lasted until the following spring, when HDZ and the Bosnian government signed the Washington Agreement, which ended the war and established (at least formally, if not in practice) the Bosniak-Croat Federation.

Brčko and Mostar from the Yugoslav Period to the End of the War

In many ways both Brčko and Mostar embodied the Yugoslav-era ideology of *bratstvo i jedinstvo* (brotherhood and unity) of national peoples and minorities. Brčko is located in northeast Bosnia south of the Sava River, which forms the border between Bosnia and Croatia. It is situated at the eastern end of the Posavina ("by the Sava River") region in Bosnia. This is an area of rich farmland and important east-west and north-south transportation crossroads in the region. By the middle of the nineteenth century Brčko was a key export point for agricultural products from Bosnia, especially the region's famous fresh and dried plums, which were shipped across Europe and even as far as the Americas.[42] Brčko's economy continued to have a heavy agricultural basis throughout the Yugoslav period, though a number of smaller manufacturing concerns were also established. Prewar Brčko was a multiethnic municipality of nearly ninety thousand residents, of whom 44 percent identified themselves as Bosniak, 25 percent Croat, 21 percent Serb, 7 percent Yugoslav, and 3 percent Other in the 1991 census.[43] As elsewhere in Bosnia, Brčko town was more ethnically mixed, both residentially and socially, while the smaller outlying villages were predominately monoethnic.[44] Brčko residents are often quick to note that their town, like nearby Tuzla, had a reputation for being a stronghold of antinationalist *Jugoslovenstvo* (Yugoslavism) prior to the war.

Mostar is the primary city in Herzegovina, the southwestern region of Bosnia, which borders Croatia's Dalmatian coast. Straddling the turquoise blue Neretva River, Mostar has also been an important transportation hub in the region. For centuries its famed bridge, which was built in 1566 by the Ottomans, was the primary crossing point over the Neretva. During the Yugoslav period Mostar developed rapidly as several large industrial concerns were established in the city, the biggest of these being the aluminum producer Aluminij and the military manufacturer Soko, which together employed more than eight thousand workers.[45] The city also benefited from a large number of tourists, both domestic and international, who flocked to its historic center and Medjugorje, the booming nearby Catholic pilgrimage site.[46] Like Brčko, Mostar was one of the most diverse cities in prewar Bosnia. In 1991, 35 percent of the municipality's 126,000 residents identified themselves as Bosniak, 34 percent Croat, 19 percent Serb, 10 percent Yugoslav, and 2 percent Other. Mostar also boasted the reputation of having one of the highest rates of mixed marriages in the former Yugoslavia, which contributed to the relatively large percentage of people who embraced a Yugoslav rather than ethnic identity in the city prior to the war.[47]

Mirroring state-level results in Bosnia, the 1990 elections produced a nationalist ruling coalition in both towns. In Mostar nationalist parties captured nearly two-thirds of the seats in the municipal assembly—led by HDZ and SDA, which between themselves took just under half the votes.[48] In Brčko nonnationalist parties performed somewhat better, receiving more than 35 percent of the vote—one of the highest percentages in the country—led by the SKBiH-SDP, which garnered a plurality. However, following orders from their respective leaders at the state level HDZ, SDA, and SDS excluded SKBiH-SDP from the ruling coalition.[49] As elsewhere in Bosnia these nationalist coalitions quickly unraveled due to mutual distrust and inability to reach political compromises. The path of social polarization and war differed in each town, however, which, as I discuss in chapter 4, has had important consequences for postwar peacebuilding.

Brčko, along with the neighboring town of Bijeljina, was one of the first cities to experience the onslaught of violence and ethnic cleansing that erupted in Bosnia in spring 1992. As noted above, the process of political disintegration in Bosnia began in earnest the previous September, when SAOs were established in Serb-majority municipalities east and west of Brčko. In response HDZ leadership in Brčko began procuring arms from Croatia and set up their own Krizni Štab (Crisis Staff) in the southwestern corner of the municipality later that month. Before the end of the year SDA also established a separate headquarters in the village of Gornji Rahić and began to recruit and train volunteers for their own defense forces.[50] Brčko's local SDS leadership remained relatively passive during this period. But this changed in February 1992 when, under the orders of Karadžić, they began calling for the ethnic division of Brčko municipality. At the same time the JNA garrison stationed in Brčko began recruiting, training, and arming local Serb volunteers. However attempts to create a Brčko-based militia met with little enthusiasm outside of outlying Serb villages. Consequently a decision was made in April 1992—by whom exactly remains unclear—to invite militias from Serbia and Bijeljina to cleanse downtown Brčko of non-Serbs and establish a corridor linking the western and eastern SAOs in Bosnia. These units attacked the city on the May 1, three days after SDA leadership rejected SDS and HDZ proposals to partition Brčko at a municipal assembly meeting.

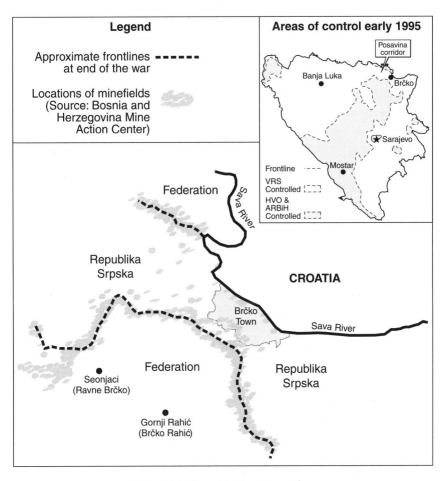

Figure 5. Brčko and the Posavina corridor

Following the attack on the downtown, Bosniaks and Croats re-treated to the southern villages of Brčko where they set up parallel gov-ernment administrations (Ravne Brčko and Brčko Rahić, respectively) and organized a joint defense against Bosnian Serb forces. After the first year of fighting little territory changed hands and both sides settled into trench warfare, with extensive minefields and fortified bunkers, more reminiscent of World War I.[51] Despite several attempts by the ARBiH and local HVO forces to break these lines, the VRS clung tenaciously to this narrow, strategic corridor of territory running through the northern half of Brčko (see figure 5). Unlike elsewhere in Bosnia, relations between Croats and Bosniaks remained peaceful in the Brčko area—even as belligerent emissaries arrived from Mostar and Sarajevo and war between the two communities spread across Central Bosnia and Herzegovina from spring 1993 until February 1994.[52] Indeed, significant numbers of Bosniaks continued to serve in HVO units in Posavina throughout the war, motivated in large part by monthly salaries of several hundred Deutschmarks (in contrast, most frontline soldiers in the ARBiH received no wages).

Recounting Mostar's wartime history is a more complex endeavor than Brčko. The earliest armed clashes took place in February 1992 between the JNA—which was using bases in and around the city as launching pads for attacks on Dubrovnik and other Croatian towns in Dalmatia—and local Croat police reserves.[53] Despite attempts to defuse the situation, including cease-fire negotiations and a ten-thousand-person peace march in downtown Mostar the following month, the JNA attacked the city in April following a large truck bomb that caused several dozen casualties. While this initial conflict was largely between the JNA and its SDS allies on one hand, and HVO and Croatian Defense Forces (HOS)—which was the military arm of the Croatian Party of Rights (HSP)—on the other, a large number of Bosniaks fought with the latter and the commander of the HVO in Mostar at the time was also Muslim.[54] In June Serb forces withdrew from the city, though they continued to shell Mostar continuously from the surrounding hills. At this time most ethnic Serb residents of Mostar also fled to Eastern Herzegovina or Serbia.

The second stage of the war in Mostar was the outbreak of hostilities between Croat and Bosniak forces, which began when HVO launched attacks on East Mostar in May 1993. Relations between the two erstwhile allies had deteriorated over the previous year as HDZ proceeded to take over political control of Mostar—which it considered the capital of the secessionist Herceg-Bosna parastate that it was establishing in Bosnia—and its military arm, HVO, moved to disarm HOS units and expel their Bosniak members, most of whom joined the ARBiH or closely aligned paramilitary formations. Despite these developments the Bosnian government was desperate to avoid armed conflict with Croats in Mostar since Herzegovina was the main route through which weapons could be smuggled to its pitifully armed military forces. But the outbreak of war in Central Bosnia ended any chance that peace could prevail between the two sides in the city.

The two conflicts devastated Mostar, tearing apart shared life in the city through "urbacide":[55] few Serb families remained; tens of thousands of Bosniaks were ethnically cleansed from the western portion of the town, while several thousand Croats east of the Neretva River fled or were driven out of their homes;[56] a military frontline running through the downtown divided Croat-controlled West Mostar from Bosniak forces on the east side; and East Mostar and the central core of the city—including the Stari Most—had been reduced to rubble by HVO artillery barrages and heavy street fighting. The Washington Agreement, which was signed in March 1994, brought an end to this conflict, though citizens of the city continued to suffer from occasional artillery bombardments from VRS forces on the eastern hills until the end of the war. As part of the agreement the European Union also promised to undertake a two-year mission, beginning in July 1994, which would assist with the physical and political reconstruction of the city.

Ending the War and Reconstituting a Country: The Dayton Peace Agreement

The Washington Agreement was a key military and diplomatic turning point in the war. Freed from their own conflict, Croats and Bosniaks turned their attention toward regaining ground captured by Serb forces at the beginning of the war. Both sides also received an influx of weapons from abroad, and military training from current and former U.S. officers.[57] As the VRS began to lose ground its commander, Ratko Mladić, tightened the noose on the remaining UN safe havens behind RS lines (Goražde, Foča, Srebrenica, and Žepa), culminating in the massacre at Srebrenica in July 1995. The tragic fall of Srebrenica was a second turning point, as it shamed reluctant Western leaders into taking a more active role in ending the war. The following month NATO stepped up airstrikes against VRS communications networks. At the same time the Croatian offensive *Oluja* (Storm) drove out Serb forces and civilians from the Krajina regions of Croatia and Bosnia.[58] Faced with rapid territorial losses to Croat and

Bosniak armed forces, as well as increasing pressure by Serbian president Slobodan Milošević to cut a deal in order to relieve sanctions that were crippling his country's economy, the RS was forced back to the negotiating table.

Several weeks of intense shuttle diplomacy by a State Department team led by Richard Holbrooke produced a cease-fire and signing of an Agreed Basic Principles document in Geneva on September 8, 1995, which established general parameters for peace talks. Prior to the beginning of the talks that November at Dayton, Ohio, Bosnian president Alija Izetbegović warned American negotiators that territorial concerns— "the map"—would be the most difficult issue to resolve.[59] This proved to be true, and the dispute over control of Brčko in particular threatened to scuttle the entire peace agreement that had been hammered out over three grueling weeks of negotiations. At the last minute, and under intense pressure from the Americans who were threatening to close down the talks and declare them a failure, Izetbegović and Milošević agreed to set aside the issue of control of Brčko to be determined by international arbitration within a year after signing the Dayton Peace Agreement (DPA).[60]

The DPA created a complex consociational system with extensive ethno-territorial autonomy, which has been described as a "classic example of consociational settlement" and "an ideal-typical consociational democracy."[61] The resulting state consists of two entities, the RS and the Bosniak-Croat Federation. The Federation is further divided into eight relatively homogenous and two ethnically heterogeneous cantons, with the latter two in turn devolving significant political authority to their municipalities (see figure 6).[62] Finally, there is the Brčko District, a post-Dayton construct that is shared by the entities territorially but possesses its own autonomous local government. Under this highly decentralized ethno-territorial framework nearly all political authority is possessed by the entities, prompting one scholar to wryly observe that Dayton Bosnia "seems to be essentially a customs union with a foreign ministry, thus indeed a government with no authority within its territory."[63]

In addition to ethno-territorial autonomy, at the state level multiple consociational measures guarantee the participation of the three constituent peoples in Bosnia's political process. There are two executive bodies:

a collective three-person Presidency consisting of one Serb elected from the Republika Srpska and one Croat and Bosniak from the Federation, and a Council of Ministers which must include at least one member from each group. The state legislature is bicameral. The House of Peoples contains fifteen members (five from each constituent people) appointed by their respective entity legislatures; the House of Representatives is elected through proportional representation with fourteen seats guaranteed to the RS and twenty-eight to the Federation. Finally, each community can

Figure 6. Dayton Bosnia

invoke veto powers on issues they deem to be of "vital national interest." Despite numerous reforms that have strengthened state institutions in the past decade this broad consociational framework still defines political relations in Bosnia.

International Peacebuilding Activities in Postwar Bosnia

The DPA also assigned an extensive role for international organizations in the postwar peacebuilding process. To begin, a large (about sixty-thousand-person) peacekeeping intervention force (IFOR) under NATO command was authorized to enforce the cease-fire, separate the wartime armies, and oversee their demobilization.[64] At the end of IFOR's one-year mandate a follow-up stabilization force (SFOR) was authorized. Though originally hewing to a minimalist peacekeeping role, SFOR gradually expanded its mission to include the arrest of indicted war criminals and support for the implementation of the DPA—especially regarding returns and freedom of movement—which was being obstructed by nationalist opposition. SFOR lasted until 2004, at which point it was followed by a small European peacekeeping contingent (EUFOR), which continues to monitor the security situation in Bosnia to this day.

The DPA also made provisions for a robust civilian peacebuilding presence. These organizations have generally acted with a great degree of independence in Bosnia, pursuing their own respective peacebuilding mandates. Foremost among the veritable alphabet soup of organizations have been (1) OSCE, which organized elections in Bosnia until 2002 and has also been involved in monitoring human rights conditions; (2) UNHCR, which has overseen the return of refugees and internally displaced persons (IDPs); (3) the United Nations Mission in Bosnia and Herzegovina (UNMIBH), in particular its International Police Task Force (IPTF), which conducted police reform and monitored human rights until 2002, when it was replaced by the European Union Police Mission (EUPM); and (4) OHR, which is charged with monitoring implementation of the DPA. Other organizations that have had a significant role in the postwar reconstruction process include the World Bank, International Monetary Fund (IMF), United States Agency for International

Development (USAID), and the EU's Customs and Financial Assistance Office (CAFAO), which have distributed international aid and pursued economic reforms in the country.

Unlike other peacebuilding missions, the UN has not played the lead civilian peacebuilding role in Bosnia. Instead this task fell to OHR, an ad hoc institution overseen by a Peace Implementation Council (PIC) consisting of more than fifty member states. In practice OHR has often maintained a significant degree of autonomy in agenda setting and policy execution from the PIC, especially under the activist leadership of High Representatives Wolfgang Petritsch (1999–2002) and Paddy Ashdown (2002–6). In the beginning though, the language of the DPA provided clear limits on OHR's mandate, declaring it responsible for "coordinating the activities of the civilian organizations and agencies in Bosnia," while also respecting their "autonomy within their spheres of operation," and refraining from "interfering" with military operations.[65] This weak mandate reflected, in large part, American insistence that OHR be given little authority over other civilian organizations and no influence in military affairs.[66]

Postwar peacebuilding in Bosnia can be roughly divided into three periods. The first two years were characterized by limited goals and a lack of on-the-ground capacity—with the exception of Mostar and the EUAM mission.[67] NATO, for instance, focused on demobilization of armed forces and controlling the Inter-Entity Boundary Line (IEBL) which divided the two entities. Meanwhile civilian organizations prioritized physical reconstruction and holding national (1996) and local (1997) elections. Little progress was made on returns, which were fiercely resisted by local politicians. As it became clear that nationalist obstruction was hindering efforts to make even minimal progress toward peacebuilding goals, a consensus began to emerge that this passive approach was doing little to reduce political instability and the possibility of renewed conflict. Starting in the summer of 1997 the first signs of a change in course started to come into view. British military forces began undertaking operations to apprehend figures indicted for war crimes by the ICTY. And OHR and SFOR provided overt support for political initiatives undertaken by Biljana Plavšić and her allies in the RS, who broke with hardline elements in SDS that spring. Then, at a December 1997 PIC meeting in Bonn member states granted OHR wide-reaching powers to make "binding decisions"—including the ability to impose legislation and dismiss elected officials if deemed necessary.[68]

The introduction of these "Bonn powers" marked a decisive shift to a second, activist phase of intervention in Bosnia, during which time OHR steadily took on a greater role in planning, coordinating, and implementing policies. During this period international officials pursued a two-track peacebuilding agenda. The first was to more aggressively challenge the authority of those who were obstructing implementation of the DPA. The second High Representative, Carlos Westendorp (1997–99), used his new powers to sack officials—including elected politicians—who blocked returns and resisted the implementation of political agreements, a policy that would accelerate under his successors. Taking a greater role in ensuring implementation required an expanded on-the-ground presence as well, as it was necessary to "develop a localized power capacity to challenge the writ of the ethnocratic order ensconced locally by ethnic cleansing and wartime criminality."[69]

The second focus of this period was a concerted effort to create and develop more effective central institutions (statebuilding). Initially under Westendorp the use of the Bonn powers to facilitate statebuilding was limited to basic reforms such as the introduction of a single state currency and common license plates.[70] His successor, Wolfgang Petritsch, went even further in his efforts to develop state institutions that would contribute to the "functional integration" of the two entities.[71] This process reached its apotheosis during the term of the fourth High Representative, Paddy Ashdown, when the two entity armies were unified, a statewide tax authority established, and the judicial system overhauled to increase state competencies.

This activist peacebuilding and statebuilding agenda was not without its critics, several of which argued that Bosnia's problems stemmed less from nationalist politicians or the state's institutional structures than the unhealthy and outsized influence that unelected international officials played in the political process.[72] In particular they asserted that OHR frequently overstepped its authority by imposing laws and dismissing democratically elected Bosnian politicians who resisted its mandates. The result was that Bosnia more resembled an international protectorate than a sovereign state. As long as OHR and other international organizations continued to interfere in what were essentially domestic political considerations, this line of argument went, Bosnia's elites had little incentive to pursue difficult but necessary political compromises.

In January 2006 a new High Representative closely associated with this point of view, Christian Schwarz-Schilling, replaced Paddy Ashdown, thus marking a transition to the third, and current, phase of international intervention in Bosnia. Schwarz-Schilling immediately declared that OHR would no longer attempt to dictate politics in the country. Instead Bosnia's politicians would have to take "ownership" of the political process themselves and find compromises on reforms necessary for membership into the EU. This change in policy proved to be an immediate disaster. A previously negotiated agreement on constitutional changes unraveled and was defeated in a vote in Parliament in April 2006. Plans for police reform also collapsed in acrimony that summer. The politicians most responsible for these failures—Haris Silajdžić and Milorad Dodik—parlayed their opposition to these reform measures into electoral victory six months later after conducting sharply divisive nationalist campaigns.[73] In an abrupt about-face Schwarz-Schilling was sacked in 2007, but a weakened OHR has irrevocably lost the ability to advance further peacebuilding reforms since then. Meanwhile, as noted at the beginning of this chapter, Bosnia has fallen into a downward spiral of political stagnation and mounting nationalist rhetoric, with political elites now openly challenging the political structures established at Dayton.[74]

These recent developments have weakened the argument that Bosnia's problems are primarily a product of the perversities of international intervention. Indeed, without internationally imposed reforms such as the introduction of a common currency and license plates, and the multiyear reform and monitoring of police forces, the development of social and political conditions necessary for even the modest number of ethnically cleansed people who have returned to their prewar homes would never have occurred. Yet these and other measures have typically been resisted by leaders of each community in whichever entity, canton, or municipality they dominate politically and demographically. What has emerged from the precipitous decline in the political situation in recent years is a renewed appreciation for the problems inherent to Dayton Bosnia's ethno-territorial consociational framework, which has institutionalized ethnic divisions at all levels of the system, enabled political obstructionism, and fueled the destructive pursuit of exclusive control over still contested territories.[75] As former High Representative Miroslav Lájčak (2007–9) has argued, "Bosnia has become a prisoner of Dayton."[76] It is these institutions—and the integrative alternative developed in Brčko—to which we now turn.

3

Institutions

As noted in the previous chapter, Bosnia's ethno-territorial consociational compact is the product of contentious negotiations between the three warring parties that culminated in the DPA in 1995. Mostar is the embodiment of this model, as there alone has it been comprehensively extended down to the level of a single city, the scale at which everyday interaction takes place and is mediated by political institutions. Conversely, in many ways Brčko is the antithesis of the ethno-territorial approach adopted in Bosnia. As I outline below Mostar's institutional framework has not contributed to peace in the postwar period. Instead, is has hardened ethnic divisions and bolstered the position of the most obstructionist political elements in the city. In contrast the integrative approach pursued in Brčko has proven to be more successful to date in mitigating conflict and creating an effective multiethnic government. This chapter concludes with some more general observations about the ineffective and illiberal aspects of ethno-territorial forms of consociationalism in Mostar and Bosnia more generally.

Mostar under the Interim Statute

Mostar at the end of the war was a completely partitioned city, separated into Bosniak and Croat halves by the Neretva River in the northern and southern stretches, and the former military frontline running along the Boulevard of the National Revolution and Šantić Street in the center of the city. Parallel political regimes and public utilities and services had been established, and communication between the two halves of the city was almost nonexistent. The task facing the incoming EU mission in the city was, in short, daunting. The Memorandum of Understanding signed by the EU and the two sides in July 1994 was, in contrast, ambitious. It charged the EUAM with a series of reconstruction "aims" and "principles" that would lead to democratic elections and the re-creation of a "single, self-sustaining and multiethnic" city administration before the end of its two-year mandate.[1] By the end of the EUAM's first year physical reconstruction efforts were moving forward. Progress toward political reunification, however, was much slower. It wasn't until early 1995 when an advisory group consisting of West Mostar mayor Mijo Brajković, East Mostar mayor Safet Oručević, Milan Bodiroga (representing the interests of the remaining ethnic Serbs in the city), and other local and regional figures was established and negotiations on a unified city administration began in earnest.[2]

Prior to the peace talks at Dayton the three sides agreed on a set of general principles for an Interim Statute that would establish a unified city administration. As spelled out by an annex to the DPA, Mostar would be organized according to a two-level municipal system. First, the entire territory of prewar Mostar would be unified under a joint city administration responsible for urban planning, infrastructure, public transportation, and the city airport. The joint city administration was also given responsibility over whatever finance, tax, and economic policies were not regulated by Federation or cantonal law. Second, Mostar would be divided into six separate city-municipalities, which would have jurisdiction over all other "local responsibilities."[3] Real administrative power, in other words, would reside with those who controlled the municipalities.[4]

One key point of contention that remained unresolved was the size of a proposed central zone, which would be directly administered by the city. This was a highly divisive issue with territorial, political, and symbolic significance because the central zone represented "the only part of the city not under the management of a Croat or Bosniak majority municipality, but solely under the administration of the unified city administration. As such, the normal functioning of the central zone would reinforce the authority of the city administration."[5] Bosniaks advocated an expansive central zone that would encompass Mostar's urban core, including parts of West Mostar. Croats were opposed to the whole idea of a seventh, shared municipal unit in the center of the city, but recognizing that they could not stop its introduction insisted that its territory be limited to the Bosniak-controlled portions of Mostar east of the former military front line.[6]

After two months of intense haggling following Dayton, EUAM head Hans Koschnick, in his position as final arbiter of the negotiations, issued a decree delineating the size of the central zone on February 7, 1996. Though smaller than called for by Bosniaks it was still substantial, and extended into West Mostar in several key places. Koschnick's decision was immediately denounced by HDZ. Within minutes rioters from West Mostar occupied and trashed EUAM's offices at the Hotel Ero. Outside, Koschnick's armored car was surrounded and attacked with rocks by an angry mob while West Mostar police stood by. He remained trapped in the vehicle for over an hour until IFOR troops finally arrived and broke up the protests. Following these attacks Italy, which had just taken over the EU Presidency, arranged an emergency summit in Rome. At this summit the EU acquiesced to Croat demands to decrease the size of the central zone.

The Interim Statute, which was published following the Rome conference, was a complex consociational settlement that divided Mostar into six ethnically organized municipal districts—three Bosniak (North, Stari Grad, and Southeast) and three Croat (West, Southwest, and South)—and the small central zone (see figure 7).[7] Above this was the joint city administration with the limited powers previously outlined. The executive office of the city administration consisted of a mayor and deputy mayor, each from a different community (i.e., one Bosniak and one Croat), who swapped positions every six months. Composition of both the city council and individual municipal councils were determined by a rigid quota system based on the prewar population in Mostar, which meant that no single ethnic group would be able to obtain a majority. The thirty seats of the joint city council were divided equally among Bosniaks,

Croats, and Others—the latter category consisting of ethnic Serbs, Roma, or mixed heritage residents—with twelve seats elected from a citywide list and three from each of the six municipalities.[8] In similar fashion the councils of the city municipalities were also apportioned ethnically according to the prewar population, which theoretically precluded either Croats or Bosniaks from obtaining a majority in five out of the six municipality councils.[9] Finally a vital interest clause ensured that legislation could only be passed with the majority support of Bosniak and Croat deputies at both the city and municipal levels.

In theory these various consociational power-sharing measures insured the need for consensus. In practice they promoted political obstructionism and institutionalized the ethno-territorial division of the city. As the 2003 report from OHR's Commission for Reforming the City of Mostar ruefully observed: "Unfortunately, virtually all of the provisions of the Interim Statute of the City of Mostar remained mere declarations on paper, and none were implemented in accordance with the original intentions contained in the Statute."[10]

There were several reasons for this. One problem was that the rigid electoral quotas did not reflect the demographic or political realities on the ground. As a consequence of the war the presence of ethnic Serbs in Mostar had been dramatically reduced as most families either left voluntarily or were driven from their homes. Moreover, OHR estimated that less than six thousand had returned to the city by the end of 2003.[11] Croat and Bosniak parties quickly learned to game the system by promoting token Serb candidates to stand for election under their banners thereby capturing these seats for themselves. Given their dependence on the parties for their position, such figures had little independence or political power. Thus while on paper the Interim Statute gave Serbs a meaningful role in the political process—based on their prewar demographic presence in the city—this never translated in practice and their influence remained marginal.

A second issue was that the Interim Statute did not define what constituted a vital interest, thus this veto mechanism could be used to block virtually any decisions made by the joint city administration. Consequently the "city council failed to exercise properly even the limited responsibilities accorded to it."[12] Indeed, the council rarely convened to debate or vote on pressing issues. At one point it went a year without meeting.[13]

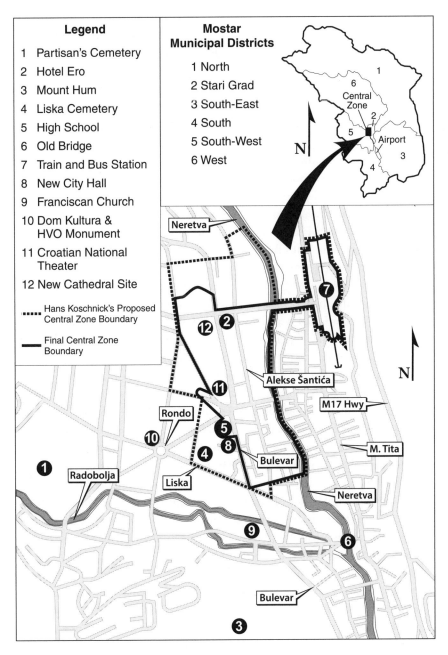

Legend

1 Partisan's Cemetery
2 Hotel Ero
3 Mount Hum
4 Liska Cemetery
5 High School
6 Old Bridge
7 Train and Bus Station
8 New City Hall
9 Franciscan Church
10 Dom Kultura & HVO Monument
11 Croatian National Theater
12 New Cathedral Site

····· Hans Koschnick's Proposed Central Zone Boundary

—— Final Central Zone Boundary

Mostar Municipal Districts

1 North
2 Stari Grad
3 South-East
4 South
5 South-West
6 West

Neretva

N

Central Zone

Airport

N

Neretva

Alekse Šantića

M17 Hwy

M. Tita

Rondo

Bulevar

Radobolja

Liska

Neretva

Bulevar

Figure 7. Postwar Mostar

Not surprisingly, then, the central zone—and the common city institutions that were supposed to be established within it—never functioned as intended. Instead Mostar remained a politically divided city with parallel governing institutions housed in different buildings and funded by separate budgets.

There was a different problem at the municipality level where HDZ refused to implement the vital interest clause in municipalities it controlled, thus shutting out Bosniak councilors from the decision-making process. After years of obstruction by Croat municipalities OHR finally issued a decision imposing this mechanism, though to little effect.[14] The refusal to implement the vital interest veto was part of a broader pattern of obstruction within Croat controlled municipalities. Following the 1996 elections HDZ announced the formation of a "Union of Croat Municipalities" that would jointly administer the three Croat majority municipalities without Bosniak input: "We will make an association of these three Croat municipalities into one. The municipal council will be for the communities of Croat municipalities . . . to administer a Croat territory according to the measures of the Croat man."[15] This plan ran in direct opposition to the Interim Statute, which internationals in Mostar quickly pointed out, therefore it was never formally instituted. Informally, however, HDZ did go about governing the three municipalities precisely as if they were a single entity. Indeed, little effort was made to hide this fact, as their municipal offices were all located within the same building in West Mostar.[16]

In addition to consolidating governance of these three municipalities, HDZ and its allies also initiated a number of projects aimed at further Croatizing West Mostar's spaces and thus cementing control over their half of the city. Street names were changed, with prominent Croatian politicians, artists, military heroes, and historical figures replacing Yugoslav-era names—and the color of the signs changed from blue to red of the Croatian flag. Monuments to fallen HVO soldiers were erected, as was a towering cross atop Mt. Hum, which overlooks the entire city. And massive construction projects, such as the rebuilt Franciscan church with a 107-meter bell tower, a Croatian national theater, and a new cathedral, were initiated along the former frontline.[17] Meanwhile prominent Yugoslav-era monuments such as Partisan's cemetery were left to fall into disrepair, and other significant prewar public spaces, like the city's Dom Kultura (House of Culture), were repurposed as exclusively Croat venues.[18]

The 2004 OHR-Imposed Institutional Reforms

In response to the ongoing failure to establish a functional city government, OHR Mostar began outlining a process for reforming the Interim Statute in 2002. However the new High Representative, Paddy Ashdown, brushed aside these plans for a year, fearing that they would interfere with countrywide economic reforms he was pursuing at the time.[19] Finally in April 2003 OHR Mostar was given the green light to establish an official commission, composed of local political elites with negotiations mediated by OHR officials, which was tasked with drafting a new statue that would provide for a unified city administration. After talks bogged down that summer Ashdown issued a decision creating a second commission chaired by a special envoy, Norbert Winterstein.[20] That December the commission issued its report, accompanied by a proposed draft statute. When the Mostar city council refused to adopt the plan Ashdown again issued a decision imposing the statute in early 2004.[21]

The new city statute abolished the administrative responsibilities of the six city-municipalities, thereby reestablishing Mostar as a single unit of government and strengthening the authority of the central city administration. Somewhat confusingly and contradictory to these aims, however, the city-municipalities have been reconstituted as "city areas" with city administration branch offices.[22] Though the statute declares that the "sole purpose" of these city areas is to improve the range of services available to city residents in their own neighborhoods, the practical effect is the informal perpetuation of these former municipal units as (ethnic) spaces of administrative governance. The city-municipalities also continue to serve as electoral districts, with three delegates from each unit (eighteen) elected to the council (and the other seventeen chosen through citywide elections), thus preserving the organization of Mostar along ethno-territorial lines as a constituent element of the electoral system.[23] As a result, seventeen of the eighteen councilors elected through municipal constituencies in the 2008 elections belonged to parties representing the demographic majority in East and West Mostar, further perpetuating ethnic division in the city.[24]

The new statute also preserves most of the key consociational power-sharing measures found in the Interim Statute. The president and vice president of the council still must come from different ethnic groups, as must the council president and city mayor. National interests and the need for grand coalitions are also secured through both vital interest veto rights and the requirement that all core decisions—that is, the budget, (indirect) election and dismissal of the mayor, voting on symbolic issues such as street names, and amendments to the statute—also must be passed by two-thirds majority. Finally, the previous quota system for the city council has been replaced by a complicated formula that specifies both a minimum (four) and maximum (fifteen) number of representatives (out of a total of thirty-five) from each of the city's three constituent peoples, thus ensuring that no one group can dominate the council. However Serbs remain such a marginal demographic presence in Mostar that they never receive more than their guaranteed minimum. In practice, consequently, the new electoral rules have established a soft quota system resulting in a city council composed of fifteen Bosniaks, fifteen Croats, four Serbs, and one representative from a nonconstituent community. The mayor is indirectly elected by a majority of the city council, thus ensuring—in theory—the need for cross-ethnic support.

Continued Political and Social Division

Unification of the city under this new statute is, to put it most generously, still very much a work in progress. A more realistic assessment is that it has largely been a failure due to resistance by powerful political interests and inadequate oversight of implementation by international officials. While there is now a single city administration, and parallel institutions have been officially abolished, the "unification of public services [has] stalled at the formal level, with the old divided services under a common name but still operating separately."[25] Additionally, the city's budget remains informally divided, as the rival nationalist parties have continued the practice of utilizing parallel accounts within municipal departments.[26] As the head of SDP in Mostar told me, "The statute is not something that has been accepted and works in practice, it exists only on paper."[27]

One of the more salient illustrations of this fact is that city authorities still lack control over certain neighborhoods and activities. In the former Old Town municipality surrounding the Stari Most, for example, few businesses—which profit greatly from tourism—pay taxes to the central city administration. Nor do police regularly patrol that part of the city. Instead this neighborhood continues to be controlled by politically connected syndicates running protection rackets.[28] One of these rackets is led by Semir Drljević, the former head of the Old Town municipality prior to his removal by OHR in 2000. Currently president of the "Club of Jumpers from the Stari Most" and the local Bosniak war veterans association, Drljević takes great delight in using his control over the annual bridge jumping contest to thumb his nose at Ljubo Bešlić, Mostar's ethnic Croat mayor.

For example, while observing the preparation of festivities for the 2007 jumping contest—the 441 Tradicionalni Viteški Skokovi sa Starog Mosta (441st Traditional Knights Jump from the Old Bridge)—I noticed that a new word, *Viteški*, meaning "Knight," had been appended to paraphernalia advertising the event. The number 441 was a reference to the age of the bridge, which was built in 1566. The previous year the annual contest was advertised as the 440 Tradicionalni Skokovi sa Starog Mosta (440th Traditional Jump from the Old Bridge). Discussing this curious word change with bridge jumpers and former wartime fighters, I discovered that the 441st Viteška was one of the names of the ARBiH brigade that fought against Bosnian Croat forces along the frontline running through downtown Mostar during the war. Moreover, Drljević was one of the commanders of this brigade during the war. The renaming of the diving contest by Drljević and other organizers was thus a conscious ethno-territorial strategy that marked the bridge jumping event and the place in which it was held, the Old Town, as exclusively Bosniak space and hence unwelcome to ethnic Croats in the city. Further reinforcing the point was the presence of a large flag of the wartime Republic of Bosnia and Herzegovina draped from a nearby bridge on the day of the contest.

Shortly before the contest a local web portal predominately read by Croats in Mostar ran a column highlighting Drljević's wartime history and the significance of the name change. This generated a lively discussion on its online forums, and in coffee shops and bars in West Mostar, with Drljević's appropriation of the contest for ethno-territorial purposes precipitating a negative response toward the event and Bosniak political figures on the "other side" of town.[29] Consequently not a single ethnic Croat from the city participated in the diving contest, and the mayor and other prominent HDZ officials from Mostar ultimately boycotted the event. Meanwhile Drljević's action was tacitly approved through quiet, approving jokes and comments amongst many residents of the Old Town and East Mostar.

Mostar's politicians have also proven unwilling or unable to adapt to the new power-sharing system, rendering the city "increasingly ungovernable."[30] Political deadlock gripped the city for more than a year following municipal elections in 2008 as Croat and Bosniak parties were unable to reach agreement on the election of a new mayor, division of control over municipal departments, or a city budget for 2009. The impasse arose because HDZ reneged on a 2004 deal with SDA to support the latter party's candidate for mayor following the 2008 elections.[31] Eventually OHR was forced to step in and issue a decision ensuring that city monies were disbursed to maintain the continued operation of basic services such as the police, hospitals, and fire department.[32] HDZ's Ljubo Beslić was finally reelected mayor of Mostar in December 2009 following procedural changes to the city council voting process again imposed by OHR.[33]

The city continues to be plagued by political dysfunctionality to this day. Indeed it was the only municipality in the country in which local elections were not held in 2012 due to the inability of city councilors to agree on necessary changes to the electoral system following a ruling by Bosnia's Constitutional Court that the use of the former city municipalities as electoral districts was unconstitutional because of large differences in population across the six units.[34] Following the expiration of their governing mandates that November the mayor and city council informally agreed to continue working in their former capacity in the absence of new elections. However, this decision was countermanded by the High Representative, Valentin Inzko, who sent government officials a letter enjoining them from any decision making activity until they resolved the dispute.[35] Thus at the time of writing Mostar remained trapped in a politically absurd netherworld with no legitimate local government in place.

Another telling example of Mostar's continued political dysfunctionality is the opulent new City Hall, which was built along the Boulevard of the National Revolution on the site of a Yugoslav-era elementary school. Shortly before its scheduled opening in March 2012 a monument to Croatian soldiers who died during the war was erected on the grounds next to the building—with mayor Beslić's approval—prompting Bosniak councilors and department heads to boycott the ceremony and all subsequent events in the building.[36] Weeks later a large, unauthorized monument to Bosnian war veterans was erected in the middle of the night. In response the mayor and Croat politicians boycotted work in the new building as well.[37] Meant to symbolize Mostar's progress toward political reunification, the padlocked doors of the empty City Hall instead stood as an appropriate metaphor for just how little had been accomplished to date.

Given all of these problems it is not surprising that residents of Mostar have little confidence in local institutions. In a 2008 poll that asked citizens to identify the institutions they trusted the most, more than half of the respondents from Mostar (52 percent) chose none of the listed options. Trust in the local police (14 percent) was especially low—and contrasted greatly with Brčko where 69 percent of respondents identified police as the most trusted institution in the District.[38] Since then pessimism in Mostar has only increased. In a 2012 poll of city residents—conducted for OHR and other international organizations in Bosnia to gauge public sentiment following the Constitutional Court decision and city hall crisis—77 percent of respondents indicated that the situation in Mostar was worse than in 2004. Moreover 83 percent of those polled stated that they "do not trust at all" or "mainly do not trust" local authorities in Mostar.[39]

The Arbitral Tribunal Process and Early Institutional Reforms in Brčko

As noted in the previous chapter, the warring parties were unable to resolve Brčko's status during the Dayton peace talks, instead agreeing to submit the dispute to international arbitration. Roberts Owen, an American lawyer who had advised the State Department during peace negotiations and drafted the bulk of the DPA, was chosen to be the chief arbitrator of a three-person team, along with one representative each from Bosnia's two entities. The task of the Arbitral Tribunal was to rule on the "the disputed portion of the Inter-Entity Boundary Line [IEBL] in the Brčko area."[40] Throughout 1996 the RS vacillated between grudging cooperation and refusal to participate in the proceedings, causing Owen to delay a ruling until February 1997. Meanwhile local authorities in RS Brčko obstructed all attempts by non-Serbs to return to their prewar homes. In the weeks leading up to a decision leaders from both the RS and Bosniak parties threatened the resumption of war and "chaos in Bosnia" if their side was not awarded Brčko town.[41] Recognizing the continued intensity of passions Owen issued a First Award that delayed a final decision on the dispute for another year and directed OHR to appoint an international "supervisor" over the Brčko area to serve for a period of no less than one year.[42]

Neither the RS nor Federation arbitration representatives (Vitomir Popović and Čazim Šadiković, respectively) agreed with Owen's decision—for understandably different reasons. Therefore it and all subsequent awards were written and signed solely by Owen. Remarkably the RS did not dispute this maneuver, which ran contrary to UNCITRAL arbitration rules under which the tribunal was supposedly operating.[43] Owen claimed that a deal was reached at Dayton to suspend the UNCITRAL rules and allow for the presiding arbiter to make a unilateral decision in the absence of agreement among tribunal members and cited a letter by Slobodan Milošević to this effect.[44] The questionable legality of this move led to some discomfort in the international community, but ultimately it was accepted that "power and necessity are sometimes a law unto themselves."[45]

The First Award was an unusual ruling that had significant repercussions for the future of international intervention and peacebuilding in Bosnia, just two of which are highlighted here. First, Owen decided that the tribunal's jurisdiction extended beyond the narrow question of the precise location of the IEBL, the position argued by both the Federation and RS:

> The Tribunal is mindful that the RS has contested this broad view of the Tribunal's authority and has argued strenuously that all the Tribunal may do is fix the final position of the IEBL in the Brčko area. In reality, however, as previously noted, this view seriously understates the scope of this dispute. At Dayton the parties argued—and are continuing to argue—about what laws and political structures are to control the lives of the people of the area, and the Award must be framed in that context.[46]

In placing Brčko under international supervision and calling for the reform of local institutions, Owen made clear his view that the ultimate concern of the tribunal was what kind of political authority would emerge in Brčko, not merely who would control the territory. Second, the decision gave powers and responsibilities to the supervisory regime that were without precedent at the time in Bosnia. Its general mandate from Owen was to oversee "Dayton implementation throughout the Brčko area," and "strengthen local democratic institutions in the same area." Additionally, following municipal elections scheduled for the fall, it was enjoined to create "a multiethnic administration in the Town of Brčko." To facilitate these tasks, the supervisor was given vast powers to "promulgate binding regulations and orders" that would supersede "any conflicting law."[47]

The first supervisor, retired American ambassador Robert Farrand (1997–2000), arrived in Brčko on April 11, 1997. Despite the formal powers he possessed he initially found it difficult to generate progress on returns of Bosniaks and Croats to their homes, or on reforms of governing institutions in RS Brčko. Following the controversial municipal election in RS Brčko that September (discussed in greater detail in chapter 5), OHR set about the task of creating multiethnic institutions. This election, in which prewar Croat and Bosniak residents of RS Brčko were allowed to vote, resulted in a narrow majority for Serb nationalist parties. Farrand decided to use the results as a rough guide for establishing the ethnic composition of the new municipal government. In early October he issued three supervisory orders establishing a new multiethnic administration, police, and judiciary in RS Brčko.[48] Fiercely resisted by SDS, these initial attempts to introduce multiethnic institutions remained little more than declarations on paper until the following spring, when Bosnian Serb opposition parties united with the handful of Croat and Bosniak parliamentarians in the RS National Assembly to elect Milorad Dodik as prime minister of the entity. Working together with Dodik and RS president Biljana Plavšić, OHR Brčko was gradually able to sideline several of the most obstructionist SDS interlocutors in the city (for more on this see, chapters 4 and 5).

Encouraged by this limited success Owen decided to delay a final decision on Brčko's status for one more year in order to give the RS a chance to fulfill its obligations on returns and the creation of multiethnic institutions, with the warning that:

> Given the RS's systematic non-compliance with (indeed, defiance of) the Dayton Accords in the Brčko area for much if not all of 1997, the Tribunal's

final IEBL decision in late 1998 or early 1999 will surely diminish the RS's position in the Brčko area unless the RS by that time has carried the burden of demonstrating very clearly that it has truly reversed course and committed itself to an apparently permanent program of full Dayton compliance and revitalization of the area.[49]

Finally, at the end of this Supplemental Award he put both parties on notice that absent sufficient cooperation by either side, the conversion of the entire prewar Brčko *opština* into a "neutral district" beyond the control of either entity would be "seriously considered."[50]

The Creation of the Brčko District

Roberts Owen was true to his word. A year later, on March 5, 1999, he issued a Final Award declaring that the entire territory of Brčko would become "a new institution, a new multiethnic democratic government to be known as "The Brcko District of Bosnia and Herzegovina" under the exclusive sovereignty of Bosnia and Herzegovina."[51] The two entities would jointly hold the territory of the District in "condominium" but they would have no legal authority within its borders:

> Upon the establishment of the new District, the entire territory, within its boundaries (i.e., the pre-war Brcko Opstina) will thereafter be held in "condominium" by both entities simultaneously: The territory of the RS will encompass the entire Opstina, and so also will the territory of the Federation. Neither entity, however, will exercise any authority within the boundaries of the District, which will administer the area as one unitary government.[52]

Owen noted that RS authorities had continued to obstruct returns and resisted the formation of multiethnic institutions in RS Brčko. Thus failing to show progress required by the Supplemental Award, he had no choice but to "require a change of government."[53] In retrospect it seems that Owen had this solution in mind from the beginning. Besides signaling his interest in this approach in both the First and Supplementary Awards, he had also pushed during negotiations at Dayton for transforming Sarajevo into a neutral multiethnic "district" of the state.[54]

In contrast to the rest of Bosnia, where the division of the country along ethno-territorial lines has been instituted in the pursuit of the consociational goal of ethnic autonomy, the Brčko District has been purposefully designed with the aim of achieving political and social integration of ethnically divided territory. This principle is clearly outlined in the Final Award, which states, "The basic concept is to create a single, unitary multi-ethnic democratic government to exercise, throughout the pre-war Brcko Opstina, those powers previously exercised by the two entities and the three municipal governments."[55] Owen also mandated that international supervision of Brčko continue until the supervisory regime is able to certify that all conditions of the Final Award are met. As we shall see in chapter 7, these decisions were quite controversial and engendered a series of legal and political battles between the District and OHR Brčko on one hand, and the entities and OHR Sarajevo on the other.

Unification of the three ethnically controlled territories in Brčko was a difficult challenge, even though OHR already had two years of experience in carrying out a similar process in RS Brčko. First, it required the merger of the three separate municipal authorities (RS Brčko, Gornji Rahić, and Ravne Brčko) into a single District government (see figure 8).[56] Second, the Federation and RS police forces and judiciary also needed to be dismantled and reconstituted as unified District institutions. Third, creating a single District-wide political and legal system also entailed drafting a statute and rewriting the entire legal corpus in the Brčko area, which was a contradictory hodgepodge of Yugoslav and entity-based laws. Perhaps the most ambitious task was the unification of the separate school systems. Education is one of the most contentious issues in Bosnia, and integration has been fiercely resisted in the few remaining ethnically mixed communities in the country, as it was when first proposed in Brčko in 2000. However, the following year OHR Brčko successfully integrated the District's schools under a single multiethnic curriculum, which has operated without serious incident in the decade since. This remains the only integrated school system in the country.[57]

Unlike Mostar there are no formal guarantees of proportional ethnic representation in the District Assembly or civil service jobs. Instead political parties adhere to an informal "ethnic key" principle whereby Bosniaks and Serbs each hold roughly 40 percent of the positions in the municipality while Croats fill the remaining 20 percent.[58] Also, while the entities are

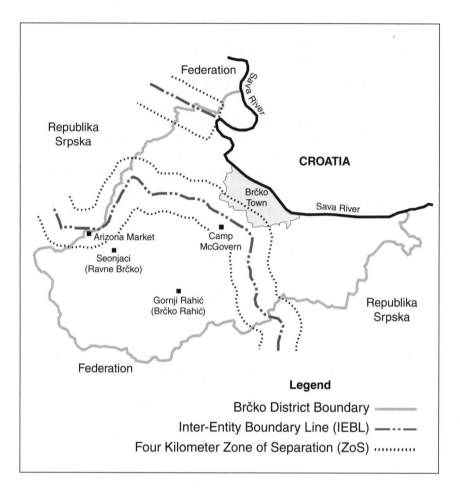

Figure 8. The Brčko District

forbidden from interfering in the District's internal affairs, Brčko residents are free to choose the entity in which they wish to claim citizenship and vote in for entity and national elections. Finally, in addition to legally dissolving the IEBL that ran through Brčko, *mjesne zajednice* ("local communities," which are similar in scale to large neighborhoods) no longer function as the lowest level of administrative units in the District—though they are free to register as nongovernmental organizations—further undermining potential alternative sources of ethno-territorial division.[59]

Institutional and Social Integration with Proportional Power Sharing: Achievements and Shortcomings

Overall the integrative institutional approach adopted in Brčko has been quite successful to date. The police, courts, schools, and administrative institutions are not just fully integrated, they also exhibit a high level of professionalism compared to the rest of Bosnia. This has not gone unnoticed by District residents: polls conducted in the District show that these institutions consistently receive high marks for trustworthiness and overall approval relative to other governing institutions in the country. In a 2003 poll conducted by the National Democratic Institute (NDI) 73 percent of Brčko residents registered "trust" in the District police and 67 percent in the District justice system, while 61 percent indicated they were "satisfied" with the work of the District government and departments. In contrast only 43 percent of those polled indicated trust in Bosnia's government and parliament.[60] A more recent EUFOR poll (2009) found that 66 percent of Brčko residents expressed satisfaction with the District's status (significantly, this poll also revealed little difference across ethnicity in approval).[61] Such support for the District's status is crucial for any lasting success in Brčko as it provides a relative sense of security for people of all ethnic backgrounds, thereby facilitating reconstruction and reintegration of the town.

Support for the District's integrated education system is also remarkably high. In a 2004 poll nearly 90 percent of District residents agreed with the idea that "children with different national backgrounds should attend the same school."[62] A 2006 OSCE report on the state of education in Bosnia also noted that "residents in Brčko District are consistently the most satisfied with education in BiH."[63] Indeed, according to the OSCE roughly 5 percent of all students in Brčko's schools come from outside the District, including the neighboring town of Gunja in Croatia, driven in large part because parents "believe the quality of secondary education is better" in the District.[64] This is not to say that education in Brčko is without its difficulties. For instance, a common complaint amongst teachers I have spoken with is that they are given inadequate training to deal with the complex interactions regarding instruction in each of the three recognized languages.[65]

The successful integration of schools in Brčko is important because they provide a setting for constructive, daily socialization across ethnic lines for the current generation of youth who have no personal memory of the war. Indeed, informal discussions I have had over the years with former students of the District's secondary schools indicate that they are the central place in which cross-ethnic friendships are forged among youth in Brčko. Again, the contrast with Mostar is stark, as all schools but the Gymnasium (academic high school) remain segregated. And even the Gymnasium's unification is far from complete as the persistence of separate classes in Mostar for all subjects means that the school "has a unified management, while preserving ethnic segregation and the ethos of segmental autonomy. The materialization of a new form of school that is concurrently 'shared' and 'separated' creates a new type of school geography in B&H, one based on the ideology of ethnic symmetry and polarization of youth."[66]

All of the above is not to say that Brčko's multiethnic institutions have operated without problems. The District Assembly has often found it difficult to agree on a handful of key personnel hires, such as the chief of police. And several instances of corruption in hiring, public tender contracts, and land use decisions have come to light since the first elections in 2004. In response OHR Brčko felt it necessary to introduce a series of supervisory orders regulating the conduct of hiring civil servants in the District. Even so corruption remains a concern. In October 2011, Brčko's second mayor, Dragan Pajić, was charged with abusing his position for personal gain, just a month after he resigned from office due to violation of the District's conflict of interest laws.[67] More serious for the District's future are dozens of lawsuits (totaling nearly 400 million KM) by companies that have invested in Brčko and which accuse the government of failures in fulfilling contractual obligations such as the prompt approval of necessary permits. While many of these cases stem from legitimate complaints, discussions with local and international officials indicate that several may also be part of an elaborate kickback scheme in which contracts are intentionally written to include undeliverable promises on the District's part, thus providing grounds for a lawsuit asking for monetary damages.[68]

Despite these problems it is a stretch to claim that the District is "drowning in corruption and mismanagement," as one prominent think tank has recently claimed.[69] First, corruption is widespread in Bosnia—and indeed in most countries which have experienced violent conflict—so this is less a failing specific to the District than an illustration of the inherent difficulty of solving systemic corruption in a postwar environment. Second, District authorities have a great deal more money—and responsibility—than other cities in the country, which rely on entities, cantons, or the state for funding and management of many public services. In contrast, the District runs and pays for its own education system, judiciary, police, hospitals and health care system, and social welfare policies. This creates more opportunities for malfeasance at the municipal level, whereas elsewhere in Bosnia cantonal or entity government offices offer the most lucrative possibilities for looting of public resources. Moreover one needs to consider how Brčko compares to other parts of Bosnia. International oversight regarding the activities of local officials—and greater independence of the District's police, courts, and auditors—means that there is greater transparency in Brčko, and that cases of malfeasance are more likely to be uncovered and prosecuted than elsewhere in the country. It does not necessarily follow, though, that the problem of corruption in the District is worse. Indeed, more telling in my view than the fact that a former mayor of Brčko has been indicted, is that so few political figures of equal or greater prominence have been prosecuted for similar crimes elsewhere in Bosnia—even when significant evidence of malfeasance exists.[70]

Residents of Mostar, for example, can—and do—recite a litany of problems with corruption in their city, from dodgy land deals, to the need to pay large bribes for specific services or permits, to tax avoidance schemes, and nepotism in hiring practices. For instance, under the Interim Statute the city's urban planning department had no ability to control the issuance of building permits even though this was supposed to be one of its core competencies, consequently "illegal building throughout the city became one of its biggest problems and generators of illicit wealth."[71] And it is widely known even today that the quickest way to be assured of a necessary permit or decision from city authorities if one is lacking in the requisite *štela* is not to go through official channels, but to pay for the services of one of the city's well-connected criminal intermediaries.[72] Despite this, prominent elected officials and public employees in Mostar have never been prosecuted for corruption, let alone seriously investigated. It is scarcely believable that this is because the city's officials are that much cleaner than in Brčko. I would go even farther and suggest that the lack of investigations or prosecutions is, rather, indicative of a deeper, more systemic culture of corruption in Mostar than in the District, where genuine efforts to tackle the problem are being made.

As I noted in chapter 1, the Brčko District is more of a hybrid in which the pursuit of broad social and territorial integration has been balanced by various power-sharing measures, including an electoral system and District Assembly voting procedures which hew more closely to consociational principles. This is especially the case following recent changes to the District statute by OHR Brčko. Elections for the assembly are conducted through an open-list proportional system, with the mayor indirectly elected by assembly members, as in Mostar. Initially there was no provision for veto rights in the assembly. Instead the stipulation that a three-fifths majority was required for votes on contentious issues ensured that in practice no single ethnic group could push through decisions without some degree of support from the other two. However this was changed in May 2008 when then-supervisor Raffi Gregorian (2006–10) amended the statute—following lobbying by several District politicians—to include mild veto provisions requiring support from at least one-third of councilors from each constituent people to "prevent outvoting" on sensitive subjects such as religion, culture, education, monuments, language, budget and spatial planning.[73]

Unfortunately there have been signs that the District's electoral framework may be less than ideal. Two points in particular stand out. First, as in Mostar, indirect election of the mayor by District Assembly members prevents voters in having a direct say in this important position, and discourages candidates from advancing political platforms that might appeal to a broader spectrum of the electorate. Second, the proportional system offers few incentives for parties or candidates to attempt to draw cross-ethnic support from voters. These two factors lead to a dynamic in which coalition negotiations tend to take place after rather than before elections where they could promote the emergence of more moderate political platforms, as is the case with centripetal or aggregative electoral processes.[74] Additionally, this process also fuels corruption in the District as postelection negotiations over the mayor and positions in government often revolve as much around corrupt horse trading of favors and patronage as they do around common political goals.[75] Further complicating matters are tensions between local political elites and the priorities of their parties' entity-based leadership.

All of these factors came into play following the 2008 elections, when difficult postelection negotiations ultimately produced an unwieldy "concentration" government involving all of the parties that gained seats in the District Assembly, which was headed by the aforementioned Pajić.[76] Still, the transition from an ethnic Bosniak to Serb mayor represented an impressive degree of political maturity in the District, especially when contrasted with the year-long political deadlock that engulfed Mostar following its election that year. More optimistically, following the 2012 election a relatively uneventful and short bargaining process led to the election of Brčko's first Croat mayor, Anto Domić, from HDZ. This political event was quite remarkable given that ethnic Croats are the substantially the smallest of the three constituent peoples in the District by population.[77]

The Pernicious Effects of Ethno-Territorial Consociationalism in Mostar and Bosnia

Perhaps one of the clearest lessons that can be discerned from examining the effects of political institutions on everyday life in these two cities is that the adoption of an ethno-territorially based consociational framework in Mostar has been a critical factor limiting the progress of peacebuilding efforts in the city. First, it has reproduced ethno-territorial division as each of the six city-municipalities—and, later, city areas—have been effectively captured by one of the two communities. Second, it has also empowered the most obstructionist local actors, thus fostering instability and political dysfunctionality rather than cross-ethnic accommodation. Finally it has entrenched ethnicity as the dominant cleavage in social life and political affairs and inhibited the development of alternative political and social associations.

In this Mostar is a microcosm of Bosnia as a whole, as the ethno-territorial consociational institutions agreed on at Dayton have also not produced a stable state, but rather engendered the fragmentation of the country into a series of squabbling ethnocratic territories.[78] When a coalition of elites in the country do reach a compromise, such as the package of constitutional reforms agreed on by the three main nationalist parties (SDS, HDZ, and SDA) in autumn 2005, their rivals engage in ethnic outbidding to derail the process and improve their position at the next polls.[79] The systematic privileging of ethnicity at all levels of the state has also marginalized parties that run on nonethnic or multiethnic platforms and has stymied attempts by civil society activists to promote forms of political and social association that crosscut the dominant ethnic cleavages.[80] Instead political elites from all three groups have continued to pursue divisive policies aimed at maintaining control over what they perceive as their ethnic spaces.

The adoption of ethno-territorial consociationalism in Bosnia has also provided the necessary bases for the reproduction of political power by nationalist parties. It insulates them from genuine electoral competition by creating a safe demographic margin and restricts political participation by defining "legitimate" politics within an exclusively ethnic framework. At the same time it allows elites to keep people in a continual state of fear by invoking threats to their own territorial-political autonomy or highlighting the discrimination that coethnics face in other ethnocratic spaces in Bosnia. It also facilitates the control of economic resources and public enterprises by nationalist parties and their allies, and entrenches them in administrative apparatuses.[81] The parties in turn use their command of public offices and assets to provide patronage—for instance, jobs, business contracts, and plum privatization terms—in order to solidify their political standing. The result is a near-perfectly closed system for reproducing ethnonationalist political control. These dynamics have prompted the observation by one Bosnian political scientist that in practice Bosnia resembles a *"democracy of ethnic oligarchies* rather than a *democracy of citizens."*[82]

This phenomenon is, I argue, an outgrowth of the structural logic of ethno-territorial consociational compacts. Put simply, advocates of these forms of consociation tend to mistakenly view territorial arrangements as fairly inert features of a political system—mere containers in which or between which political and social processes take place, rather than constitutive elements of such processes in their own right. Arend Lijphart, for example, claims that whether or not ethno-federalism is an appropriate policy choice for generating ethnic autonomy in consociations is a pragmatic decision, dependent on the geographical context of ethnic settlement patterns.[83] But a key lesson from Mostar and Bosnia is that territorializing ethnic identity and political power profoundly transforms social and political relations by erasing the distinction between ethnic and territorial conflicts.

Additionally, Mostar and Bosnia illustrate the difficulty in reconciling ethno-territorial consociational arrangements with "liberal" forms of consociation championed by John McGarry and Brendan O'Leary. The fundamental problem is that ethno-territorial consociations fuse together ethnic and territorial principles. Consequently the basis of political identity and electoral politics rests on an ethnically spatial, rather than individual, foundation. Since ethno-territorial structures, unlike identity, are fixed and clearly demarcated, the result is that where individual citizens reside effectively defines their political status as ethnic subjects—and thus significantly (pre)determines how they may participate politically. Recall, for example, how city-municipality electoral constituencies in Mostar under the new statute have effectively blocked the election of candidates representing minority populations in East and West Mostar.

To give another example of the illiberal character of the ethno-territorial consociational system in Bosnia, consider the constitutional provisions that effectively disenfranchise those who live in the "wrong" entity in the country. According to Article V of Bosnia's constitution an ethnic Serb living in the Federation is prohibited from running as the Serb candidate for the Bosnian Presidency or being selected as a member of the House of Peoples, and vice versa for an ethnic Croat or Bosniak who resides in the RS. A corollary of this provision is that such individuals are also blocked from participating in the vote for their designated ethnic representative in the three-person Presidency. In 2005 the Council of Europe's Venice Commission argued that this fusion of ethnic and territorial principles violates Protocol 12 of the European Convention on Human Rights—of which Bosnia is a signatory—concerning discrimination. In 2009 the European Court of Human Rights agreed, and ordered that these constitutional provisions be changed. To date, however, reforms have been blocked by political disagreements among the various nationalist parties.[84]

To be clear I am not offering here a critique of consociationalism in toto, as this critique does not apply to consociational compacts that promote ethnic autonomy primarily through nonterritorial measures, as is the case with Northern Ireland under the Good Friday Agreement, for example. I am also not arguing that territorial methods of recognizing and institutionalizing difference in ethnically plural states are inevitably problematic and should always be avoided. Nor do I believe that it is possible—or even desirable—to attempt to submerge all ethnic differences in the name of some grand nation-building project. Rather my point is that territorial arrangements can be as important as electoral systems in shaping the "rules of the game." Moreover, as the case of Mostar illustrates, the combination of ethno-territorial division and consociational power-sharing measures is especially ill-suited for mitigating ethnic conflict and developing effective institutions in communities at the city level and below, the scale at which most everyday political and social interaction takes place.

4

WARTIME LEGACIES

As William Faulkner once observed, "The past is never dead. It's not even past." This is an especially appropriate aphorism for Bosnia as past events continue to profoundly shape political and social relations in the postwar period. In chapter 1 I noted that one of the most important, yet least understood, aspects of peacebuilding is the influence of wartime social and political processes. That events which took place during the war continue to matter in its aftermath is clear. But precisely when and how these legacies shape peacebuilding in the postwar period remains something of a black box. In part this is a problem of evidence—information about wartime processes is often fragmentary, hidden, or contested—and in part it is a problem of method—how do we demonstrate plausible links between events and processes across time and space?

The cases of Brčko and Mostar show just how difficult it can be to identify meaningful wartime legacies. On the surface the most significant legacies of the war appear to be the ones the two towns have in common: both were sites of extensive violence and ethnic cleansing; both remained highly contested spaces even after the fighting ceased; and in both nationalists who came to power during the war and opposed political or territorial compromise appeared to be deeply entrenched. Indeed, by most accounts Brčko seemed to be a more intractable problem than Mostar at the end of the war. It is no surprise then that, given their comparable wartime histories and levels of ethnic tension in the immediate aftermath, both cities were singled out by international and domestic observers as potentially combustible, divided cities in need of special attention during the peacebuilding process.

Yet for all their evident similarities the unfolding local and regional dynamics of the war and immediate postwar period produced political conditions in Brčko that were more favorable for compromise and reform than in Mostar. Specifically, in the former the legitimacy of each of the three main nationalist parties in Bosnia was severely weakened in the eyes of a significant portion of the local population, while in the latter the war brought about unchallenged supremacy for the Croat nationalist party HDZ and its mafia allies.[1] These differences had a profound effect on postwar peacebuilding trajectories, but the impact was by no means predetermined. Dissatisfaction with ruling nationalists in Brčko might not have been converted into political action if international officials had not successfully identified and cultivated key potential opposition figures. Likewise, without strong economic and political support from Croatia until Franjo Tudjman's death in 1999 Croat nationalists in West Mostar might have found it more difficult to maintain such a strong grip on power. It is not enough, then, to treat legacies of war as static variables—one needs to trace the conjunction of specific legacies with concrete postwar processes, which I attempt to do in the rest of this chapter.

Damaged Brands: Nationalist Parties during the War in Brčko

In Brčko the SDA in particular suffered from a lack of legitimacy due to two perceived mistakes before and during the war. The first was SDA's decision to form a governing alliance with SDS and HDZ following the elections in 1990. As noted in chapter 2, SK-SDP won a plurality of votes in municipal elections in Brčko.[2] Despite this the party was unable to put together a governing coalition as the three national-ist parties reached an agreement to form a ruling coalition in the local government, following orders given by their respective leaders at the state level.[3] This decision by the SDA was widely criticized by Bosniaks in Brčko given the subsequent attack on, and ethnic cleansing of, the city by Serb forces.

The second event, which crystallized the view that SDA had failed to protect Bosniaks at the beginning of the war, was the decision by the president of the party's Brčko branch, Mustafa Ramić, to appear on local television with the commander of the nearby JNA base on May 1, 1992, the date that Serbian paramilitary forces swept into the town and began rounding up and killing non-Serb residents. In this appearance Ramić told residents not to flee Brčko but to stay calm and remain in their homes while local authorities regained control of the situation. In his defense it seems that he was in effect a prisoner of Serb security forces at that time and thus coerced into making this statement.[4] Regardless of this fact SDA has never recovered politically from the perception that Ramić's announcement cost the lives of an untold number of residents in Brčko town who heeded the call to remain in their homes rather than flee, and to this day SDP remains far more popular than SDA in Brčko. In the first District election in 2004, for example, SDA won just 10 percent of the vote—little more than half the total gained by SDP.[5] Eight years later SDA failed to crack 10 percent of the vote, while SDP remained the most popular party in the District.[6] The continued popularity of SDP in Brčko is also explained in part by the central role its local leadership—in particular Mirsad Djapo, who became the District's first elected mayor in 2004—played in negotiating an exchange in September 1992 of several hundred Bosniak civilians in RS Brčko for residents of Bukvik, a Serb majority village just south of the front lines which had been captured by the ARBiH the previous month.

In a similar fashion HDZ was weakened in Brčko by widespread suspicions that political leadership in Croatia and Herzegovina repeatedly sold out Posavina Croat interests during and after the war. Since the early stages of the conflict rumors have abounded that Bosnia's HDZ leader at the time, Mate Boban, cut a deal in 1992 with Radovan Karadžić to give up parts of the Posavina region in exchange for territorial concessions by the RS elsewhere in Bosnia. To this day news stories purporting to have uncovered incontrovertible evidence of the "betrayal" of Posavina continue to make headlines in Croatia and Bosnia.[7]

The belief that HDZ was willing to abandon Croats in Brčko was also fueled by orders to end the military alliance with Bosniaks along the Posavina corridor when war broke out between the Croat and Bosniak armies in Central Bosnia and Herzegovina in 1993—this despite the fact that Croat armed forces in the Brčko area were devoid of manpower and consequently heavily reliant on Bosniaks who served in local HVO units throughout the war. To put this in perspective, according to official records from June 1993 (during the height of the Croat-Bosniak war in Bosnia) more than 20 percent of HVO forces in the Posavina region were of Bosniak ethnicity.[8] In the end local authorities in Brčko ignored orders from Herzegovina to terminate their alliance. As the former HVO military commander in the region recounts: "We had no reason to start a conflict with Bosniaks. We had joint interests to preserve the free territory. . . . There were instructions that we abandon this joint defense. And there were also attempts on the part of Bosniaks to provoke tensions. But thank God there was enough reason on both sides."[9] From that point forward there was a general distrust of HDZ among Croat elites in the region. Ivan Krndelj, a prominent local politician who became deputy mayor of the multiethnic administration in RS Brčko in 1997, and eventually left HDZ the following year, put it to me this way: "The struggle was always there between Posavina and Herzegovina—useless struggle. Politicians [in Herzegovina] didn't know their job . . . they always looked after their own interest, and they scratched us off."[10] Conflict between Croats in Brčko and HDZ's Herzegovina-based leadership also mirrored dissatisfaction toward HDZ held by many in Posavina, Sarajevo, and Central Bosnia.

Of the three nationalist parties SDS came out of the war in the strongest position, dominating the political landscape in RS-held Brčko. Yet even the standing of SDS was much more precarious than it appeared on the surface. This was especially the case among the prewar Serb population in the city. Again this dynamic can be traced back to the wartime period, in particular disaffection caused by irregular militias from Serbia and other regions of Bosnia that fought in the area in the early stages of the conflict. These militias were not just responsible for some of the worst incidents of ethnic cleansing during the war, they also engaged in widespread looting and resisted all attempts by the local civilian authorities to control them, prompting the head of the RS Brčko War Presidency council at the time, Djordje Ristanić, to bring the problem to the attention of RS leadership in Pale: "A special feature of the Brčko front is organized and individual crime in the form of looting. This has assumed such proportions that individuals have lost their lives and been wounded in their desire to steal. . . . The result of the looting is that Brčko is now a devastated town. This has led to the fall of combat morale, significant demoralization of the Brčko population and the absurdity of the whole war."[11] Foremost amongst the militias rampaging through Brčko were Arkan's Tigers from Serbia.[12] After more than a month of complaints to authorities in Pale and Serbia the police chief of RS Brčko, Dragan Veselić, traveled to Belgrade in June 1992 to discuss the matter directly with Franko "Frenki" Simatović, the Serbian secret police official overseeing the militias.[13] Driving back after the meeting he was killed when his car was struck by a train at a railroad crossing near the Bosnian border. RS Brčko authorities saw this thinly disguised assassination as a clear warning to mind themselves and not interfere with the activities of outside military forces. A semblance of local control in RS Brčko was only established in spring 1993 after militia forces had moved on to other regions.

A second source of tension between local elites in Brčko and SDS's national leadership was disgust by the former about the scale of corruption and personal fortunes accrued by the latter. Several leading figures in RS Brčko, including Ristanić and his close ally Žarko Čošić—who took over as police chief following Veselić's murder—were supporters of the short-lived September 1993 VRS mutiny in Banja Luka. This little-known event revealed significant morale problems in the VRS, and broader resentment against war profiteers in the SDS who were building massive fortunes despite the general economic collapse in the RS. On September 10 members of the 16th Banja Luka Brigade took control of key buildings in the city center and arrested the local head of the SDS, Radisav Vukić.[14] Following this they released a statement that bitterly attacked SDS leadership:

While we were fighting . . . skillful manipulators, with the blessing of the existing authorities, increased their private empires and carried out their depraved political dreams in the safeness of the rear. Then, with a pompous promotion by the mass media, and by throwing philanthropic crumbs to the people and the army, they have become the saviours of the Serbian nation overnight. . . . We have decided to launch a battle against all our fellow citizens who have been involved in shady businesses or have allowed them, thus betraying the interests of the Serbian people.[15]

After a week of negotiations between the coup leaders and Radovan Karadžić the conflict ended when the latter agreed to pardon all those involved and promised to have a state commission look into the charges of corruption. Despite this compromise tensions between SDS leaders who profited from the war and those who supported the aims of the September 1993 rebellion continued into the postwar period, with important consequences for postwar peacebuilding in Brčko.[16]

The main power base for SDS in Brčko in the postwar period was the tens of thousands of ethnic Serb refugees and IDPs who were resettled in the city in the final months of the war and during the spring of 1996 when thousands of Serbs fled suburbs in Sarajevo that were scheduled to be returned to the Federation.[17] However support for SDS was less solid than it appeared at first glance as the allegiance of this socially marginalized population was based as much on fear and coercion as political loyalty. In particular authority over the Ministry for Displaced Persons and Refugees in Brčko gave SDS two powerful weapons that could be selectively wielded in order to manage the IDP and refugee population: first, it controlled the distribution of rationing cards that granted access to much needed basic food provisions. Second, the ministry was also in charge of allocating housing permits, which allowed people to settle in "abandoned"—that is, ethnically cleansed—properties in town. As a result of extensive physical destruction in RS Brčko, in the immediate aftermath of the war there was not an adequate amount of housing stock to accommodate all of the refugees and IDPs, thus this lever was especially powerful as any person who went against the wishes of Mladen Savić, the SDS strongman who controlled the ministry and was also a IDP from Sarajevo, would quickly find themselves and their family tossed out into the street.[18] More generally, conditional access to humanitarian assistance was one of the primary ways in which SDS ensured political compliance and support in Brčko. For example, prior to the 1997 election the RS Brčko Red Cross Center, which was controlled by SDS supporters, broadcasted "at least two announcements in the local media suggesting that residents who did not register were "traitors" and would suffer unspecified negative repercussions."[19]

The Cultivation of Moderate Local Elites in Postwar Brčko

The significance of these weaknesses among the three ruling nationalist parties in Brčko is that it offered international officials more fertile ground to cultivate alliances with local moderates—or at least more pragmatic nationalists—who were willing to work with them to implement peacebuilding reforms. For example, in May 1998 Ravne Brčko mayor Mio Anić, Ivan Krndelj, and several other leading Croat politicians in the area joined the newly founded, moderate political party, the New Croatian Initiative (NHI).[20] In Anić's opinion this split was inevitable: "I always disagreed with the policies over there [Herzegovina]. It was always a problem and if it weren't for the war we would have parted years earlier, because they always had different views than us."[21] Discontent with HDZ's Herzegovina-oriented political priorities, these local Croat political elites supported the creation of a multiethnic administration in Brčko and cultivated good relations with OHR. They were also instrumental in keeping HDZ and its mafia allies from taking control of the Arizona Market, a massive black market that developed in the Brčko region after the war, and which quickly became the largest economic concern in the region.[22] In exchange they were protected from political and personal retaliation by the supervisory regime in Brčko, which blocked an attempt by HDZ to remove them from their positions later that year.[23]

Several further events contributed to this postwar breakup. One was the push by HDZ for a boycott of the September 1997 municipal election, in which former residents of the territory of the prewar Brčko *opština* now under RS control were eligible to participate.[24] The resulting low turnout disadvantaged Croats when OHR Brčko used election results as a rough guide for the ethnic composition of the multiethnic institutions that were subsequently established in RS-Brčko that December.[25] A second irritant was HDZ's evident disinterest in the ongoing arbitration proceedings. From the beginning Croat politicians in Brčko argued that all of the Brčko area should be made a neutral district or separate territory under UN administration, seeing this option as the best chance to avoid being dominated by either Bosniaks or Serbs in the region.[26] HDZ's leadership offered only minimal backing for this position, fueling fears in Brčko that the party would not hesitate to forgo any claims to the area if it suited their interests. The final precipitant was the election of Ante Jelavić as president of the HDZ in May 1998. Jelavić represented hard-line nationalist interests in Herzegovina who advocated the creation of an independent Croat entity in Bosnia, a policy that if achieved would mean abandoning Croats outside of Herzegovina.

Most important for the peacebuilding process in Brčko was the role played by local Serbs who were willing to buck SDS's obstructionist policies. In this they were helped by Biljana Plavšić, a vice president of the wartime RS—and supporter of the Banja Luka rebellion—who became president of the RS after Karadžić was forced to resign as part of the terms of the DPA, as well as other figures in the region who had also been sympathetic with the events of September 1993. It would be a mistake to characterize Plavšić or most of her supporters as moderates (indeed, she was later indicted by the ICTY and pled guilty to committing war crimes in 2002). Rather what united them in opposition to SDS was disgust with corruption among the party's elite and the belief that SDS's uncompromising attitude would result in the RS's complete loss of Brčko in the ongoing arbitration proceedings.[27] Indeed, in Brčko cooperation with opposition leaders often meant cutting deals with the very same people who were responsible for ethnic cleansing during the war, people such as former militia leader Ljubiša "Mauzer" Savić who, if not for being a key interlocutor in Bijeljina and Brčko, would have almost certainly been indicted for war crimes.[28]

In spring 1997 a political rift emerged in the RS when Plavšić—supported by the international community in Bosnia—broke with her hardline colleagues Karadžić and Momčilo Krajišnik and declared her support for the acceptance and implementation of the DPA.[29] Plavšić had important allies in Brčko, including Savić, Ristanić, Čošić, and Andrija Bjelosević, who was a prominent postwar police commander. On August 28 Bjelosević, Čošić, and other police loyal to Plavšić attempted to take over the police station in Brčko, with backing by IPTF and American SFOR troops. This maneuver failed in the face of organized resistance from Karadžić and Krajišnik supporters, hundreds of whom were bused in from towns in the eastern RS.[30] Following the failed police station raid several of these figures were forced to temporarily flee Brčko, though they later returned to help vet personnel in the integrated police force that was initiated at the end of the year.[31]

In the aftermath of this failed effort SDS moved to shore up local support by initiating a campaign to Serbianize the landscape of RS Brčko, unveiling a statue of Draža Mihajlović, a World War II Četnik general who led ethnic cleansing campaigns against Croats and Muslims in Bosnia, building a monument to the "Serb defenders of Brčko" in between the central municipal buildings downtown, and constructing an Orthodox church in the formerly Bosniak-majority suburb of Meraje (see figure 9).[32] Work on the latter continued throughout the fall and into the following year despite a supervisory order to halt construction.[33] Ultimately OHR Brčko decided not to push the issue, lest intervention provoke further violence.

The party also worked to reassert control over the police and municipal government by replacing dozens of local officials with more pliant proxies:

> Pale initiated a series of actions designed to reconsolidate its hold over Brčko. This involved a crackdown on police and others who were not considered sufficiently loyal to Pale. We have it on good account that 30 special police were sent from Pale to Brčko to hunt down pro-Plavšić supporters among the Brčko police. . . . On September 24th, most of the Executive Board of the Brčko Municipal Assembly were replaced by Pale proxies.[34]

However, the fact that (1) the majority of local politicians who made up the RS Brčko executive board were viewed as insufficiently supportive of SDS's politics, and (2) a significant number of local police were willing to participate in an operation to take over police stations from Pale-aligned hardliners demonstrated the party's relatively fragile standing in Brčko at the time. This was also illustrated by SDS's need to bus in supporters from other towns in order to generate a powerful countermobilization.[35] Consequently, as I outline in greater detail in the next chapter, after the municipal election the following month OHR decided to push forward with plans to reform institutions in RS-controlled Brčko, with Robert Farrand issuing a series of supervisory orders calling for the creation of a multiethnic city administration, judiciary, and police. Though SDS complained vociferously about the decisions and attempted to obstruct implementation as much as possible, there was no further mass violence.

Peacebuilding efforts gained further momentum when Serb opposition parties united with the handful of Croat and Bosniak parliamentarians in the RS to elect Plavšić supporter Milorad Dodik as prime minister of the RS the following January, which led to the dismissal of obstructionist SDS figures such as Mladen Savić from their positions in various RS ministries in Brčko. With the removal of Savić and other Pale-aligned officials, OHR Brčko was able to begin making progress in effecting returns of Bosniak and Croat families to their homes, starting with returns to the southern suburbs located in the Zone of Separation (ZOS), where Serb refugees from Croatia and the Federation had been resettled by SDS in an attempt to create a "biological barrier."[36] Additionally, OHR was able to gain support for its plans from several key local political figures in RS Brčko such as Siniša Kisić, who eventually became the Brčko District's first appointed mayor.[37] In 1998, for instance, Kisić played a key role in convincing angry Serb IDPs to refrain from attacking the first Bosniak returnees to RS-controlled neighborhoods in Brčko town such as Klanac, Meraje, and Gluhakovac.[38] Looking back on his decision to work with OHR Kisić notes:

> Among Serbs there is always a story about who is a greater Serb. I am a Serb by birth, but as I said then, "this is not my occupation." . . . The easiest thing to do in an unstable situation is to make obstacles or make things more difficult. But that is not a long term policy. That is a policy for one day, one month, for a TV station or newspaper to broadcast my view for three days and then it's over, and what next? So this is what the situation was in 1997 and all the years that followed.[39]

Kisić became central to OHR's peacebuilding efforts over the years—both as a spokesman who could explain and sell reforms to Bosnian Serbs in Brčko, and a politician with sufficient standing to allow OHR to claim that its policies were supported, to a degree, by all three communities.[40]

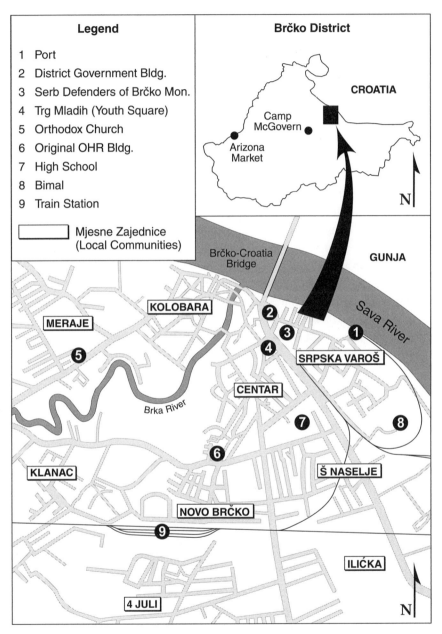

Figure 9. Downtown Brčko

SDA and the "Betrayal" of Mostar during the War

The war brought a significant decline in SDA's status amongst Bosniaks in Mostar, for similar reasons as HDZ in Brčko. Specifically, there was widespread bitterness that leadership in Sarajevo had "betrayed" Bosniaks in Mostar prior to the outbreak of the Bosniak-Croat war in May 1993 in exchange for peace and the continued flow of military supplies though Croat-controlled West Herzegovina. While SDA as a party was not completely eclipsed, as it was in Brčko, the local leaders who emerged from the war owed their legitimacy in large part due to the perception that they resisted the abandonment of Mostar by Sarajevo.[41] They were, in short, SDA members more as a matter of convenience than conviction, and several, including Safet Oručević, East Mostar's mayor until 2001, eventually joined one of SDA's main political rivals, SBiH.

There is a good deal of evidence that SDA headquarters in Sarajevo did indeed decide that Mostar was not worth risking a confrontation with HDZ. During the summer of 1992 HDZ and HVO intensified efforts to push aside Bosniaks and tighten political and military control over the city. The president of SDA in Mostar, Ismet Hadžiosmanović, acquiesced to this development under instruction from Alija Izetbegović.[42] However in September several leading Bosniak figures in the city began to rebel against his leadership and founded the Muslim Cultural Circle, which advocated firm political resistance against Croat actions in Mostar. Izetbegović initially denounced the group following a failed attempt to negotiate a power-sharing arrangement during a visit in October.[43] As tensions in the city escalated Hadžiosmanović's position became more precarious; shortly after Izetbegović's visit, Oručević and his allies effectively sidelined him by taking control of SDA's regional board—which included Mostar and the broader Herzegovina region—and directing political activity through this body rather than the Mostar SDA board. By the end of the war Oručević would become the unrivaled Bosniak leader in the city.

It is unclear but seems likely that the decision to cast aside the SDA leadership in Mostar eventually had Izetbegović's tacit approval. Oručević's rapid political rise is a bit of a puzzle. Not outwardly pious, a generation younger than Izetbegović, and the owner of a slots and billiards joint before the war—such establishments were often run by people with connections to the Yugoslav underworld—he was not a typical SDA politician. Izetbegović normally selected as local SDA leaders people who had either a personal or familial connection to him through the group Mladi Muslimani (Young Muslims), an Islamist association which had been persecuted under the Yugoslav regime. The brothers of both Ismet Hadžiosmanović, and Mustafa Ramić in Brčko, for example, had been in Mladi Muslimani with Izetbegović. It seems, however, that Izetbegović's need for Oručević's personal connections and particular expertise was great enough to overlook these concerns.[44] By January 1993 Oručević was negotiating the procurement and transportation of weapons with HVO on Izetbegović's behalf under the title "logistics coordinator under the president."[45]

Political Clashes between Bosniak Elites in Mostar and Sarajevo and the Rise of Hardliners

Led by Oručević, Bosniak political elites in Mostar were initially strong supporters of efforts to establish a joint municipal government and develop the shared central zone in the city in the early years after the end of the war. The problem was that this position was not shared by SDA leadership in Sarejevo, which was frequently willing to treat Mostar as a bargaining chip in the broader battle for political positioning in the Federation. Nowhere was this more apparent than the negotiations at Rome in February 1996, which produced a much reduced central zone in the city:

> Many Mostarians, particularly on the east side of town, felt that . . . SDA had sold out the idea of a unified Mostar by signing the Rome Agreement and accepting a diminished central zone. Safet Orucevic, the mayor of east Mostar submitted his resignation, which Bosniak SDA president Alija Izetbegovic refused to accept. In March, Izetbegovic sent an open letter of explanation, perhaps also of apology to the citizens of Mostar, for the deal brokered at Rome.[46]

These and other actions created friction between Sarajevo and Oručević and his allies in Mostar. In a remarkable interview with the political journal *Slobodna Bosna* shortly after he resigned from SDA in 2000 Oručević condemned the party's policies toward the city:

Regardless of what SDA policy will be in the future, I will cooperate with it only if it is good for Mostar and works for the reintegration of Bosnia-Herzegovina. The policy of the SDA in the past was often contrary to the interests of Mostar citizens. One example of this has been the struggle over apartments. In Mostar as in Sarajevo this is the key issue. The struggle to hold on to apartments in Sarajevo, over which a tacit agreement was reached with the opposition, has worked directly in favor of HDZ extremists in Mostar. All this time we have been unable to return a single person to the western part of Mostar. I was forced to struggle simultaneously with HDZ extremists and with those people in the SDA who do not care about the return of all to their homes. . . . If the SDA continues to behave contrary to the interests of Mostar and to its citizens' desire to see it unified, it will be difficult for it to retain any influence in Herzegovina.[47]

Within a year Oručević—worn out by constant clashes with politicians in Sarajevo—left for a lucrative consulting position in Austria, while hardliners more interested in maintaining exclusive Bosniak control over East Mostar than building a unified city administration began to fill the void.

The Wartime Emergence of Mostar as the Bastion of HDZ and Bosnian Croat Nationalists

In contrast to the situation for SDA, hardline elements in HDZ emerged from the war in an unchallenged position of authority in Mostar. Moreover, as elites from the surrounding region of Herzegovina took control of leadership positions in both the Croatian and Bosnian branches of HDZ, the interests of Croats in West Mostar increasingly became defined as one of the most important issues for the broader Croat community in former Yugoslavia, resulting in an alignment of local, national, and regional interests in Mostar.

This was not, however, a preordained outcome. The first step in the process occurred in February 1992 when Mate Boban replaced Stjepan Kljuić as the head of HDZ in Bosnia. As noted in chapter 2, Kljuić supported the vision of a multiethnic and indivisible Bosnia while Boban, who was from West Herzegovina, advocated the creation of Herceg-Bosna, an independent Croat state with Mostar as its capital. Boban's ascension was facilitated by several influential figures in Franjo Tudjman's new government in Croatia who originally hailed from the Herzegovina region. Foremost among them was Minister of Defense Gojko Šušak, an émigré living in Canada prior to the war. An unswerving supporter of Herceg-Bosna, Šušak ensured that the "Herzegovina lobby" received full political and monetary support from Zagreb until his death in 1998.[48] To give a sense of Šušak's personal involvement in politics in Herceg-Bosna both before and after the war, consider that it was he, and not President Tudjman or Foreign Minister Mate Granić, who signed the DPA's annex on Mostar on behalf of Croatia.

There is a further political context to Croatia's support for Herzegovina. As members of the Croat "diaspora," Bosnian Croats are allowed to vote in Croatian elections. Consequently voters from Herzegovina were—and continue to be—a key electoral base for HDZ, having tended to vote overwhelmingly for the party through the years. The result of these strong personal and electoral ties to HDZ and the Tudjman regime was that for several years after the war the political and economic interests of Croatia and Croat-dominated Herzegovina were closely intertwined. As an internal analysis by OSCE in 1997 bluntly concluded, Herceg-Bosna was "a region that in every respect, from military and security matters to business ties, is part of Croatia."[49]

Further bolstering Croat hardliners' status in Mostar was the military (HVO) and closely aligned mafia-based paramilitary forces such as Mladen "Tuta" Naletilić's "Convicts' Battalion," which was so named because its members included a number of well-known criminals from the prewar Yugoslav underworld. Tuta, who had served time in prison for various offenses during the Yugoslav period, recruited criminal associates from the region to fight under his command. Initially the ethnic composition of the Convicts Battalion was mixed, but with the ascent of Boban and his secessionist politics in the spring of 1992, Bosniak members gradually left and formed their own private militias in East Mostar. According to former militia members in East Mostar who I interviewed, throughout the rest of the war these ostensible enemies conducted a lucrative trade in food, drugs, tobacco, medicine, weapons, and people.

Tuta's militia and the HVO gained a great deal of respect early in the war due to their prominent role in the defense of the city against JNA forces following the outbreak of hostilities in 1992. However HVO and Tuta's militia were not the only Croat forces who fought against the JNA. In addition to them a significant part was played by HOS led by Blaž Kraljević, a Herzegovinan émigré who returned from Australia in 1990 to fight for Croatian independence from Yugoslavia. As noted in chapter 2, HOS was the military arm of the HSP, a self-styled neo-Ustaša party. Ante Pavlević, the head of NDH in World War II, had promoted an ideology in which Muslims in Bosnia were—despite their religious differences—cultivated as allies and even described as the most pure of Croats, the "flower of our Croatian nation."[50] Consequently HSP advocated an undivided Bosnia shared by Croats and Muslims, and a military alliance between the two communities in order to defeat Bosnian Serbs and the JNA.

This position clashed with Boban's plans for an independent Herceg-Bosna, which he began to put in motion following a May 1992 meeting in Austria with Radovan Karadžić, where the two leaders agreed to the division of Bosnia. This prompted Kraljević to draft a public proclamation denouncing the meeting as a betrayal of Croat and Bosniak interests in Bosnia, stating, "We implore all citizens of Bosnia and Herzegovina, especially Croats and Bosniaks, not to take into account any statements or agreements between Mate Boban and Radovan Karadžić. Neither speaks in the name of Croats and Bosniaks. They do not represent what the Croats and Bosniaks want. . . . HOS and the TO are defending, and will defend, Bosnia and Herzegovina."[51] At the same time Kraljević began cultivating closer ties with Bosniak leadership in Sarajevo, going so far as to accept an appointment as a commander in the ARBiH in July. Shortly afterward he initiated an assault against Trebinje, the main Serb-controlled town in Herzegovina.[52] In a preemptive strike against their growing rival, HVO and Tuta's militia killed Kraljević and his deputies in an ambush just outside of Mostar on August 9, 1992. Within two weeks HOS forces were brought under HVO command and all Muslim members disarmed and expelled.[53] Following Kraljević's assassination HDZ and its military-mafia allies in the region would not be seriously challenged during the war again—either militarily or politically.

Violent and Nonviolent Croat Nationalist Resistance to the Reintegration of Mostar

This political-military-mafia nexus was vehemently opposed to the dismantling of the Herceg-Bosna parastate as required by the Washington Agreement and DPA, and resisted all measures leading to the creation of a single, multiethnic city administration in Mostar.[54] As Hans Koschnick observed in a report following his first year as the EU administrator in Mostar, "Local HDZ leaders in their majority are of a particular nationalistic brand and furthermore intimately connected with the local military commanders and some even with gang leaders . . . their financial means, their command of the police and their links with organised crime as well as their access to the local media as propaganda instrument make them fearsome 'warlords.'"[55] Six months later Koschnick would learn just how far hardliners were willing to go in order to spoil the peacebuilding process. Following the release of his draft Interim Statute in February 1996 a mob ransacked the EUAM headquarters in the center of town and rioters attacked his armored car with bullets and rocks as he tried to flee.[56] This was not the first time the he had been targeted. In September 1994 a rocket propelled grenade from West Mostar was fired into his apartment at the EUAM headquarters. Fortunately he was downstairs eating dinner in the cafeteria at the time.[57] As I noted in the previous chapter, the EU responded to the violence by giving in to Croat demands to reduce the size and administrative authority of the planned central zone.

Croat nationalists also conducted a violent campaign against political moderates in the city prior to the municipal election four months later. Shortly before the vote the leader of the multiethnic United Democrats coalition, Josip "Jole" Musa, an ethnic Croat who lived in West Mostar, was forcefully evicted from his office. That same week a supporter's café was destroyed by a bomb and four Croat members of the coalition dropped out of the race following death threats.[58] Three months later Musa was wounded in a machine gun attack on his apartment. Despite these and other incidents, OHR's panglossian response was that the election was "without doubt a success" for both Mostar and the EUAM.[59]

There was also a renewed wave of evictions of the few remaining non-Croat families in West Mostar following the election, often facilitated by West Mostar police and former members of Tuta's Convicts' Battalion.

UNHCR documented seventy-one cases of evictions during the year—nineteen of which occurred from November 22 to December 12.[60] Violent events such as explosions, gunfire, and evictions continued to accelerate in the city in early 1997. As the UN IPTF mission noted in a report that spring, "The general environment in Mostar has been one of unchecked violence, with little police or political action being taken to create a sense of normalcy, peace and security."[61] Violence by Croat extremists came to a head in February 1997 during the Muslim holiday of Kurban Bajram (Eid al-Adha) when West Mostar police fired shots into and beat an unarmed crowd of Bosniaks who were marching toward the Liska Street cemetery to pay respects to individuals who died when Bosnian Serb forces attacked Mostar in 1992. One person was killed and twenty-one people injured. SFOR troops and IPTF police monitors watched passively a few hundred meters away as the violence unfolded. In the weeks following the attack an additional twenty-eight Bosniak families were forcefully evicted from their West Mostar apartments and nineteen more families fled due to fear of further violence.[62] A SFOR armored personnel carrier guarding the former frontline was also damaged by anti-tank rockets fired from West Mostar.[63]

A comprehensive UN report after this incident determined that West Mostar police had been given prior notification of the planned procession to the cemetery. It also identified five officers who drew their weapons or fired on the crowd. Following the report international officials pressured West Mostar authorities to dismiss the five officers and initiate criminal proceedings against them. The next month a West Mostar lower court convicted three of the officers of the crime of "participating in the mistreatment of citizens in the course of performing their duties," but gave each of them suspended sentences.[64]

Violence was not the only means by which Croat hardliners in Mostar obstructed peacebuilding efforts. More common was the simple refusal to implement agreed-on measures, as discussed in chapter 3. Shortly after he resigned, a chastened Koschnick observed, "It is not enough to have an agreement or a contract. . . . An agreement here is one thing, life is another. In Bosnia the highest authorities sign an agreement and four weeks later ignore it."[65] Despite Koschnick's warning, international officials in Mostar continued to prioritize negotiations and signing of new accords over ensuring the proper implementation of previous agreements. As the International Crisis Group (ICG) noted in 2000, "A constant parade of international bureaucrats continues to descend on Mostar, demanding change, carrying out mediations and negotiations, and signing still more agreements which the HDZ has no intention of honouring."[66] Another HDZ strategy was to declare an international official "persona non grata" in the city and refuse to meet with him as happened to the head of OHR Mostar, Martin Garrod, in 1998. Garrod left Mostar shortly thereafter, though OHR insisted that his departure was unrelated to this incident.[67]

Poisoned Political Relations

Following the deaths of Šušak (May 1998) and Tudjman (December 1999) the situation in Mostar began to improve somewhat. In 1998 Tuta and his lieutenant Vinko "Štela" Martinović were indicted for war crimes by the ICTY.[68] In January 2000 HDZ lost to SDP in parliamentary elections in Croatia and the following month Stipe Mesić was elected president. Mesić, who became Croatia's first prime minister following the 1990 elections, had resigned from HDZ in 1994 in protest over the party's Herzegovina-oriented policy. After taking over as president he immediately reduced financial support to shadow Herceg-Bosna institutions in Bosnia. Before the end of the year he also sacked several generals connected with the Herzegovina lobby.[69] HDZ also did poorly at the polls in Bosnia's fall 2000 general elections, leading to the formation of a ruling coalition in the Federation called the Alliance for Change, which for the first time since the end of the war excluded HDZ and SDA from power.

Facing the withdrawal of support from Croatia and the loss of political patronage opportunities and funds due to being excluded from the new governing coalitions in Bosnia, HDZ hardliners withdrew from Federation institutions and called for the formation of an autonomous Croat self-government centered around its Herzegovinan strongholds. Members of the association of Croat Military Invalids of the Homeland War (HVIDRa), an extremist veterans' group founded by Tuta, also threatened ethnic Croats who were cooperating with the Alliance for Change coalition with violent retribution.[70] This last gasp attempt to hold on to power was immediately opposed by High Representative Wolfgang Petritsch who removed HDZ's president, Ante Jelavić, from his position as the Croat member of the Bosnian presidency in March 2001. The following month international auditors backed by SFOR troops raided, and then subsequently shut down, Hercegovačka Banka, the primary entity through which the Croat separatist movement and parallel institutions were financed.[71]

Due to this decisive intervention by international officials, and the lack of support from Croatia, the attempt to establish an autonomous Croat entity in Bosnia eventually failed. In the decade since this failure determined opposition to peacebuilding reforms in Mostar by HDZ has, despite foot dragging, lessened. In particular the use of violence to block returns of displaced families to West Mostar and stymie efforts to create unified institutions in the city has all but ceased. This does not mean that an acceptance of shared life in the city has taken root, though. Croat politicians, for instance, continue to resist efforts to integrate schools in the city. Another illustrative case is the Liska street cemetery, a prewar park that was used as burial grounds for citizens of all ethnic backgrounds during the JNA siege of the city in 1992 due to the fact that existing cemeteries were too exposed to artillery and snipers. Over the past decade Croat officials in West Mostar have encouraged and even paid for Croats to remove bodies and rebury them in Catholic cemeteries leaving hundreds of empty holes behind.[72] They have also attempted to have the entire cemetery exhumed so that the space could be restored as a park.[73] One specious line of argument which has been forwarded is that the wartime cemetery is unsanitary. But a petition circulated in West Mostar in 2003 captured the underlying tension this multiethnic space causes:

> We are dissatisfied and bitter that seven years since the war ended there has not been found an appropriate political, human and moral solution which would resolve one painful, sad and lasting scar from the war, and this scar removed from Liska park. . . . We believe—out of deep respect for all who were killed in the whirlwinds of war or died of natural causes and were buried in the park at that time—that regardless of which people they belonged to, they must finally find peace in their own cemeteries.[74]

Leaders of Mostar's Islamic community have rejected proposals to ethnically homogenize Liska by removing their dead to cemeteries in East Mostar, arguing that the space should stand as a symbol of the administratively unified city.[75] To this day the fight over the cemetery's future continues.

More broadly, the effects of the Croat intransigence linger on and continue to poison politics in Mostar. Most significantly, as noted above, HDZ's actions fueled the emergence of obstructionist Bosniak forces. Thus by the time I began conducting fieldwork political dynamics had flipped, with international officials working in the city identifying local Bosniak politicians and criminal networks as the biggest impediment to reform and implementation of the new city statute introduced in 2004.[76] This has continued to the present day with SDA and several prominent Bosniak figures in the city, such as Mufti Seid Smajkić, demanding the reinstatement of the Interim Statute—calls that have only intensified following the ruling that the city's current statute is unconstitutional.[77] A key source of Bosniak opposition is the belief that ethnic Croats now constitute a slim demographic majority in the city, and that Croat politicians are motivated by this advantage to dominate city politics to the detriment of Bosniak interests.[78] For example, as noted in chapter 3, HDZ refused to honor a 2004 agreement with SDA to support the latter party's candidate for mayor in 2008, despite the fact that it received less votes in the latter election. Bosniak officials and residents also complain about the lack of investment and services in East Mostar under HDZ mayor, Ljubo Bešlić.[79] Considering the history of violence and political obstruction by Croat nationalists in Mostar in the early years following the war the fear that Bosniaks are "losing" the city under the new statute are understandable. Moreover many in the city are also still concerned that Sarajevo-based politicians remain willing to sell out Bosniak interests in Mostar in exchange for other political considerations.[80] Given the legacies of the war and the earlier postwar period in the city it is likely that this climate of mistrust will continue to persist for the foreseeable future.

5

SEQUENCING

As the reader may have noticed, there is a significant difference in the timeline of international intervention in Mostar and Brčko. As part of the terms of the Washington Agreement it was decided that Mostar would be temporarily administered by the EUAM, which formally commenced operations in the city in July 1994—even as fighting continued elsewhere in the country—until December 1996, when it turned over political oversight to OHR. Conversely the OHR supervisory regime in Brčko was not established until April 1997, over a year after the war ended. Prior to this, the most significant international presence in the Brčko area were American SFOR troops patrolling the IEBL and its demilitarized ZOS, which split the prewar municipality in half.

Peacebuilding in the aftermath of war is a difficult task, requiring patience, time, and sufficient resources for social relations to stabilize and new institutions to take hold and function properly. Thus all else being equal—which of course it isn't—one would expect Mostar to be further along in this process given the head start it had over Brčko. This has not turned out to be the case. One reason for this apparent anomaly concerns the sequencing of peacebuilding reforms, in particular political and economic liberalization. In Mostar international officials followed the liberal peacebuilding model of rapid democratization and market reforms. Liberalization prior to institutionalization was a boon to nationalists, locking them in positions of political power and providing a veneer of democratic legitimacy, while further cementing the results of ethnic cleansing throughout the city. In Brčko the temporal ordering was reversed as multiple supervisors fought off outside pressure to speed up privatization and hold early elections. This made it more difficult for nationalist parties to manipulate the privatization process to their benefit, facilitated the implementation of more thorough and durable institutional reforms, and gave alternative political forces time to develop bases of support prior to the first District elections in 2004.

The Failure of Early Elections in Mostar

Mostar was not just the site of the earliest international peacebuilding efforts in Bosnia with the establishment of the EUAM in 1994, it also led the way in political liberalization, holding the country's first postwar election in June 1996. At the time the city was plagued by political and social instability: Bosniak families were still being forcefully evicted from apartments in West Mostar on a weekly basis; EUAM chief Hans Koschnick had been violently attacked in February following the release of his blueprint for a new city administration; and the resulting compromise Interim Statute—which was formally introduced at the end of that month—had not even begun to be implemented. Despite these problems the EU stayed firm to the goal of a quick election, which it viewed as a necessary step prior to closure of the mission. The EUAM's director of reconstruction, John Yarwood, claims that the organization thought it best to hold the election before implementing a new city statute.[1] However it is unclear whether this was Koschnick's idea or whether he was under pressure from the EU Council Presidency to proceed in this manner. The United States was also keen that the municipal election in Mostar be held as scheduled lest delays there provide any impetus for delaying the general election in Bosnia scheduled for September 1996, less than two months before U.S. presidential election.

At the February 1996 emergency conference in Rome the EU agreed to extend its mission in Mostar for six months (until December 1996) but insisted that the election go forward at the end of May as planned.[2] The framework for the election, which had been agreed on at Dayton, stipulated that "any person age eighteen or older who is identified in the 1991 census as a permanent resident of the municipality of Mostar and who still has his or her permanent residence in the City of Mostar at the time of the elections shall be eligible to vote for and be elected to the City Council and the City-Municipal Councils."[3] This was a somewhat odd decision as it meant that those who had been ethnically cleansed from Mostar during the war—roughly over half of the city's prewar population—would be denied the right to vote. Hence it was not much of a surprise that only weeks before the election was to take place Bosniak parties threatened a boycott if arrangements were not made to accommodate voters who were living as refugees in other countries. To meet these demands the election was delayed one month to allow OSCE, which was overseeing the process, time to set up polling stations in Bern, Bonn, Oslo, and Stockholm, cities where a large number of Bosniak refugees from the Mostar were residing. However OSCE did not make similar arrangements for the roughly twenty thousand displaced ethnic Serbs—most of whom were living in Serbia or the RS—instead insisting that they travel to Mostar if they wished to vote in the election. Given opposition to the election by RS leadership and the genuine fear most Serbs felt about traveling through Federation-controlled territory only months after the war had ended, this effectively blocked them from participating in the election.[4] Consequently, despite the efforts of Mostar's Yugoslav-era mayor, Radmilo Andrić, only a couple of hundred ethnic Serbs participated in the election.[5]

A second flaw was that election rules were organized according to the principle of voting "where they were" during the 1991 Yugoslav census rather than allowing citizens the choice of either "voting where they were" or "where they currently lived" as in the countrywide elections later that fall. Thus while refugees scattered across Europe were ultimately allowed to vote, IDPs residing in Mostar at the time of the election were denied this right, even though many had no plans to return to their former homes. This rule especially irritated Croats whose numbers in the city had swelled during the war as families from Central Bosnia were settled into hastily constructed "Bobanvilles"—named after Mate Boban, the wartime president of Herceg-Bosna who encouraged the resettlement of Croats into Herzegovina—on the outskirts of the city.[6] Indeed, most international and local officials believed that Croats held a slight demographic advantage in Mostar in the immediate postwar period due to this resettlement policy.

In the event, the SDA-led coalition achieved a narrow electoral victory winning 49 percent of the vote, with the HDZ list garnering 46 percent. The multiethnic United Democrats coalition received 3 percent of the votes, with the remaining scattered among a handful of other parties and individual candidates.[7] While it is likely that the dominance of the two nationalist parties roughly reflected the degree of polarization that still existed between the communities only months after the conclusion of the war, Croat nationalists in the city also took no chances, violently attacking United Democrats candidates and supporters (see chapter 4).

While the overall vote between SDA and HDZ was close, SDA benefited from the electoral rules established under the Interim Statute. As discussed in chapter 3, in recognition of Mostar's diverse prewar ethnic composition the consociational framework reserved sixteen seats for ethnic Croats, sixteen for Bosniaks, and five to "others," with the latter category including those who identified themselves as Serb, Yugoslav, Roma, or Jewish. Shrewdly, East Mostar's mayor, Safet Oručević, maintained good relations with the United Democrats and also recruited Serb candidates to run for his SDA-led coalition. As a result SDA gained all five of the seats reserved for others in the initial election, giving the Bosniak coalition a clear majority in the new municipal assembly.[8]

HDZ's response to the election was to deny its relevance.[9] West Mostar mayor Mijo Brajković argued that it "did not imply any practical changes" other than legitimating the legal status of the Croat part of Mostar.[10] This was a perceptive observation. The credibility of the EUAM mission in the city was in shambles following Koschnick's abandonment by the EU in the face of Croat nationalist violence in February. Additionally, rather than maintaining a significant presence in the city in order to facilitate the implementation of the Interim Statute, the EU began the process of closing down EUAM and WEU immediately after the election, creating a further political vacuum.[11] Correctly reading the political situation, Brajković and the newly elected HDZ councilors refused to implement any of the terms of the Interim Statute and blocked the formation of a joint city administration. They also attempted to establish a separate Union of

Croat Municipalities, which aimed to fuse together administratively the three Croat dominated municipal districts in West Mostar. When international officials in the city objected to this blatant disregard for the Interim Statute they simply ignored their protestations and continued governing West Mostar under the informal Heceg-Bosna political structures which still existed in Croat-controlled sections of Herzegovina.

Oddly, international officials decided to schedule a second municipal election in Mostar the following year to coincide with municipal elections across the rest of Bosnia that September—despite the failure of the first to facilitate a functional political outcome in either the city administration or the municipalities. This too did little more than further benefit HDZ, which again refused to accept consociational power-sharing measures in the West Mostar municipalities it dominated. In turn, Bosniak politicians saw little incentive to unilaterally adhere to the terms of the Interim Statute and began dragging their feet on returns and implementation of the power-sharing procedures in the three municipalities they controlled.

Early elections did not just legitimate the authority of the most obstructive segments of the Croat political spectrum in Mostar, it also contributed to the gradual erosion of the position of moderate Bosniak leaders in the city, in particular East Mostar mayor Safet Oručević, who was a strong supporter of the Interim Statute and the reunification of Mostar. With electoral success in 1996 and 1997 came expectations that Oručević was not able to meet due to obstruction by HDZ. Specifically, his inability to deliver sufficient advances on tangible issues such as returns of Bosniaks to their West Mostar apartments and the creation of a unified city administration undermined his political standing and facilitated the emergence of more hard-line figures such as Zijo Hadžiomerović, who took over leadership of the Mostar branch of SDA shortly after Oručević left the party in 2000.

Indeed, as noted in the previous chapter, by the time I was conducting fieldwork, political dynamics had flipped in Mostar, with international officials in the city identifying Hadžiomerović and the Mostar branch of SDA as a bigger impediment to reform and implementation of the new city statute than HDZ.[12] Early elections are obviously not the whole story here. Oručević's political standing was also undermined by influential members of the SDA leadership in Sarajevo with whom he frequently clashed, and the international community, which often undercut his authority by negotiating directly with those officials rather than local politicians in Mostar (see chapter 6). Nonetheless conducting local elections prior to the existence of a workable institutional framework ensured that more moderate Bosniak figures in Mostar like Oručević would share blame for the inevitable political dysfunctionality that followed.

Cementing Ethnic Division through Privatization

As with elections, privatization of public enterprises and property in Mostar began shortly after the war, with several prominent examples preceding both the introduction of relevant institutions and a proper legal framework. At the time these activities drew little scrutiny from internationals in Bosnia. In part this was because rapid privatization of public assets was a linchpin of the liberal economic transition model pushed by organizations such as the World Bank and USAID, which spearheaded the privatization process in the country. For instance, in a 1997 report the World Bank argued that "the rapid pace at which the rest of the world privatized during Bosnia and Herzegovina's civil war places a high priority and places a short time frame on privatization work."[13] Another reason that rapid privatization was encouraged is that it was treated primarily as a matter of technocratic reform.[14] As a result the political challenges of conducting privatization in the aftermath of war were given short shrift:

> The agency [USAID] has appeared largely untroubled by the fact that . . . virtually the only locals with resources to buy state-owned enterprises were members of a rather unholy alliance among the ruling parties, the increasingly powerful mafia, and elements of the old socialist-era nomenklatura. Nor has there been much concern that . . . Bosnia's privatization programme . . . would tend to reinforce ethnic divisions and provide opportunities for the wealthy, the corrupt, and the politically-connected to consolidate their power.[15]

Crucially, this technocratic approach also meant that the privatization process in Bosnia was largely unconnected from broader political and economic reforms being pursued by OHR and other international organizations at the time.

To say that the conditions in which early instances of privatization in Bosnia took place were chaotic is an understatement. It was not until 1998 when a comprehensive set of laws governing privatization—drafted with the assistance of USAID—was introduced in the country. The resulting institutional framework was mindbogglingly complex as there were twelve privatization agencies: one for the RS, one for the Federation, and—bizarrely—one in each of the latter's ten cantons. With little international supervision or funding these agencies lacked transparency and political independence. The legislation was also rife with contradictions and conflicts of interest. Managers were permitted to direct the privatization process for their own companies. Predictably these very same managers, or their political allies, often ended up controlling the newly privatized firms. In one randomized study of privatization in the eastern RS, for example, fourteen out of seventeen companies privatized through public auction ended up in the hands of their previous directors or prominent local SDS leaders.[16] The voucher-based privatization system also bolstered the ruling nationalist parties' ethno-territorial aims in Bosnia as the entities were "allowed to distribute a disproportionate numbers of vouchers to 'their' war veterans, which discriminated against citizens who had fled or been driven from their homes during the war."[17]

As elsewhere in Bosnia, rapid privatization in Mostar ensured control of companies by ruling nationalists or their allies, who then diverted revenues into party or personal coffers. It also cemented wartime ethnic cleansing. The best example of this was the giant aluminum producer Aluminij, one of Bosnia's most profitable companies and the country's largest exporter. During the Yugoslav era Aluminij had a diverse workforce that reflected Mostar's multiethnic population. At the beginning of the war Aluminij's factory was damaged by the JNA and ceased production. Following the JNA's withdrawal from Mostar in 1992 HVO took control of the plant and appointed a new, exclusively Bosnian Croat, board of managers led by HDZ's Mijo Brajković, who later became West Mostar's mayor. Aluminij's new management immediately dismissed all ethnic Serb and Bosniak employees. When the firm reopened in 1997 it also refused to rehire these workers, going so far as to physically bar them from entering the premises. Despite intense pressure from international officials it largely continued with a hiring policy which favors Croats. According to figures compiled by Amnesty International, more than 93 percent of Aluminji's nearly one-thousand-person workforce was ethnically Croat in 2003.[18]

At the same time that Aluminij renewed production the executive board initiated a questionable privatization process, which resulted in ownership of the firm by the Croatian company TLM Šibenik (12 percent) and Aluminij's Croat management and employees, who were given voucher shares in the company based on unpaid wages accrued when the plant was shuttered. While Croats were compensated for this entire period (fifty-three months), former Bosnian Serb employees received no shares, and Bosniaks were only compensated for the period prior to the start of Croat-Bosniak war in Mostar in May 1993.[19] Thus in practice this cocapitalization scheme reinforced control of Aluminij by HDZ and provided a key source of funding for Herceg-Bosna, the informal parastate that continued to rule Croat-dominated territories in the Federation for several years after the war ended. Indeed, Brajković admitted that in the year following Aluminij's reopening the firm contributed more than $450,000 a month in revenues to West Mostar's coffers alone.[20] Aluminij's restructuring did not happen in a vacuum. Privatization and recapitalization in Mostar could not have taken place without significant assistance and foreign investment from Spanish, German, American, and Swiss companies and the Spanish government. In fact, former EAUM chief Ricardo Perez Casado arranged for technical assistance and investment from Spain, for which he received a medal from Gojko Šušak in 1997.[21]

By the end of the 1990s international officials in Bosnia began to recognize that privatization in the absence of functional legal and political institutions was enhancing the position of nationalist parties and sustaining the ethno-territorial division of the country, while providing little economic benefit. In 2000 USAID halted its support of privatization efforts in the Federation, and OHR ordered an independent audit of Aluminij's privatization. While the report released the following year highlighted several irregularities in the process it concluded that "for political and practical reasons" the privatization of Aluminij should not be annulled.[22] Outraged, Bosniak politicians in the Federation refused to accept the report's findings, arguing that it "would mean that the greatest plunder in the Federation of BiH would be legalized."[23] After four more years of contentious negotiations an agreement was finally reached in 2005 to restructure ownership of the company—splitting the 88 percent share of the company not owned by TLM Šibenik equally among workers and the Federation government—and conduct another round of privatization for the company's state- and worker-owned shares. To date, however, further political wrangling has prevented this agreement from being fully implemented.

Deferred Privatization and Economic Development in Brčko

While postwar peacebuilding in Mostar resulted in early elections and the rapid privatization of public resources, to the extent that both developments preceded the creation of functional institutional frameworks, Brčko followed a path of intensive and lengthy institution-building prior to political and economic liberalization. Interestingly, this was not a planned outcome, but rather the result of independent decisions made by Brčko's first three supervisors—often in direct conflict with instructions from distant superiors and outside advisors.

Privatization was a particular point of contention. One of the earliest orders Robert Farrand issued on arriving in Bosnia was an indefinite ban on privatization within RS Brčko.[24] This greatly disappointed his State Department superiors in Washington, DC, who were pushing for rapid privatization in order to spur economic development in the area. However, Farrand held firm on his decision, even after the Arbitral Tribunal's 1998 Supplemental Award "authorized and encouraged" him to "establish a program of privatization of state-owned and socially-owned enterprises in the area."[25] His reasoning was that absent credible institutions and a definitive legal framework privatization in Brčko would consist of little more than the looting of public resources and entrenchment of local warlords.[26]

Following publication of the Final Award in 1999 Farrand extended his ban on privatization to the Federation-controlled part of Brčko. He also declared null and void all transactions that had been conducted in violation of his original order, following evidence that such activities had continued to be pursued in RS Brčko.[27] Despite this order several further capital for debt privatizations—which were little more than schemes to transfer remaining assets from public companies in Brčko to private entities in the RS and Serbia—were attempted in Brčko. In part these activities reflected a refusal to acknowledge the fact that the RS no longer had political authority in the District, and in part it was simply a case of local managers, who had achieved their positions by dint of political connections rather than any business expertise, seeking to enrich themselves before losing control of their companies. In response to these actions, OHR Brčko again annulled such transactions in the summer of 2001.[28]

Finally, in late 2001, Brčko's third supervisor, Henry Clarke, ordered District authorities to create an office to oversee privatization efforts.[29] Established with the assistance of OHR and the German development agency GTZ, the District privatization office and tender commission set about identifying an initial batch of companies for privatization, with the first successful case being the sale of Bimal—a vegetable oil processing facility—the following summer. As part of the agreement, the European firm that purchased Bimal pledged to invest 9 million euros in the plant and hire more than a hundred new workers from all three ethnic communities by the end of the first three years of operations. Bimal is now owned by the Austrian agricultural conglomerate Studen & Co Holding, which also purchased Brčko's privatized flour mill, Žitopromet, and built a large sugar refinery in the District in 2008. In total Studen employs more than four hundred people through these three companies and its logistics center in the District.[30] International oversight of the privatization process in Brčko continued even after the District privatization office was set up. Indeed, prior to the formation of the first elected District government in 2004, staff from the economic department in OHR Brčko insisted on carefully vetting every proposed privatization.

Delaying privatization ensured that investors in Brčko benefited from institutional structures that were not only rational on paper, but also effectively administered:

> By the time of the first privatization negotiations in 2002, Brcko District had an independent, reformed and fully-functioning judiciary—applying completely new civil and criminal codes that later became models for the rest of Bosnia and Herzegovina. The District government was becoming known for its business-friendly attitude and procedures, having abolished many unnecessary regulatory obstacles before the rest of the country. Brcko also had a modern bankruptcy law and judges were being trained in the new procedures.[31]

Even with these advantages, however, privatization in the District has not been without its hiccups. Several privatized firms are struggling economically, while others have not met their obligations for employment and investment.[32] And while the District has continued to attract foreign investment, like the 90 million KM sugar refinery, the global economic downturn and concerns about corruption in the District have begun to sap investor confidence in recent years.[33] Unlike in Mostar, though, delayed privatization in Brčko did not reinforce ethnic division but has rather contributed to the development of a unified economic space that has led to relatively more mixed workplaces in the District. This is significant because ethnographic research elsewhere in Bosnia has highlighted workplaces as a key site for promoting cooperative interethnic relations in the postwar period.[34] It is also no small accomplishment given countervailing dynamics in the rest of the country.

In addition to pursuing a go-slow strategy regarding privatization, Brčko's supervisors also resisted implementing orthodox liberal economic advice from USAID consultants concerning the privatization of natural monopolies. Henry Clarke highlights this decision in an analysis of the privatization process in Brčko published with the Woodrow Wilson Center:

> Another risk Brčko avoided was the privatization of natural monopolies. I strongly opposed privatization of the Brčko port, which is a vital but underdeveloped transportation link for the whole country—and the only river port ready for multi-modal operation. I saw no pressing need to privatize Brčko's water supplies or electricity distribution. Privatization of such monopolies would also require a regulatory regime in order to protect the public, and we did not have one.[35]

As I discuss in chapter 6 a crucial element of this story is not just Clarke and his predecessors' recognition of the importance of institutions, but also the political independence afforded supervisors to buck political and economic prescriptions from distant superiors and consultants that were inappropriate for the specific conditions they encountered on the ground.

Delayed Elections and Political Moderation

This last observation also applies to political liberalization, though here the story is a bit more complex. It is commonly asserted that elections in Brčko were delayed until 2004, when the first District government was elected.

However this is not completely accurate. As elsewhere in Bosnia a municipal election took place in RS-held Brčko in September 1997. What is not widely known is that Robert Farrand in effect chose to annul the election, which was plagued with controversy.[36]

This election posed several difficulties due to the unresolved status of the IEBL in the area. Foremost was the question of whether all Bosniak and Croat residents of the prewar Brčko *opština* should be allowed to vote in the RS Brčko municipal election—as advocated by the Federation—or only those who had lived in what was now RS-controlled territory north of the IEBL? As this question had not been addressed in the Arbitral Tribunal's First Award, the decision fell to OSCE, which was in charge of election rules in Bosnia. In May OSCE opted for the latter option, a controversial decision that in effect legitimated the territorial division of the Brčko area for the time being.

Two months later a second controversy erupted when OSCE's Election Appeals Subcommission (EASC) invalidated the registration of more than thirty-two hundred voters in RS Brčko due to widespread fraud by SDS.[37] This ruling set off alarm bells in the RS, for even with OSCE's earlier decision to limit possible Federation voters to those who had lived in what was now RS Brčko prior to the war, it was not clear which side would be able to muster more votes. Ethnic Serbs had constituted approximately 20 percent of the prewar residents in Brčko town. Therefore, even though RS authorities had resettled thousands in the downtown during and shortly after the war, it was possible that Federation parties would still be able to gain a majority in a cleanly run election in RS Brčko. Such a possibility was clearly unacceptable to the RS. In the wake of the riots in Brčko that August (see chapter 4) an emboldened SDS declared it would boycott elections throughout the RS unless OSCE reversed the original EASC decision. Just days before the elections OSCE acquiesced and reinstated more than twenty-six hundred voters whose registration had previously been denied, citing "errors" in the original procedures.[38] Other OSCE officials with direct knowledge of this case, however, claim that the head of OSCE, American diplomat Robert Frowick—operating under orders from the State Department—cut a deal with SDS to allow the registration of these voters in exchange for calling off the boycott, which it promptly did following the decision.[39]

The result of all of these political machinations was a narrow victory by Serb parties.[40] What is most interesting, though, is what happened after the election took place as Robert Farrand essentially ignored it when he went about creating new multiethnic institutions through supervisory orders in RS Brčko that fall—though the results were used as a rough guide for determining the ethnic composition of the municipal government.[41] The RS Brčko municipal Assembly was marginalized in favor of a reconstituted Executive Board, consisting of an ethnic Serb mayor and Bosniak and Croat deputies, and new heads of the five municipal departments, which were selected through negotiation with local elites from each of the three communities. During the next seven years OHR Brčko and other international organizations in the area methodically worked to build up multiethnic institutions in RS Brčko—and then the District—through supervisory orders and informal tactics of consultation, sanction, and negotiation with local elites.[42]

A critical point in this institution-building process was the creation of the District. As noted in chapter 3 this was a complex and difficult endeavor that involved the merger of three separate municipal authorities, and the development of a new police force and judicial system independent from their RS and Federation antecedents. However this also presented an opportunity for thorough vetting of candidates for the new positions due to excess staffing after consolidation. OHR Brčko took advantage of this by requiring all inherited personnel from the previous municipalities—including the judiciary and school teachers—to go through a rigorous reapplication and hiring process. Only after a careful review of applications, interviews, and consultation with local political leaders were selections made. While this did slow down the process—recruitment was not completed until January 2002—it did facilitate the promotion of more competent and moderate civil servants.[43]

This approach was not without its critics in Bosnia—both domestic and international—who called for new municipal elections and for power to be turned over to local officials as soon as possible, especially after the founding of the District in 2000. In early 2001 SDS publically requested the organization of the first poll in conjunction with general elections scheduled across the rest of Bosnia in 2002. Behind the scenes Farrand's successors, Gary Matthews (2000–2001) and Henry Clarke, were receiving similar suggestions from OHR Sarajevo and the State Department. As with privatization, they resisted these calls, citing insignificant time to establish effective institutions and allow for the emergence of political leaders ready to represent District rather than entity interests: "The Supervisor's view is that the question of when the time will have come to hold District elections must be assessed in view of the fact that the District is still in the process of becoming fully established. . . . Moderate, objective and widely supported political movements capable both of winning an election and adequately representing their constituents have yet to appear on the local political scene."[44] Ultimately Clarke was successful in persuading his superiors to delay an election in Brčko until October 2004.

Following the election a multiethnic coalition led by SDP established the first District government. Thus in contrast to Mostar, where early elections entrenched HDZ hardliners who came to power during the war and weakened the standing of more moderate Bosniak politicians, delaying the election in Brčko facilitated the emergence of alternative political figures who had proven themselves during the first four years of the District's existence. Moreover, following the 2008 election Dragan Pajić, a member of SNSD was elected mayor, while the previous mayor, SDP's Mirsad Djapo became president of the District Assembly. Though the unwieldy concentration government that Pajić headed was not without its problems (as noted in chapter 3), this transition from a Bosniak to Serb mayor was an achievement in its own right—and stood in stark contrast to events in Mostar following its 2008 municipal election. Perhaps even more significant was the election of Brčko's first Croat mayor, Anto Domić, in 2012, which highlighted the ability of the smallest of the three main ethnic communities in the District to play a meaningful role in the political process. These democratic and relatively uneventful transitions of political power in a formerly bitterly contested territory that had been divided into three separate ethnocratic municipalities a decade prior represent a remarkable achievement, and highlight the wisdom of international officials in Brčko who resisted calls for rapid political liberalization following the establishment of the District in 2000.

6

Peacebuilding Practices
and Institutions

At this point the finding that rapid economic and political liberalization had negative effects in Mostar is not terribly surprising. There are many examples of similarly detrimental outcomes to such policies in the peacebuilding literature. Perhaps a more interesting and important question concerning sequencing is why the lengthy and intensive institution-building approach undertaken in Brčko did not suffer from a lack of legitimacy and support from the local populace? As noted in chapter 1, critics of the institutionalization before liberalization model warn that peacebuilding interventions often come to be perceived as authoritarian and undemocratic, perceptions that in turn undermine the legitimacy of international officials, and local participation in the peacebuilding process. Yet despite the vast authority wielded by the supervisory regime it generally received broad support from District residents over the years. Moreover productive participation by local elites in the reform process was greater than anywhere else in Bosnia. How did international officials in Brčko manage to achieve this?

Successful postwar peacebuilding requires a strong international presence at the local level, a meaningful engagement with local actors, and sustained commitment of resources and personnel. In Brčko the broad supervisory powers established by the Arbitral Tribunal concentrated decision-making authority and policy formulation responsibilities in OHR Brčko's hands to a far greater extent than elsewhere in Bosnia. This clear place-based hierarchy gave the supervisors significant influence over other Brčko-based international staff, improving the coordination of policy activities. It also imparted greater legitimacy to peacebuilding efforts in the eyes of political and economic elites in Brčko, both due to the supervisory regime's relative independence from outside interference and the development of dense daily interactions between international and local officials. In Mostar, in contrast, the practice and organization of peacebuilding militated against the establishment of an effectively localized international presence. First, internationals in Mostar suffered from a lack of independence from distant superiors, which undercut their authority and impeded their ability to create productive working relationships with local officials. Second, as elsewhere in Bosnia the various international civilian and military organizations in Mostar lacked sufficient coordination of policy creation and execution, a problem exacerbated by shifting and poorly aligned areas of responsibility and the different nationalities of organizational heads. Finally, a lack of social and political embeddedness by international officials working in the city had a further detrimental effect on international-local relations and policy decision making.

The Supervisory Regime and the Concentration of Political Authority in Brčko

One of the most fascinating and consequential aspects of international intervention in Brčko has been the series of awards issued by the Arbitral Tribunal, the ad hoc legal institution charged with ruling on the disputed portion of the IEBL in the Brčko area. As noted in chapter 3, the First Award, which created the OHR supervisory regime in the Brčko area, gave supervisors the power to "promulgate binding regulations and orders" that would supersede "any conflicting law."[1] The Final Award two years later further expanded the mandate of OHR Brčko in the District: it was charged with writing a statute for the new District government; appointing an interim assembly; setting up a law review commission to rewrite the laws inherited by the entities; establishing an independent tax system and budget authority; constructing new, multiethnic institutions; and deciding when the IEBL had no legal significance—and thus ceased to exist—within the Brčko area. Essentially the Final Award made the supervisory regime the "final authority in the District on virtually everything."[2]

This comprehensive mandate and sweeping set of powers was central to the success of peacebuilding in Brčko. To begin it has concentrated policy authority in OHR Brčko's hands at a level unmatched in Mostar or other field offices in Bosnia. As Henry Clarke has observed about the internal dynamics of OHR elsewhere in the country during his time as supervisor, "The 2001 Office of the High Representative in Bosnia and Herzegovina was a large, centralized staff in Sarajevo, which shared little authority and information about its plans with a deliberately weak set of field offices."[3] The OHR Brčko office in contrast was relatively powerful and independent, since its source of authority derived from the Arbitral Tribunal's awards. One key benefit of this political dynamic is that supervisors were afforded greater latitude to tailor their policies to local conditions. The decisions by the first three supervisors to delay political and economic liberalization in the face of opposition by distant superiors and outside consultants (see chapter 5) are merely the two most salient examples of the utility of this political independence.

This is not to suggest that the authority of the supervisory regime has been uncontested over the years. Susan Johnson, Brčko's fourth supervisor (2004–6), was removed from office in 2006 after repeatedly defying directives from OHR Sarajevo and the State Department aimed at ending supervision in the District. Also, OHR Sarajevo persistently argued—with limited success—that supervisors are subordinate to the High Representative, and the entities have frequently fought OHR Brčko's efforts to protect the District from their predatory behavior.[4] However these disputes tended to further legitimate rather than undermine OHR Brčko's standing in the District by creating, as I outline in the following chapter, what amounted to a close patron-client relationship between it and local political and economic elites. This dynamic was a critical—though overlooked— component of peacebuilding in Brčko insofar as the resulting political alliance in turn positively affected peacebuilding efforts within the District.

Place-Based Hierarchy and Policy Coordination

The broad authority given to the supervisory regime also facilitated the co-ordination of peacebuilding activities in Brčko. This becomes clear when one compares the organization of international peacebuilding intervention elsewhere in Bosnia, which has been, by design, highly decentralized across different agencies. One of the consequences of this approach has been difficulty in effectively coordinating policy efforts in the country. As the European Stability Initiative (ESI) characterized the situation in 2000:

> The international community is a honeycomb of power centres, with multiple actors pursuing their individual goals with substantial autonomy. There are myriad international organisations, each with its own source of authority. . . . Each is answerable to a different hierarchy or constituency, with programming and funding decisions taken in isolation and at a distance from Bosnia. . . . So far as there is any organising principle among this institutional diversity, it is horizontal rather than hierarchical.[5]

In Brčko, in contrast, the Arbitral Tribunal's awards established a clear, place-based hierarchy among international organizations. Due to the supervisory regime's expansive mandate, nearly every peacebuilding activity—returns; elections; privatization; as well as police, judicial, educational, and administrative reforms—either ran through the OHR Brčko office or was dependent on close coordination with it in order to succeed. This gave supervisors significant influence over other Brčko-based international staff. Additionally, because of its initial unresolved status and the subsequent mandate to create from scratch an autonomous district, Brčko was considered a singular situation with distinct priorities and peacebuilding challenges from other places in Bosnia. Consequently most of the key international organizations in the country (i.e., UNMIBH/IPTF, OSCE, OHR, SFOR) set up separate regional offices or bases that dealt specifically with Brčko's unique set of issues.

Additionally, it is not an insignificant fact that Brčko is located in the corner of northeast Bosnia, quite distant from the capital. Even with the best weather and road conditions it takes a minimum of three hours to reach Sarajevo on a dangerous, winding road. Therefore face-to-face communication between international staff in Brčko and headquarters in Sarajevo was and remains infrequent. Conversely Brčko-based internationals tended to share densely intertwined "daily paths and projects" of experience, especially in the first three years after the war.[6] During this time, for example, daily meetings between OHR Brčko staff and representatives from SFOR, IPTF, UNHCR, OSCE, UN Civil Affairs and CAFAO were held in Farrand's office.[7] And social time was often spent together at a gym set up for international staff or one of the handful of restaurants and bars in the town. Isolated from head offices in Sarajevo and other centers of intervention, for most of the relatively large international cohort assigned to this small outpost in Bosnia the relevant social and professional communities tended to be remarkably "localized" over the years. Thus, while in theory institutional affiliation and organizational chains of command should have structured policy priorities and interaction among different officials in Brčko, in practice many Brčko-based internationals viewed themselves as part of a coherent "Brčko team," an attitude which early supervisors in particular shrewdly cultivated.[8]

Further improving coordination of peacebuilding efforts in Brčko is the fact that the relationship between civilian and military actors was unusually strong over the years. Robert Farrand has identified this as one of the key reasons for his success: "It is crucial, insofar as getting results on the ground: the alignment of military and civilian objectives on the broader scale, and then the alignment in each of these little regional areas. . . . you have to spend a lot of time talking, the different cultures."[9] While it undoubtedly helped that Farrand served in the armed forces prior to taking up a diplomatic career, thus helping him better navigate the cultural differences, there is a second reason military-civilian coordination was superior in Brčko: from the beginning it has been something of an "American" project in which both the supervisor and local military commander were always Americans. The point is not that Americans are more effective than Europeans in Bosnia. Rather, it is easier to bridge the civilian-military divide in peacebuilding environments in the absence of national differences, which, as I outline below in the case of Mostar, almost inevitably complicated matters. To give just one example, in the fall of 1997 when OHR Brčko was beginning to facilitate returns of Bosniak families to their former homes in the ZOS, Farrand was able to secure an informal agreement with the local American military commander to have his troops adjust their normally straight patrol routes in and out of RS Brčko so that they would occasionally detour through these neighborhoods—which increased operational risks, especially at night—thus serving as a deterrent against Serb hardliners who were attacking the settlements.[10]

Embeddedness and the Cultivation of Productive Local-International Relations

The cultivation of good working relationships with local elites has also been critical to the success of peacebuilding in Brčko. Henry Clarke has observed that "for Brčko, there could be no question of 'top-down' versus 'grass roots' reforms. To succeed, every major reform had to be introduced and sold at every level. . . . To that end, coordinating at the local level was essential. It is easier to lead, to coordinate and to negotiate reforms when you are meeting regularly, face to face, with all the key actors." In contrast, elsewhere in Bosnia:

> OHR in Sarajevo could develop and even impose new laws but relied almost entirely on existing Bosnian institutions to implement them. The High Representative at that time, Wolfgang Petritsch, recognized and often cited the need for "ownership" of reform by the local people, but he did not have an effective mechanism for achieving it. In Brčko, we could not guarantee "ownership," but we could make reforms work, and that did give us support for more reforms.[11]

As Clarke points out, characterizing peacebuilding efforts as either top-down or grass-roots misses the point. More important for the successful development and implementation of reforms are productive international-local relations that can only be established through regular interaction and dialogue.

To expand on this point, the Brčko experience suggests that local ownership is an overrated, or at the least misprescribed, solution for peacebuilding ailments.[12] Nowhere else in Bosnia has there been less ownership of peacebuilding reforms, in the sense of local control over policy creation than the Brčko District. What has existed, though, is a situation in which input is consistently solicited on how to best proceed with a given set of goals. Take the Brčko Law Review Commission (BLRC), which was charged with rewriting the entire legal system in the District and had almost complete freedom to draft legislation as it saw fit. From the beginning the BLRC made it a practice to organize roundtable discussions and circulate initial drafts of laws among political parties and members of the District government and judiciary as a way to generate feedback and develop consensus. A reworked draft would then be presented to the District Assembly for consideration, amendment, and adoption.[13] In this way only one law—the 2001 Law on Education, which created an integrated District-wide school system—had to be imposed by supervisory order during the BLRC's time of operation.

International and local officials also worked closely together during the implementation process. For example, a District Management Team (DMT) consisting of municipal government experts funded by USAID was established to assist local officials in the development of new District institutions in the first three years after the Final Award.[14] Osman Osmanović, who was appointed head of the District's new Revenue Agency at the time, is one of several Brčko officials who highlighted their positive working relationship with DMT during my research: "I learned from them what devotion means, working twelve hours a day till seven in the evening."[15] In a similar vein the District's first mayor, Siniša Kisić, observes that "in this period we had an active relationship with OHR. We had weekly meetings. The supervisor had his agenda and we had ours—without imposition. When I was the mayor we even had joint press conferences where the supervisor presented his activities and then I as mayor presented activities of the government."[16] In other words, reforms have worked in Brčko because local officials have been cultivated as partners—not owners—of the peacebuilding process.[17]

By partnership I do not mean to imply that local-international relations were equal in terms of power or authority, nearly all of which rested with the supervisory regime prior to the 2004 elections. Rather the international staff embedded in Brčko typically worked together on a daily basis with local actors and made a concerted effort to listen seriously to their concerns. The few times when inadequate attention was paid to local interlocutors setbacks have resulted. For example, in 2000 Brčko's second supervisor, Gary Matthews, rushed through an attempt to integrate schools with little input from District officials or public discussion with concerned parents, setting off massive protests in October, which resulted in the temporary closure of the schools until changes were reversed.[18] The following year

Matthews's successor, Henry Clarke, organized more than thirty public forums throughout the summer to discuss school integration with District citizens.[19] He also worked extensively behind the scenes with teachers and District officials to gain support for the changes. While he did end up having to impose the education law, integration of the schools that fall proceeded smoothly with minimal incidents or public protest.[20]

Political and social embeddedness has also played a role in enhancing relations between local and international officials. What I mean by embeddedness is the degree to which international officials become effectively localized in relation to the practices, networks, and institutions that mediate political and social processes at the sites in which they operate.[21] As noted above, Brčko is a remote posting in northeast Bosnia. Because it is distant from both the capital of Sarajevo and the Adriatic coast of Croatia, international officials assigned to this small outpost in Bosnia more often than not could be found—especially in the early years—putting in extra hours at the office or socializing with friends or colleagues from the District during the weekends.[22] During Farrand's tenure as supervisor, for instance, weekly strategy meetings attended by representatives from each of the major international organizations in Brčko were held every Saturday afternoon.[23] Moreover, relative to Mostar and other field offices in Bosnia, international officials have tended to stay longer at their posts in Brčko. For example, from 1994 to 2004—when Paddy Ashdown effectively sidelined the OHR Mostar office by appointing a Mostar Implementation Unit run out of Sarajevo (see below)—the EUAM and its political successor, OHR Mostar, cycled through nine different heads of office, or nearly one a year.[24] In contrast, during sixteen years of supervision in Brčko there have been only six supervisors.[25]

Extended time at a field site or office is crucial for facilitating knowledge of local political dynamics and the development of personal relationships with local elites. As Farrand, who spent thirty-eight months as supervisor, observes, "Shorter commitments of time—say, six to nine months—simply will not cut it in view of the need to establish interpersonal relations with a wide array of actors as you seek to establish your authority, based, you hope, more on suasion than diktat. Establishing such relationships takes time."[26] Unfortunately shorter commitments, and the attendant lack of social and political embeddedness, have tended to be the rule rather than the exception at the field offices of most international organizations in

Bosnia. Andrew Gilbert, for instance, observes that during his sixteen months of ethnographic fieldwork (2002–3) in Sanski Most and Prijedor, two northwestern Bosnian cities with OSCE field offices, three Human Rights Officers (HROs) and four Democratization Officers (DOs) cycled through the former city, while there were three different DOs in the latter. Only the HRO in Prijedor remained the same during this period. The consequence of this rapid turnover, Gilbert observes, is that these foreign officials' interactions with local officials and citizens was marked by "profound uncertainty and anxiety regarding the reliability and trustworthiness of the information they possessed, how it was interpreted, and where it circulated."[27]

Short-term postings, though, are just one of many factors which inhibit knowledge of local conditions and the development of effective personal relations. Kimberley Cole notes, for example, that disembeddedness is also shaped by the fact that international officials in Bosnia are exempt from much of the state's regulatory mechanisms and generally do not rely on its institutions for the provision of social goods like health care, utilities, and education.[28] One way in which officials working in Brčko developed a richer understanding of the everyday issues faced by residents in the District was the creation of a "citizen's complaint system," which was established by the DMT in 2000. Designed to provide public feedback on government services, more than eighteen hundred responses were received in the initial year, as local residents used it to report an array of problems both within and beyond the realm of official responsibilities.[29]

In addition to the complaints system, District residents would also frequently write the OHR Brčko office, providing rich insight into local concerns. Long-time deputy supervisor Gerhard Sontheim made a point to read and respond to each of these letters, directing petitioners to relevant administrative departments and asking District officials to provide updates on key cases. To give a sense of the scale of this undertaking, from June 2004 to February 2007, OHR Brčko received 912 letters. During this period complaints were primarily concerned with reconstruction assistance, though complaints about court cases, hiring decisions, tender processes, and land use decisions from the department of urbanism and spatial planning were also common.[30] Eventually the last problem was dealt with through a supervisory order removing the head of the office, prodded in part by the information provided by these letters.[31]

Undermining Political Independence in Mostar

One of the more striking aspects of peacebuilding intervention in Mostar is the degree to which international officials in the city have consistently suffered from a lack of political independence due to interference from faraway superiors with little knowledge of conditions on the ground, beginning with the EUAM and WEU missions and continuing to more recent efforts by OHR Mostar to reform the city's institutional framework. The situation for the EUAM was especially absurd. To begin, the EU administrator, Hans Koschnick had no say in selecting the composition of his staff.[32] Instead EU member states nominated their own candidates for posts, which were divvied up along national lines. Consequently the structure of the EUAM mission, including the number of departments and division of responsibilities between them, was influenced by "the need to provide acceptable portfolios for the persons nominated by the Member States."[33] Second, the EUAM was hampered by excessive micromanagement over its budget, which led to cash-flow problems and the devotion of "a considerable part of its limited staff resources" to prepare regular, detailed accounts of its expenditures.[34]

Finally, Koschnick was required to request guidance from, and submit regular reports to, a constantly shifting and ineffective set of EU actors. Officially the EU administrator was required to report to the EU Council of Ministers that had appointed him. In practice, however, the council delegated oversight of the mission to the Council Presidency and an advisory working party consisting of member state representatives. The main problem with this arrangement was that every six months the Council Presidency—and thus the staff responsible for dealing with the EUAM and making final decisions—would rotate to a new country, creating, in Koschnick's words, a "traveling circus of political responsibility."[35] The working party was also ineffective as "decisions were frequently carried over from one meeting to the next, reflecting the need to refer back to the national capitals."[36] In a remarkable resolution published following the closure of the EUAM the European Parliament expressly admitted these oversight failures, noting that the Council Presidency and advisory working group "were clearly not capable of performing the task of supervising the joint action entrusted to them by the Council."[37]

Most vexing for Koschnick was that the EU and its member states consistently undermined his independence by failing to offer the political support necessary to facilitate the ambitious goals of the EUAM mission. The starkest example of this was the EU's response to Croat opposition to Koschnick's arbitration ruling concerning the composition of the city's planned central zone. Although it was a compromise between the Bosniak and Croat positions, his decision was violently rejected by HDZ (see chapter 4). Rather than backing Koschnick, Italy, which had just taken over the EU Presidency, arranged an emergency summit in Rome. There the EU agreed to a "comprehensive solution" that acquiesced to Croat demands to dramatically reduce the size of the central zone.[38]

Incensed by the EU's refusal to support his decision—and being forced to sit at the negotiating table with the very same local authorities who had been responsible for the attacks against EUAM and WEU personnel— Koschnick resigned a week later, stating, "I have resigned as the EU states did not endorse me in the conflict with Croat authorities in the town. European states' governments demanded too much, forcing me to continue cooperation with the Croat police commander in the western part of town who had been watching his policemen jeopardizing the lives of my policemen."[39] Following an investigation of EU policy failures in Mostar later that year the European Parliament expressed regret that "Mr Koschnick did not always receive the full and unreserved political backing of the Council Presidency and EU Foreign Ministers" and acknowledged that "the work of the EU Administration was unnecessarily hampered by a whole series of omissions and shortcomings in preparations and in decision-making."[40]

Unfortunately these lessons seem to have been poorly learned as ineffective and overly intrusive oversight and a lack of political independence did not end with the closure of the EU mission in Mostar at the end of 1996. The OHR and OSCE field offices in Mostar have also seen their input routinely ignored or overruled through the years. One former senior international official in Mostar characterized OHR Sarajevo's approach as a schizophrenic combination of "management by laissez faire" and "event driven" bursts of activity. That is, his superiors would be disengaged from goings-on in the city until a dramatic incident motivated them to react, typically with some top-down directive devised in Sarajevo.[41] Former OHR Mostar head Finn Lynghjem (2000–2001) concurred, stating, "You couldn't do anything unless it came from Sarajevo . . . if you did too much it would inevitably be criticized." The result was that "almost 80 percent of my energy and time went to fighting my own people, in Sarajevo."[42] In recent years the problem has become more one of neglect. Characterizing the relationship between OHR Mostar and Sarajevo during the tenure of Miroslav Lájčak, one OHR official in the city states that "we didn't even exist for him."[43]

Perhaps the best example of this problem was the administrative unification of the city imposed by Paddy Ashdown in 2004. OHR's field office in Mostar first formulated a plan for unification and pitched it to Ashdown when he arrived in Bosnia in 2002, but he set it aside for a year to concentrate on his "bulldozer" economic reforms. As Ashdown acknowledges, this did not go over well with international officials in Mostar: "The French ambassador [OHR Mostar head Jean-Pierre Berçot] complained bitterly . . . that we were sweeping this problem under the carpet."[44] Finally, the following spring (2003) he gave OHR Mostar permission to initiate local political negotiations. However when these talks appeared to bog down that summer Ashdown quickly changed course and established a Commission for Reforming the City of Mostar, run out of OHR Sarajevo, prompting Berçot to resign in protest. Then, after his January 2004 decision to impose the commission's unification plan, Ashdown established a separate Mostar Implementation Unit (MIU) headed by a special envoy answerable directly to the High Representative to oversee reform efforts, again undercutting staff at OHR Mostar.[45] As the political officer from the office at that time put it to me, "Ironically, while trying to get rid of parallelisms in Mostar, we were establishing one of our own."[46] There was also a concerted effort from Sarajevo to suppress information about difficulties concerning implementation of the new city statute. According to one OSCE official, her superiors in Sarajevo had ordered her to cease writing reports on the political situation in Mostar in 2005 because they were seen as too negative, which complicated Ashdown's attempts to show substantial progress in the city and thus justify closing down the MIU.[47]

Diffusion of Authority, Shifting Priorities, and Coordination Problems

A second problem affecting peacebuilding efforts in Mostar has been poor coordination among international organizations. For instance, in

1996 EUAM offered 12 million Deutschmarks in funds for refurbishment of the three hydroelectric plants in Mostar on the condition that HDZ and SDA relinquish control over the structures to a unified city administration. SDA's national leadership in Sarajevo refused the offer, instead obtaining funds from the World Bank with no strings attached.[48] Even within the EUAM mission in Mostar proper coordination of activities and responsibilities was often lacking as "individual department heads tended to work independently with their own procedures."[49] Moreover, due to its weak mandate the WEU police contingent in Mostar did not adequately support or coordinate with the EU administration mission in the city: "The WEU police contingent did not assume a genuinely regulatory role, but was confined to advisory and observer duties. The EU administrator was therefore never in the position of having adequate instruments to enforce his decisions and impose them on the hardliners in the opposing factions. He therefore always lacked a vital element of authority."[50]

Internal reports by WEU give a sense of just how little power the police contingent had in relation to obstructionist paramilitary and police forces in the city. Consider the following excerpts from an August 1995 report, a year after the WEU began its mission in Mostar:

> There have been a number of incidents between West [Mostar] Police and WEU police during the week. Most were of a relatively minor nature however one occurring on Monday evening resulted in WEU and East [Mostar] police officers being surrounded by armed men from West Intervention Group. All the incidents, including this one, contravened previously agreed freedom of movement arrangements and represented a challenge to the authority of the WEU police. . . . It is not clear whether these incidents are part of a plan or misunderstandings between officers of good intention. The end result is that East [Mostar] police have stopped patrolling the Boulevard and this cannot contribute to a quick development of a unified police force.

This is a remarkably understated summary of the operational situation at the time—not to mention a charitable interpretation of the West Mostar police actions given the actual details of the incidents of the previous week, especially the armed confrontation on Monday highlighted in the same report:

At 21.40 hrs the Joint Patrol 805 (WEU and East [Mostar] police officers) vehicle was stopped between WEU police station and checkpoint C10 by the same West [Mostar] police officers. They wanted to take the interpreter and the two East [Mostar] police officers out of the car but a WEU police officer did not allow, closing and locking the vehicle's doors. After few minutes the WEU police vehicle was surrounded by about 15 West [Mostar] police intervention officers who arrived at the location in two vans. They were pointing machine guns to the WEU police vehicle. They ordered the WEU vehicle driver to stop the engine and turn off the lights. WEU duty officer and West [Mostar] police liaison officer tried to go to the location but they were stopped by West [Mostar] police officers. . . . At 22.40 hrs the vehicle was released and the East [Mostar] police chief, Mr. Djonko, came to the location and took back the East [Mostar] police officers to their police station.[51]

Though the details of this incident are dramatic, what is perhaps more telling is just how ordinary such overt obstructionism and threats of violence again international officials in the city were during the EUAM and WEU missions.

An additional factor hampering the effective coordination of peacebuilding activities in Bosnia has been the set of practices surrounding the definition of regional Areas of Responsibility (AORs). To begin, they have frequently shifted over the years—shrinking, expanding, and disappearing as international priorities or intraorganizational politics changed. While flexibility can be a virtue, mutating AORs has made it more difficult to maintain continuity in operations at the local level. Moreover, international organizations' AORs have rarely shared common geographical boundaries. Take the AORs of the Mostar-based regional headquarters of OHR, OSCE, UN IPTF, UNHCR, and SFOR in 2001, illustrated in figure 10. While all five overlapped in the city itself, there were significant differences across them as a whole, such as OHR Mostar's responsibility for Canton 10, UNHCR's extension into Central Bosnia, and SFOR's vast remit, which included Sarajevo and its surrounding environs as well as most of the Eastern RS. Given these differences it is not surprising that policy focus and knowledge across organizations has often been less than optimal in the region.[52]

Civilian-military coordination was also a persistent problem in Mostar. It is worth recalling that the EUAM mission began before the Dayton

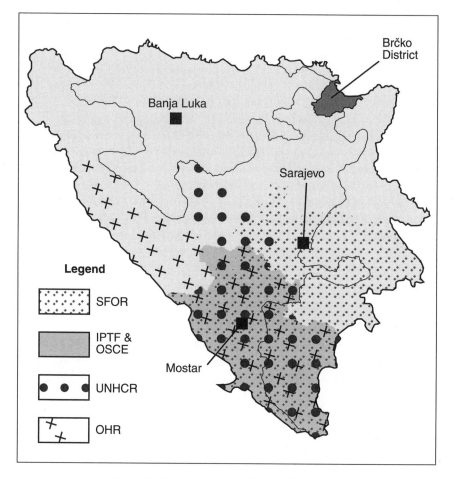

Figure 10. Mostar region Areas of Responsibility (AORs)

Agreement was signed, thus during its first eighteen months of operation the only international military presence in the area were UNPROFOR peacekeepers. However the EUAM had no control over UNPROFOR operations, nor was it within the mandate of the peacekeeping force to support the EU's efforts in the city, though it did assign a liaison officer to inform the EUAM about the military situation in the region. Combined with the limited WEU mandate noted above this meant that the EUAM lacked the authority to confront obstructionist forces in the city.

If anything, though, the situation took a turn for the worse with the arrival of IFOR forces in 1996:

> When the IFOR troops, UNPROFOR's successor after the Dayton Accords, arrived, its commander made clear that IFOR . . . would not sign a Memorandum of Understanding with the EUAM because IFOR did not feel responsible for the political process within the Federation, especially not for Mostar. In principle, IFOR would respond to military elements of the Bosniac or Croat side only in case of a direct threat.[53]

This was not a bluff. During the February 1996 riots Spanish IFOR troops took over an hour to reach EAUM headquarters and rescue Koschnick and his staff. Disregarding the possibility of violent reactions to the arbitration decision on the Interim Statute, IFOR commanders had done little to bolster their presence in the city that day. Likewise, when Croat police attacked Bosniaks who were walking toward the Liska Street cemetery to pay respects to their dead in February 1997 (see chapter 4), SFOR troops and IPTF police monitors stood aside and watched passively as the violence unfolded.

Even though Mostar was the headquarters of IFOR's (and later SFOR's) Multinational Division South-East (MND-SE), poor civilian-military relations in the city continued to bedevil peacebuilding efforts over the years. It is worth noting here that civilian-military coordination was also lacking elsewhere in Bosnia, especially in the first few years of intervention. A key reason for this, as noted in chapter 2, is that the United States insisted that civilian organizations in Bosnia have no authority over military operations in the country.[54] Another is that the United States demanded that military peacekeepers' activities also be limited, due to the Pentagon's fear of "mission creep."[55] As it became clear that nationalist obstruction—especially regarding returns and freedom of movement—was hindering peacebuilding efforts in the country, SFOR began to expand its activities in support of political initiatives undertaken by civilian organizations, such as the decision to help Biljana Plavšić and her allies in the RS in 1997. Starting that year British military forces also began undertaking operations to apprehend figures indicted for war crimes by the ICTY. However the French, who commanded MND-SE, were reluctant to adopt these more aggressive approaches, preferring to maintain a minimalist peacekeeping stance.[56] As OHR and other international organizations began to pursue a robust peacebuilding agenda in the late 1990s and early 2000s this led to a growing disconnect between civilian and military actors in Mostar.

One arresting example of this division was OHR's attempted audit of Hercegovačka Banka offices throughout the Federation in 2001. This bank was the primary conduit through which money to support the Herceg-Bosna shadow statelet was channeled, making it one of the lynchpins of the Croat separatist movement in Bosnia.[57] Insufficiently backed by SFOR in the Mostar region—which deployed only a handful of militarized police—international auditors were quickly attacked and held hostage in the banks by violent mobs of HDZ supporters. When the French commander in the region refused to send reinforcements to rescue them the auditors were forced to leave critical documents behind after their lives were threatened.[58] In contrast, in the British and American-controlled sectors of the Federation, the audit went smoothly due to the presence of robust SFOR escorts. After the incidents SFOR tried to claim that security risks had not been properly assessed in the Mostar region. This claim, though, was undercut by the fact that security at the French base in the city had been beefed up markedly prior to and during the events.[59]

In both the attack on the EUAM offices in 1996 and the botched Hercegovačka Banka audit it was also not an insignificant fact that the heads of the affected civilian organizations were a different nationality than the military commanders in Mostar at the time. Indeed, multiple international officials in Bosnia highlighted national differences as a significant impediment to the effective coordination of peacebuilding activities during interviews. This problem was especially acute in Mostar due to the city being something of a "European" project that entailed—as noted above in the case of the EUAM—a delicate apportionment of leading positions to different EU member states in a manner not unlike the use of an ethnic key to distribute power and patronage in Bosnia. These national divisions did not just affect high-profile failures such as the Hercegovačka Banka operation, they also contributed to less than optimal day-to-day communication and cooperation between and among civilian and military officials. In the late 1990s, for instance, SFOR and civilian organizations were unable to even effectively coordinate public information activities in Mostar due to cross-national tensions.[60]

The Failure to Establish Close and Effective International-Local Relationships

Peacebuilding efforts in Mostar have also been negatively impacted by the lack of close and productive relations between local and international officials in the city. As recounted in the introduction, this problem was brought into sharp relief by the fact that meetings between the two frequently took days to arrange, a situation that stood in contrast to local-international relations in Brčko. There are several reasons for this difference. First, compared to Brčko those working in Mostar tended to spend less time in the city while off-duty, instead traveling to Sarajevo (a two-hour drive on one of the better roads in the country) for greater cultural amenities or to visit friends working at the central offices, or the Adriatic coast (one hour) for the beach and sun. Indeed, I learned early on during research that it was counterproductive to offer to meet on the weekends with international officials working in the city. In Brčko, in contrast, weekends were a highly productive time to schedule interviews. This is admittedly a subjective judgment, but it is a difference that became clear during my eighteen months of fieldwork in the two cities.

Second, insufficient political independence also undercut attempts to create effective working relationships with local elites who, seeing international officials based in the city routinely ignored or bypassed, instead attempted to communicate directly with their superiors in Sarajevo. As early as 1999, for example, the OSCE field office in Mostar was complaining that Zijo Hadžiomerović, who was then angling to oust Safet Oručević as head of the SDA in Mostar, "routinely fires off complaints to top IC officials in Sarajevo without even a cc to the RC and other IOs represented in Mostar."[61] This complaint is echoed by other senior officials who worked in the Mostar field offices, such as Lynghjem, who recalled that "they bypassed us when it suited them, both the international and the national."[62] Paddy Ashdown's decision to appoint a MIU envoy answerable directly to himself—described above—is another example of this phenomenon. Moreover, the lead role played by international officials in Sarajevo over the years who would sporadically pop into Mostar for a political meeting or ceremony has also undermined efforts to create a sense of meaningful local participation—both among politicians and ordinary citizens—fueling apathy and disinterest in the peacebuilding process and a disconnect with international officials working in the city.

A third factor undermining local-international relations has been the rapid turnover in international staff in Mostar, which was widely noted by local residents and officials alike. As Ljubo Golemac, the head of Mostar's "West" municipality under the Interim Statute told me, "People would come talk with me and then I would never see them again . . . as soon as they got to know people here they would be transferred."[63] Golemac's comment echoes a key lesson Farrand says he learned during his time in Brčko: "Longevity *by itself* counts for much in the estimation of the local body politic and its leaders. In my judgment, therefore, a candidate's willingness (or lack thereof) to commit for the longer haul should be a critical factor in determining his or her suitability for the job."[64] Unfortunately, frustrated by outside interference and a lack of peacebuilding progress, officials working in Mostar have tended to move on quickly to other, more appealing, posts. Again, the difference between Brčko and Mostar in this regard was made evident during fieldwork. In the summer of 2005 I arranged preliminary meetings in the two cities. When I returned the following year the majority of my international contacts were still working in Brčko, while in Mostar most officials I had met the previous summer had moved on to other postings. This problem became more salient over time as staying too long in Mostar put one at risk of being tainted by the broader peacebuilding failure in the city, which could prove damaging to one's career.

In other cases rapid turnover of personnel, and the resulting lack of institutional memory and personal connections, was more institutionally driven. For example, the WEU police contingent rotated on a six-month basis, with neither a handover period or situation notes left behind by departing officers.[65] At times it has also appeared that a lack of prior experience or familiarity with Bosnia in general, and Mostar in particular, has been viewed as a plus for appointment to senior international positions in the city, rather than a liability. Jacques Andrieu, the head of OHR Mostar from September 2003 to May 2004, was a regional prefect from France who had never held a diplomatic post outside of the country prior to his appointment.[66] Ricardo Perez Casado, who took over as head of EUAM following Koschnick's resignation, likewise had little international experience and no familiarity with the region. According to news reports this was seen as an advantage in Brussels as he would not be "burdened by the past."[67]

7

PATRON-CLIENTELISM IN THE BRČKO DISTRICT

In the previous chapter I highlighted the embeddedness of international officials and participation in peacebuilding reforms by local officials as two factors that are crucial for understanding peacebuilding progress that has been achieved in Brčko to date. To a certain degree, though, this explanation begs the question of just how embeddedness and productive local-international relations was achieved to such a degree in the District. In this chapter I describe one of the key factors promoting these two dynamics: the emergence of a close and enduring patron-client relationship between OHR Brčko and local elites following the establishment of the District in 2000. Unlike the previous four chapters, which compare institutions, legacies, sequencing, and peacebuilding practices and institutions in Mostar and Brčko, this chapter focuses solely on the dynamics of this relationship in the latter city.

The Arbitral Tribunal's Final Award created a powerful and enduring political alliance based on shared goals between the District and supervisory regime. In essence it effectively localized the latter by embedding it in the District's institutions and giving it the responsibility of protecting this fledgling political creature from the predations of the entities. The result was the development of a patron-client relationship between OHR Brčko and District political and economic elites. My understanding of political clientelism here roughly follows Rene Lemarchand and Keith Legg, who define it as "a more or less personalized, affective, and reciprocal relationship between actors, or sets of actors, commanding unequal resources and involving mutually beneficial transactions that have political ramifications beyond the immediate sphere of dyadic relationships."[1] Patron-clientelism, to be more specific, is a conditional and instrumental relationship in which higher-status patrons use their influence and resources to provide protection or benefits for lower-status clients, who reciprocate by offering general support or assistance to their patrons.[2] In the case of Brčko, the supervisory regime's ability to play the role of patron was based on the relative political independence afforded supervisors by the Arbitral Tribunal's awards. The resulting dynamic was that OHR Brčko used its influence and authority to provide protection for the District in the latter's battles against the entities—and their frequent ally, OHR Sarajevo—with District authorities reciprocating by supporting, or at the least not actively opposing, the various peacebuilding reforms that were being pushed by the supervisory regime and other international officials within Brčko. Taking on the role of the District's patron did not just give the supervisory regime leverage over local elites, it was also central to the development of close and productive international-local relations, as successfully coordinating these efforts required constant face-to-face communication and strategizing, including regular meetings and exchanges of memos and working papers.

One could argue that the development of political clientelism preceded the Final Award. The 1997 alliance between OHR-IPTF-SFOR and Brčko-based Serb political and security figures who supported Biljana Plavšić and opposed SDS's obstructionist policies certainly contained elements of a patron-client relationship, as did the relationship between NHI and OHR Brčko in 1998 and 1999. As noted in chapter 5, for example, in exchange for political and personal protection, individuals like Brčko's second wartime police chief, Žarko Čošić, provided intelligence on SDS loyalists in the police to internationals and helped recruit personnel for the attempted takeover of the Brčko police station. Likewise Farrand's administrative, police, and judicial reforms later that year created incentives for more moderate local officials to break with SDS and support his agenda in exchange for political promotion. As it became clear that the supervisory regime would not be temporary these incentives to work with international officials increased.

The Final Award was a culmination of these trends, cementing the supervisory regime's role as the ultimate political authority in the District. However it was the immediate assault against Brčko by the entities that transformed the dynamic between the District's business and political elites and OHR Brčko into a full-fledged patron-client relationship, as only the latter had the power to protect the former against these attacks—thus preserving political independence and the accrual of economic benefits for the former. In the rest of this chapter I narrate the emergence, and subsequent decline, of political clientelism in Brčko.

Political Implications of the Final Award

On March 5, 1999, Roberts Owen issued his Final Award, which called for the establishment of an autonomous Brčko District. One of the more controversial aspects of Owen's decision has proven to be the creation of the District as a substate condominium in which the two entities share possession of the entirety of the District's territory, but Brčko itself exists "under the sovereignty of Bosnia and Herzegovina . . . subject to the powers of the common institutions of BiH."[3] To start, the condominium Owen created is at odds with the concept and existence of previous condominiums, such as the Anglo-French condominium of New Hebrides (1906–80) or Anglo-Egyptian Sudan (1899–1956). In these and other cases of international law, condominium arrangements refer to shared, joint, or divided sovereignty exercised over a territory by two or more outside states.[4] In contrast, in the Brčko District the relationship between territory and power is precisely reversed: the entities are described as having irrevocably delegated all of their political authority to Brčko's governing institutions while retaining joint ownership of the District's territory.

It has been debated whether this separation of territory from political authority was Owen's primary aim. Former OHR Brčko legal officer Matthew Parish describes the reference to Brčko as a condominium as a "legal fiction" constructed to protect the Final Award from criticism that it altered the constitution of Bosnia, which declares that the state may consist of only two entities—the Federation and RS.[5] Since all territory in Bosnia would continue to belong to one of the two entities, who then delegated their powers to local authorities in Brčko, the District could in no way be construed as a third entity. This is a valid observation, but it is clear that Owen was also looking for a way to avoid being forced to make a Solomonic decision to divide the territory of Brčko between the two opposing sides. Indeed in the First Award he declared that "rather than handing a trophy to one side or another" the more important principle before the tribunal was finding a political solution that would be most equitable for all residents of the Brčko *opština*.[6] Moreover, given the inability of the RS and Federation to work together constructively on any issue regarding Brčko, a more traditional solution creating *shared political authority* over the territory of Brčko would almost certainly have been doomed to failure from the start. The ingenious solution to this problem that Owen crafted granted both sides *shared possession of territory* in Brčko, while obliging them to delegate their political authority to an autonomous District government. This unprecedented attempt to decouple territory from political authority in the Final Award does not appear to have been a merely legal afterthought, then, but rather central to the aims of its creator.

However in solving the problem of competing political and territorial claims over Brčko in this way the Final Award created further ambiguities concerning the relationship between the District and the state. For example, just what does it mean to place the District "under the exclusive sovereignty of Bosnia and Herzegovina"? Having been created four years after Dayton, the Brčko District is of course not mentioned in the country's constitution. At the time this concern was fairly theoretical in nature. Bosnia was scarcely a state in any sense of the word. The entities held nearly all of the governing competencies one associates with a sovereign state, such as control of borders and customs, taxation, social welfare programs, armies, police forces and intelligence services. In effect the Final Award served to make Brčko independent from the "real" sovereign powers at the time—the entities. As we shall see this would change in subsequent years, especially during the tenure of High Representative Paddy Ashdown, who would pursue ambitious state centralizing reforms.

The Final Award and a subsequent Annex separated political authority from territory in a second manner that proved to be equally controversial.[7]

First, it created an independent supervisory regime with broad powers that was formally answerable to the tribunal itself. Just as significantly, the supervisory regime and tribunal oversight is open-ended, remaining in place until the supervisor notifies the tribunal that the District's institutions are "functioning effectively and apparently permanently."[8] Additionally, the tribunal reserved the right to modify the conditions of the Final Award in any way, up to granting one or the other entity complete control of the District's territory. In effect the tribunal, or more accurately the presiding arbiter, Roberts Owen, "bestowed upon itself the authority to establish an international supervisory regime, and granted that regime the power . . . to oversee the administration of the entire area."[9] Naturally, this remarkable development did not sit well with a host of interests in Bosnia, ranging from the entities to the High Representative, the latter of whom saw himself as the ultimate international authority in Bosnia and the supervisor of Brčko as his subordinate "deputy."

Contesting the Final Award

The Final Award was not a surprise to authorities in the Federation, despite their public grousing after its announcement. While they had argued for exclusive control of Brčko in front of the tribunal they had also noted that creation of a multiethnic district would be an acceptable alternative. Privately this latter option was precisely what the negotiating team expected the outcome would be.[10] On the other hand RS politicians seemed to be genuinely surprised—and outraged—about the decision. RS Brčko mayor Borko Reljić resigned in protest and the RS national assembly passed a resolution refusing to recognize the legality of the Final Award.[11] To this day the resolution continues to be the official legal position of the RS, as it has never been revoked.[12] Behind the scenes OHR headquarters in Sarajevo was also displeased with certain aspects of the award. Thus from the beginning of the existence of the District the OHR office and local authorities in Brčko found themselves at odds with important domestic and international authorities elsewhere in Bosnia.

By 1999 relations between OHR Sarajevo and OHR Brčko had already become strained, which only compounded conflict between the two offices. At the beginning of supervision in 1997 internationals in Sarajevo wanted little to do with Brčko as it was seen as an intractable problem. Therefore they were quite content to leave this "American project" alone to its own devices. But as OHR under Westendorp began to take its first tentative steps toward bolstering and creating state institutions in Bosnia the independence of OHR Brčko and autonomous decisions made by the Arbitral Tribunal began to rankle officials in the central office, who started to look for ways to reign in supervision in Brčko. Robert Farrand's strong support of the Final Award only made things worse, prompting OHR Sarajevo to accuse him of insubordination to the organization.[13]

One of the key points of contention between Brčko and Sarajevo was the source of the supervisor's authority. Immediately after the Final Award was issued the OHR Legal Department in Sarajevo began a push to have this relationship clarified according to their terms in the forthcoming Annex: "It must be understood that the Supervisor is a Deputy High Representative, and his authority is thus derived from and subordinate to that of the High Representative. That is to say, the powers of the Supervisor are not created in any way by the authority of the arbitral tribunal."[14] The legal team of OHR Brčko replied that the supervisor's powers came from neither the High Representative, nor the Arbitral Tribunal, but rather the two PIC conferences that endorsed the First and Supplemental Awards, which laid out the supervisor's responsibilities and powers.[15] Therefore, just as OHR Sarajevo claimed that the High Representative's "Bonn powers" were bestowed on him by the PIC at the December 1997 conference in Bonn, Germany, the supervisor's authority also flowed from this source, independently of the High Representative. The supervisor then was the final authority in the Brčko *opština*, but as a Deputy High Representative his actions required a "high degree of coordination" with OHR Sarajevo.[16]

A second disputed area was the delegation of entity powers and the relationship between Brčko and the state of Bosnia.[17] OHR Sarajevo contended that "any competence originating in the Entities and destined for the District must be understood to be delegated first by the Entities to the State, and then through the State to the District . . . the District thus gains more the character of a municipality, which is what it should have, rather than that of a third Entity."[18] Ostensibly, this argument was about Bosnia's "governmental matrix within which the District must be embedded."[19] However a second purpose of this position was to further establish a basis by which "the Supervisor might also be legitimately constrained in the exercise of his powers, even within his Brčko bailiwick, by the High Representative."[20] The problem for OHR Sarajevo was that this position clearly contradicted the Final Award, which states that the entities have directly delegated their powers of governance to the District authorities—a fact that OHR Brčko quickly and insistently pointed out.[21] Hoping to force Roberts Owen or OHR Brčko to change their mind on this issue OHR Sarajevo conducted a behind the scenes campaign to undermine the Final Award, circulating memos in Bosnia, Washington, DC, and EU offices in Brussels that questioned its constitutionality. The head of OHR Legal in Sarajevo also wrote to Owen personally, challenging the constitutionality of his decision, charges which Owen archly rebuffed.[22] Eventually an exasperated Robert Farrand wrote to OHR Sarajevo asking "if the parties (i.e., the Federation of BiH, Republika Srpska and BiH) are complying with the Final Award and not challenging it in a court, on what grounds and for what purpose is OHR-Sarajevo (Legal) raising questions about its constitutionality?"[23]

As neither side was willing to back down from these positions, OHR Sarajevo began to pursue alternate methods to assert its authority over the Brčko office. One of its primary sources of leverage was control of the flow of money. While the supervisor claimed independence from Sarajevo in decision-making authority, funds for operations still went through the central headquarter's financial department before being dispersed to the regional offices. Under Westendorp's successor, Wolfgang Petritsch (1999–2002), OHR began to put this power to use, slowing down and denying hiring of staff needed in Brčko to implement the Final Award. A second method of interference was to raise objections to OHR Brčko policy proposals, which were routinely forwarded to Sarajevo for review as part of the practice of coordination between the two offices.[24] The tension between OHR Brčko and headquarters in Sarajevo at this time was unique only in its degree of intensity, as centralization also chafed at officials in other OHR field offices.[25] However the ambiguity concerning political authority gave relations between the two offices a distinctly sharper edge.

Perhaps nowhere was the pattern of interference by OHR Sarajevo greater or more transparent than with the BLRC, which was established by OHR Brčko in June 1999 and charged with drafting a District statute and reforming the entire legal system in the District, from the writing of new laws to reforming the judiciary. It was funded by an American government grant of $1 million. However this money was administered by OHR Sarajevo, which would delay or withhold distribution of funds as a bargaining tactic.[26] The head of BLRC was an intense and driven lawyer named Michael Karnavas. According to multiple interview sources he had famously poor relations with OHR Legal staff in Sarajevo, which he regarded as lazy, inefficient, and barely competent.[27] The final straw in this relationship is said to have been a crack Karnavas made at a meeting with OHR Sarajevo officials in the summer of 2001 in which he stated that the most dangerous place to be in Bosnia was standing outside the gates of OHR Sarajevo at 5:00 p.m. on a weekday, because one was likely to be crushed by the hordes of employees rushing to leave their offices.[28] Shortly after this Sarajevo forced Henry Clarke to fire Karnavas and prematurely close down the BLRC in October 2001, months before its mandate and money was scheduled to run out. This decision greatly hampered efforts to complete the legal reforms demanded in the Final Award, with negative effects lingering on for years.[29] Nonetheless by this time few in Sarajevo, Washington, DC, or Brussels were inclined to shed tears for the District or OHR Brčko.

Starving the District

Roberts Owen had hoped that having the entities share the territory of the Brčko District in condominium would provide an incentive for them to cooperate over common areas of interest.[30] Ironically, this is precisely what has often occurred—though to the detriment, rather than benefit, of the District. In fiscal matters, in particular, political and economic interests in both the RS and Federation have repeatedly found common ground in attempts to undermine the independence of District authorities.

Financial sustainability, both in the form of creating institutions and developing stable sources of income for the newly formed District, was a pressing priority following the Final Award. Of immediate concern for OHR Brčko and local authorities was abolishing the three ethnically based payment bureaus that controlled financial transactions since the beginning of the war in 1992. These bureaus were relics of the Yugoslav-era, state-monopoly banking system and oversaw all public and private financial activities. They were also highly corrupt and dominated by nationalist parties in Sarajevo, Mostar, and Banja Luka.[31] As long as they continued to operate, the District would be subject to the whims of these outside interests. Therefore in April 2000 Farrand issued a supervisory order that gave the Brčko District Revenue Agency control over their operations in the District's territory.[32] This action was fiercely contested by both the entities and OHR Sarajevo, which was working to reform the payment bureaus by—it hoped—the end of 2000. Arguing that it would interfere with their reform efforts elsewhere in Bosnia, OHR Sarajevo refused to sign off on the order. When State Department officials in Sarajevo and Washington, DC offered only tepid support Farrand resigned.[33]

His successor Gary Matthews was pressured to amend the April supervisory order and allow the payment bureaus to coordinate their actions with Brčko until the end of the year.[34] He agreed to this in June, thinking it would "produce constructive negotiations with the entities over their obligations to fund the district."[35] Almost immediately Matthews began to realize he had been outmaneuvered as both entities refused to fulfill their funding obligations to the District. For the RS this was both a political and economic decision: manipulating the flow of funds gave it continued leverage over political developments in Brčko; but the RS was also insolvent, surviving only on international donations.[36] The Federation also had a significant budget shortfall, and influential political and economic interests in neighboring Tuzla and Posavina cantons saw withholding funds from the District as payback for alleged revenue losses they were incurring due to the continuing existence of the massive, unregulated Arizona Market in Brčko.[37]

Regardless of the different motivations, by September the District was nearly broke.[38] Desperate, Matthews negotiated agreements with the entities the following month that resulted in the partial release of funds.[39] In January 2001 the payment bureaus were finally abolished and the District was able to take control of revenue collection and distribution.[40] However the entities' punitive financial policies over the course of the year had severely stunted economic and institutional development in Brčko. The hard lesson learned by OHR Brčko and local officials was that the entities could not be counted on in any way to support the political or economic autonomy of the District. Pleading for emergency funds from international donors to keep the District afloat financially that January, Matthews bitterly observed, "It was never envisioned when the District was proclaimed . . .

that it would have to pull itself up entirely by its bootstraps. Alas we can hold out no hope that the Entities will do anything for Brčko on their own initiative, despite the dictates of the Arbitration Award."[41]

It was during the payment bureaus affair, however, that a new dynamic of political alliance and contention began to coalesce. In matters concerning the relationship between the District and the entities or emerging state institutions—which were dominated politically by the entities—both OHR Brčko and District authorities realized that absent close cooperation the District's interests would be ignored at best, and intentionally damaged at worst. Invoking the authority granted to it by the Final Award, OHR Brčko took on the role of patron defending the District from encroachments from both the entities, which were supported, all too often, by OHR Sarajevo. Under High Representative Paddy Ashdown (2002–6) in particular, the latter increasingly saw Brčko as an impediment to its planned reform efforts and thus found itself politically allied—at least in actions, if not motivations—with the entities on a range of issues.

These emergent political networks hardened during battles over economic reforms and tax harmonization that raged between the District and entities from 2001 to 2003. By 2001 Brčko had established itself as a favored entry point for cross-border trade due to marginally lower taxes and customs fees and the development of an efficient and relatively uncorrupt customs point at the Brčko-Gunja (Croatia) bridge-crossing.[42] According to the head of the District Revenue Agency at the time this was a conscious strategy adopted by the District during the payment affairs controversy:

> In September 2000 there was a meeting in Brcko and the Revenue Agency prepared new tax laws. We took the entity laws which were most favorable for the District. We made a mix of laws which were lowest. One law from the Federation, another from the RS . . . taking the most favorable rates from each entity, so they could not accuse us of making a third rate which is the lowest. But in this way we came up with the lowest [overall] tax rate in BiH.[43]

At the time customs revenue was not shared, but belonged to the governing authority—in this case the District—of each individual customs point. Therefore these revenues made up a key portion of the District's budget.[44]

However in the view of the cash-strapped entity governments Brčko was stealing precious revenues from them. During IMF sponsored tax reform talks in the summer of 2001 they complained vociferously about the District and demanded that it impose several fee increases in the name of "tax harmonization." Henry Clarke, who had arrived in Brčko just three months earlier, was taken aback by "the surprising zeal of the two entity reps for political speeches, and especially for attacking Brčko District. In response to direct challenges, the Supervisor was obliged to explain why there is a Brčko District." Even more worrisome from his point of view was "the unwillingness of the entities to consult Brčko District in their efforts to harmonize taxes, followed by their demand, *often backed by the international community*, that the District must accept without question whatever they want to do" (italics mine).[45] Little did Clarke know that conflict between the District and entities would only intensify.

Brčko-based oil distributors in particular had become major importers and sellers of oil products in Bosnia. Besides channeling a significant amount of revenues through the District's customs point their success also cut into the profits of politically connected, entity-based oil cartels. In October 2001 both the RS (formally) and Federation (informally) imposed prohibitions on oil distribution in their territories from nonentity companies and enforced this with police checkpoints on the main roads leading out of Brčko.[46] Then in December Croatia restricted all traffic of vehicles over six tons from using the Brčko-Gunja bridge-crossing, citing engineering safety concerns. However it shortly became clear that the decision by Croatian authorities was part of a deal made with the entities to halt the importation and sale of oil by Brčko merchants when the Council of Ministers (CoM)—Bosnia's weak executive authority that is dominated by the entities—issued a temporary decision the following month omitting the Brčko-Gunja bridge from Category 1 international crossing point status, thereby effectively cutting off international trade of oil products through this route.[47]

In a June 2002 meeting in Brčko the chairman of the CoM, Dragan Mikerević, explicitly told OHR Brčko and Sarajevo representatives that the bridge would remain closed until Brčko increased certain taxes to levels found in the RS and Federation. OHR Brčko was livid at this economic blackmail, but Sarajevo told them to "play the political game" with the entities if they wanted to receive support from the rest of the international community in Bosnia. The District duly amended its tax legislation and—under a heavy-handed suggestion from High Representative

Ashdown—reached a further agreement with the CoM in October to pay 2.5 million KM to cover a funding gap for the State Border Service.[48] In exchange the CoM agreed to set up a "body for coordination and cooperation with the Brčko District," a promise it promptly ignored.[49] After extended foot dragging by the CoM, the Brčko-Gunja bridge-crossing was finally fully opened up for oil products transportation in June 2003—a year and a half after the dispute first began.

By this time officials in the State Department and OHR Sarajevo were actively planning for the end of supervision. In April 2003 Sarajevo organized a meeting to discuss this topic with OHR Brčko.[50] Concerned with continued entity interference, Clarke argued that such talk was premature: "Since both Entities will be unlikely to comply financially, and since, by its actions, the RS does not yet fully acknowledge that the Awards and Brčko laws (including Supervisory Orders) take precedence over RS laws on the territory of the District, we are not close to meeting the Tribunal's requirements."[51] Clarke, though, would remain supervisor for only a few more months. His successor Susan Johnson (2004–6) was given indication from Sarajevo and Washington, DC that her position would be brief: she was instructed to hold municipal elections in the fall and terminate supervision as soon as possible afterward.[52]

The "Transfer of Competencies" Dispute

All three supervisors prior to Johnson were retired ambassadors, while she was an active duty senior foreign officer in the State Department. By 2004 OHR Brčko's opponents had come to the conclusion that the status of her predecessors was a significant factor in the problematic independence of the supervisory regime in Brčko. Therefore Johnson was chosen in part on the assumption that as a lower ranked, active-duty diplomat she would prove to be more responsive to the priorities of outside centers of power than the responsibilities of her office. This turned out to be a mistaken calculation. Despite Ashdown's private and public exhortations to "normalize"—that is, to reduce—Brčko's autonomous status and wind up the supervisory regime, Johnson soon came to the same conclusion as the previous supervisors: absent more robust institutional mechanisms regulating relations between the District and the emerging state structures Brčko would continue to be threatened by the predations of the entities.[53] In the face of opposition from her government and OHR Sarajevo she wholeheartedly embraced the supervisor's role of patron charged with protecting the District's political and economic interests.

Of particular concern for Johnson and District authorities was the position held by the entities—and strongly supported by OHR Sarajevo—that it was not necessary to obtain the District's consent in cases where the two entities agreed to sign an Inter-Entity Transfer Agreement (IETA) transferring certain governing competencies to the state. OHR Sarajevo's prime consideration, articulated in a March 2005 legal brief, was political: allowing the District to "pick and choose which among the state-building reforms it will embrace . . . would have the effect of imperiling future reforms."[54] OHR Brčko and the District took the countervailing view that the entities were indeed free to transfer powers to the state in the territories they administered, but that "such agreements . . . have no effect on the powers of governance exercised by the District Government within the territory that it administers."[55] They were especially worried about the previous year's IETA, which established a new state-level Indirect Taxation Authority (ITA) and adopted a statewide value-added tax that replaced the previous highly corrupt system of customs fees and excise taxes. Since Brčko lacked voting rights and representation on the entity-dominated ITA board it would have no say in calculating its rates of contribution to the state, or the amount of revenues that would be returned. After fierce battles over finances with the entities the previous four years, both local officials and OHR Brčko feared that this development presented a grave risk for the future political autonomy of the District.[56]

This disagreement attracted the attention of the Arbitral Tribunal in February 2005 when Johnson and District officials asked Roberts Owen to visit Brčko and discuss the Final Award's stance on the transfer of competencies issue personally. While there Owen indicated his general agreement with the District's position on the matter.[57] In spite of this in April OHR Sarajevo forwarded its legal brief to Owen and asked him to give his opinion on the matter. Owen instead decided that the relevant parties' views should be presented before the tribunal and set up a procedural conference on the matter in June. Concerned by this turn of events, Ashdown wrote to Owen pointedly reminding him that "these issues possess a significance for Bosnia and Herzegovina as a whole—and for its ambitions to join the European Union—that extend well beyond what may seem to be at stake."[58] Undeterred by this warning Owen went ahead with the conference, at which an apoplectic OHR Sarajevo objected—to no avail— that the tribunal had no jurisdiction to consider the matter.[59] After several months delay, during which time the interested parties submitted written briefs, Owen decided in January 2006 that the tribunal did have jurisdiction to rule on the dispute, though under pressure from OHR Sarajevo and the State Department he paused the legal process to allow meetings of an informal working group to see if a compromise could be negotiated.[60]

Susan Johnson's strong support for the District in this matter, and refusal to agree with Ashdown's insistent claims that the conditions for ending Supervision had largely been met, earned her fierce criticism from OHR Sarajevo. As then-mayor Mirsad Djapo put it to me, "Everyone was against us—the High Representative, the state representatives, everyone. Only Susan supported us."[61] While there had always been tension between the Brčko office and headquarters it was acknowledged by long-time OHR officials in both offices that the rivalry turned particularly nasty after she arrived. In part staff in Sarajevo began to see Brčko's concerns as not just complicating their preferred reform policies in Bosnia, but also potentially delaying the overarching goal at the time of ending OHR's presence in Bosnia as quickly as possible. But others pointed to the High Representative's inability to conceive of Johnson as an equal due to her gender as also part of the problem. As one of Ashdown's British compatriots in OHR remarked: "Paddy is one of those old-fashioned Liberals that is not terribly progressive concerning these things."[62] Whatever the reason, Johnson's refusal to back down won her no friends in either Sarajevo or the State Department; in September 2006 she was ousted from her position as supervisor.

OHR Sarajevo and the State Department had been looking to replace Johnson for some time, but finding a replacement had proven to be difficult. In spring 2006 they approached Raffi Gregorian. Gregorian had previously worked on defense reform in Bosnia and had also been a member of the State Department's Bosnia desk in Washington, DC, thus he was well acquainted with the country's politics, and in particular the ongoing tensions between OHR Sarajevo on one hand and the supervisory regime on the other. In Gregorian OHR Sarajevo and the State Department finally found an official who could be made more responsive to their wishes, in part due to the fact that he was not a career foreign service officer.[63] A few months after taking over as supervisor Gregorian was also offered the position of Principal Deputy High Representative (PDHR), based in Sarajevo. He accepted this offer in February 2007 despite, as his former legal officer has observed, the inherent conflict of interest that this created: "As Supervisor he [Gregorian] was mandated to act in the District's best interests, but as PDHR he was bound to be faithful to the long-held OHR line on the transfer of competencies controversy, and a broader desire to close the BFAO [Brčko Final Award Office—i.e., OHR Brčko] or at least reduce its activities."[64] Susan Johnson had also been offered the position of PDHR but had refused, as she too believed that it presented a fundamental conflict of interest.[65]

Meanwhile, tribunal proceedings on the transfer of competencies dispute had progressed haltingly since June 2005. As noted above, at the beginning of 2006 Owen paused the process to allow the United States to pursue settlement negotiations aimed at reaching a compromise on the issue by strengthening the formal relationship between the District and Bosnia's state institutions. However these discussions went nowhere. In the meantime squabbling among the entities led to a temporary interruption in the distribution of ITA revenues in the spring, which was followed months later by an unilateral decision to lower the District's coefficient.[66] Outraged, District authorities requested the tribunal proceedings resume course in July, which Owen granted two months later despite the consternation this caused in Sarajevo and Washington, DC. By the beginning of 2007 staff in OHR Sarajevo was beside itself with these developments. Expressing the frustration with Owen in OHR at the time, one official in the organization sarcastically commented to me: "The strategy now seems to be to hope that Owen dies soon, and then this whole thing will go away."

Instead Gregorian moved to bring the tribunal proceedings to an end. In April 2007 acting in the role of PDHR he allowed OHR Sarajevo to file a brief that again contested the District's claim before the tribunal and questioned the legitimacy of the tribunal's jurisdiction to hear the case. He also wrote Owen ex parte calling for the proceedings to be suspended, a request that Owen refused.[67] Gregorian then pressured lame-duck High Representative Christian Schwarz-Schilling (2006–7) to sign two decisions that fixed contributions to and revenues from the ITA at a relatively favorable rate for the District for a five-year period.[68] Accompanying these two decisions was a brief "fact sheet" in which OHR claimed that "Brčko authorities" had been "consulted" and were "in favor" of the decisions, therefore it was "unnecessary for the Arbitral Tribunal to either accept jurisdiction or render any decision on the merits" of the ongoing dispute.[69] In response Owen agreed that absent any objections from the parties the tribunal would discontinue the hearings.[70]

The problem, however, was that District authorities had neither been consulted nor believed that the fundamental issue of the transfer of competencies had been adequately resolved. Though they were pleased that the District would receive a fair share of ITA revenue over the following five years they wanted the tribunal proceedings to continue, not just because they believed that a favorable ruling on the transfer of competencies issue would bolster their political protection from the entities, but also because they viewed OHR's decisions to be a temporary measure that would leave them vulnerable to the same problem in five years. To this effect the District authorities instructed their legal counsel to draft a letter to the Arbitral Tribunal which stated:

> OHR did not seek the consent of the Brčko District prior to the issuance of the HR Decisions . . . it is clear that the HR decisions do not constitute a mutually agreed settlement accepted by all interested parties to this case, nor can they purport to have the effect of resolving the District's claim in the place and stead of the Brčko Arbitration Tribunal. Instead the HR Decisions at best represent a form of "interim measure."[71]

A copy of the letter was forwarded to the OHR Brčko office prior to submission to the tribunal, a routine procedure that reflects the close relationship between the supervisory regime and District authorities that had developed since 2000. However immediately after receiving the letter a furious Gregorian threatened to fire Brčko's mayor, Mirsad Djapo, and any other officials involved in the negotiations if it was submitted to the tribunal.[72] Ultimately District authorities bowed to these threats and the letter was never sent.

Nonetheless, the details of the District's objections reached Owen the next month through informal backchannels. What incensed Owen, however, was that the fact sheet and the two decisions "gratuitously included" two "erroneous" and "unnecessary" paragraphs that asserted OHR Sarajevo's longstanding position that only the entities had the authority to agree on a transfer of competencies to state institutions.[73] Alarmed about the future sustainability of the District given that even the head of the supervisory regime was now working to undermine the District's autonomy, and determined to push back against what he saw as a dangerously incorrect interpretation of the Final Award, Owen issued a sharp rebuke in the form of an Addendum to the Final Award. The final paragraph of the Addendum, which I quote extensively below, broadly fixed Brčko's political authority vis-à-vis the entities along the lines desired by the District:

> The Tribunal feels obliged to make clear that its endorsement of the High Representative's settlement arrangements do not constitute approval of one specific legal assumption that seems to be implicit in the operative OHR documents. Specifically, the 3rd paragraph of the two OHR Decisions implies that under the Final Award, if and when the two entities should transfer to the State their own powers with respect to indirect taxation (as the entities did in fact on 5 December, 2003), that action would automatically take away from the Brčko District its equivalent powers with respect to indirect taxation thus giving the state sole control of such taxation. See also the suggestion in the 1st paragraph of the OHR Fact Sheet that the automatic legal result of the Entities' actions of 5 December, 2003, was that "Brčko lost" all of its authority with respect to indirect taxation. Lest these statements be taken as a correct understanding of the intent of the Final Award, however, the Tribunal feels obliged to express an important caveat as to the legal impact of a two-Entity transfer of power to the State without an equivalent transfer by, or the consent of, the Brčko District. The caveat is as follows: So long as the Entities continue to exist under the BIH Constitution, any purported two-Entity transfer to the State, made without an equivalent transfer by, or the consent of, the Brčko District, would be contrary to and illegal under the Final Award if that transfer had the effect of significantly diminishing the District's ability to function as a single, unitary, multi-ethnic, democratic government for the Brčko Opština.[74]

The response to this Addendum by OHR Sarajevo and the State Department was concern and anger. First, it came as a complete surprise, as Owen had not warned any of the interested parties before he released this new ruling. Moreover, OHR Sarajevo was furious because it thought there was a political understanding that the ITA dispute should be resolved outside the tribunal—as had been Gregorian's intention with the two decisions—in order to avoid a ruling in the District's favor on the transfer of competencies.[75] Not only did the Addendum undermine these efforts it also, in their view, walked right up to declaring, in effect, the District a third entity. With understatement the U.S. ambassador to Bosnia, Douglas McElhaney, wrote to Washington that the tribunal's decision "threatens to . . . undercut our broader objectives in Bosnia."[76] OHR's lawyers sought to downplay the ruling, noting that the legal benchmark of "significantly diminishing" the District's functions was a narrow and difficult standard to prove. In an attempt to further marginalize the Addendum, OHR did not initially inform District authorities of its existence, nor did the U.S. embassy disseminate a translated copy as it had done with previous tribunal documents.[77]

However, by the end of the year both the State Department and OHR Sarajevo came to the belated realization that it would be necessary to more definitively resolve Brčko's political status within Bosnia before closing down OHR—a shift prompted in part by concerns over a sharp deterioration in the political situation in the country since the previous fall. Thus after years of insisting that it was past time to shut down supervision it declared in February 2008 that successful resolution of the District's status vis-à-vis the state and entities was one of the five key objectives that would need to be met before it ended its presence in Bosnia.[78] The form this eventually took was a constitutional amendment which legally enshrines the District's status within Bosnia and also guarantees access to the Constitutional Court if future disputes with the entities arise. After a year of difficult negotiations and bargaining the proposed amendment was passed by Bosnia's parliament in March 2009.[79]

Though hailed by OHR as providing an important "guarantee" for the District's multiethnic institutions,[80] the amendment falls well short of ensuring that Brčko will be able to successfully defend itself against the entities once supervision is definitively terminated. First the Constitutional Court is an increasingly compromised institution. Subject to political pressures from the entities that control appointments for the majority of judges, it is widely derided for procedural irregularities and legally dubious decisions. Indeed, just months prior to the passage of the constitutional amendment the U.S. embassy in Sarajevo bluntly observed that the court "is not up to the task of defending the rule of law in Bosnia."[81] Second, in an effort to win the support of Milorad Dodik—who was the prime minister of the RS at the time—for the amendment, a provision was included which stipulated that in order to refer a dispute to the Constitutional Court not only would a majority of the District Assembly have to be in favor of this action, but also "at least one-fifth of the elected councilors from among each of the constituent peoples."[82] In effect this amounts to a potential ethnic veto, which could be used—as it has been elsewhere in the country—to block action by the District in the event that it finds itself threatened by one or more of the entities. Given repeated efforts by the RS to undermine the independence of the District and its institutions in recent years (discussed further in the Conclusion) this could prove to be a significant problem for Brčko in the postsupervision period. Indeed, Roberts Owen signaled his opposition to this provision for precisely this reason, but his objections were overruled by the State Department, which argued that a deal needed to be cut with Dodik in order to assure the passage of the amendment.[83]

The Decline of Political Clientelism and the Deterioration of Local-International Relations

As I have outlined in this chapter, one of the more remarkable elements of the evolution of contested political authority over the District is the degree to which the supervisory regime found itself ever more closely allied with District authorities in power struggles against the entities and other international officials in Bosnia. Especially fascinating is the continuing relevance of the Arbitral Tribunal, a seemingly ephemeral legal entity created in an informal last-minute bargain at Dayton, which has no paid staff or institutional home and in practice consists of no more than an extremely dogged U.S. lawyer who continues to insist on adherence to the Final Award he crafted more than a decade ago—despite efforts by most international interests in Bosnia to sideline him and the supervisory regime that he created to implement his decision. Of all the distant loci of power and authority that continue to shape the landscape of the Brčko District, this is surely the most unusual. But the decision at Dayton to forgo a negotiated compromise and resolve Brčko's status through international arbitration meant that the battle over this city in northeast Bosnia would be fought on legal as much as political terrain.

The tension between the tribunal and OHR Brčko on one side and the broader "international community" on the other is one of two fairly long-lived dynamics of political alliance and contention that have emerged in the aftermath of the Final Award. The second is the series of internecine conflicts between the District and entities. While there are substantial competing economic interests that tend to pit Brčko against the entities, the conflicts over the District's place in Bosnia reflect the fundamental fact that the country's political framework has done little to mitigate wartime ethno-territorial divisions. Thus in many ways Brčko remains a potential proxy for nationalist leaders who wish to continue to pursue their ethnocratic projects through other means.

The payment bureau funding crisis, oil distribution embargo, and ITA dispute threatened not just the political independence of the District, but also economic development in the area. Brčko's supervisors from Farrand through Johnson devoted considerable resources toward the defense of business interests in Brčko, seeing economic development as key to the sustainability of political reforms in the District.[84] During the oil embargo, for example, OHR Brčko was in constant contact with Tomislav Antunović, a Brčko-based Croat businessman with one of the largest petroleum distribution networks in Bosnia, updating him about the progress of negotiations and reporting incidents of harassment against his truckers to authorities in Sarajevo. In return for this clientelist protection business elites from all three communities became strong supporters of the supervisory regime.[85] For instance, in fall 2006, when OHR's departure from Bosnia appeared imminent, Antunović, Jovica Stevanović—the managing director of Italproject, the private corporation that managed the Arizona Market at the time—and other leading businessmen in Brčko were discussing proposals to extend the mandate of the supervisory regime beyond the end of the organization's existence. The reasoning behind this was that they believed that the continued presence of OHR Brčko remained necessary for economic and political protection against the entities and the attraction of further foreign investment.[86]

The transfer of competencies denouement caused significant damage to this patron-client alliance, as Raffi Gregorian's actions to short-circuit the arbitration proceedings convinced officials in Brčko that supervision no longer guaranteed that the District had a patron ready to defend its political autonomy or economic interests. In the words of the District's mayor at the time, Mirsad Djapo, "I think that [decision] was a mistake. He was in a hurry to finish his supervision and show success. I never supported it."[87]

Further stressing previously close international-local relations was a significant decrease in daily interaction with local officials during Gregorian's tenure. By the end of 2007, he was spending most of his time in Sarajevo, focusing on issues seen as "external" to the District, such as the constitutional amendment, and visiting Brčko only a couple of days a month. This reorientation toward a remote form of oversight run out of Sarajevo did not go unnoticed by local officials, several of whom suggested to me that it led to a noticeable decline in supervision. As one District councilor observed:

> He [Gregorian] had a completely different concept than the previous supervisor, Susan Johnson. She made an effort to find the causes and deal with the causes of problems, and not deal with the consequences. It seems to me that she relied more on information that she collected personally. Q: Because she was in the District? A: Yes. She had so many frequent and direct contacts with people here. I think that Raffi Gregorian frequently used either incorrect or unchecked information. Decisions that are made upon such information are usually wrong.[88]

The negative effects of remote supervision and a lack of accurate information can be seen in the decision to intervene in coalition talks in Brčko following the 2008 elections. The concentration government headed by SNSD politician Dragan Pajić was promoted by Gregorian after he informally vetoed a proposed multiethnic coalition that would have excluded SDP. In Pajić's words, "He insisted that SDP be in the government. And the result of that is what we have today. And he also insisted that I be the mayor. Although I didn't have the greatest number of votes, so he directly influenced the formation of this government."[89] This was a somewhat odd decision. First, as Pajić himself notes, he did not receive the most votes among Serb candidates for mayor, nor did his party do near as well (13 percent) as the SDS-led coalition in the elections (19 percent). Additionally, Pajić, who had been a doctor and hospital administrator in Brčko before moving into the pharmaceutical import business, was perceived as a corrupt figure by ordinary residents and politicians alike.[90] Therefore few in the District were surprised when he was charged with abuse of his position and removed from office three years later.[91] As one OHR official confided to me, however, the office, which, in addition to suffering from the effects of remote supervision had also experienced dramatic cuts in staff over the previous two years, had "no clue" about Pajić's reputation. Another OHR official suggested to me that there may have been another reason Gregorian pushed for a coalition headed by Pajić: he hoped that this would help in gaining RS prime minister Milorad Dodik's support for a constitutional amendment on the Brčko District. Shortly after the concentration government was formed Dodik did in fact drop his objections to the amendment.[92]

Another consequence of the shift to remote supervision was that District officials became less willing to work constructively with the supervisory regime, leading Gregorian to resort to personal threats and supervisory orders to get his way—the vow to fire any official who reported his actions to the Arbitral Tribunal being the most salient example. In May 2007 he fined a District Assembly councilor from the party SBiH, for making an obscene gesture on television.[93] That December he suspended the salaries of every member of the District government and assembly because the latter was late in adopting an annual budget, despite the fact that the District's statute contains provisions for the use of an interim budget in this event.[94] This penalty was repeated the following year when the assembly failed to submit a draft budget within an accelerated timetable he demanded.[95]

This more confrontational and distant approach chafed local officials. As one District councilor recounted, "I think Raffi's actions were not similar to civil authorities. His activities were like the army, when you have an obedient soldier. He just imposed procedures."[96] Consequently, by the end of Gregorian's tenure local political and economic elites I talked to who formerly championed a continued supervisory presence in the District now viewed OHR Brčko with indifference or hostility. This shift was also reflected in public opinion polls. Prior to his time as supervisor the OHR Brčko office was consistently supported by District residents. In 2003, for example, more than 63 percent of those polled expressed trust in it as an institution.[97] In contrast, by the summer of 2010, immediately prior to Gregorian's departure, only 15 percent of those polled in Brčko supported OHR's continued presence in the country—a lower percentage of support than even in the RS.[98] Interestingly, this deterioration of local-international relations following a shift to remote supervision was predicted in a June 2006 OHR Brčko report written for the PIC in which Susan Johnson presciently observed:

A resident Supervisor remains an essential component of effective Supervision until the regime is concluded. The Arbitral Awards expressly envision a resident, dedicated Supervisor, thoroughly familiar with the Arbitral Awards. There are good reasons for this. The role of the Supervisor is for the most part a mediator, facilitator, coach, referee, and arbiter of disputes. This requires direct, detailed, first-hand political, economic, social and cultural knowledge of the District. Only a resident Supervisor will have the necessary local expertise to manage the District's complex inter-ethnic relations and undertake his or her legal duties effectively. There is a strong desire from the domestic District institutions that the Supervisor remain resident. Changes at this late stage in the process would be inherently destabilizing, and would likely make achieving an orderly close out much more difficult and time consuming.[99]

With the arrival of Gregorian's replacement, Roderick Moore, in September 2010 international-local relations improved, to a degree. Several members of the District government and assembly positively contrasted Moore's diplomatic skill and patience with his predecessor during interviews the following summer, for instance. Despite this, however, it was clear that the previously close and productive patron-client alliance between local and international officials in Brčko was a thing of the past. First, supervision remained a remote affair: following Gregorian's precedent Moore also resided in Sarajevo and rarely visited the District. According to one official in Brčko who agreed to speak with me about this matter off the record, Moore visited the District only fourteen times over a two-year period from August 2010 (when his mandate started) until the end of July 2012. As this observation suggests, on-site presence and regular interaction matters. Moreover, people pay attention to such things.

In addition to this, after years of budget cuts it was unclear just how active a role OHR Brčko could have played in shepherding necessary reforms in the District during Moore's tenure. In interviews in summer 2011 local officials from across the political spectrum highlighted the need for amendments to the District statute that would clarify certain remaining legal ambiguities. However by then there was no longer an international legal officer employed at OHR Brčko who could assist the government in this process.[100] Lacking both capacity and intimate knowledge of current developments in the District—which is the product of intensive daily interactions with local officials—created a sense that, in the words of then

District deputy Mayor, Anto Domić, "now it is more like OHR doesn't exist than it does."[101] This is unlikely to change in the future, especially following the suspension of active supervision in Brčko in August 2012. Suspension—a compromise between countries which want to close OHR and those who argue that it is still necessary given recent political tensions in the country—involves leaving the supervisory regime in legal force but ending active oversight and closing the OHR Brčko office.[102] As such, it presages the definitive end of supervision in the near future.

Perhaps the breakdown of political clientelism in recent years should not be a surprise. As James Scott observes, such relationships are highly dependent on a patron's leadership, resources, and ability to satisfy clients' demands.[103] Still, it was only with great effort that hostile international officials outside Brčko were able to fracture the political alliance between the Arbitral Tribunal, OHR Brčko, and the District. Hence until recently the supervisory regime was a highly imperfect lens for reflecting the policy interests of its putative superiors in Sarajevo and Washington, DC. In contrast the occasional and only partially overlapping political and economic interests that brought the entities and OHR Sarajevo together against the District meant that theirs was a much more fragile and diffusely co-ordinated relationship. These structural differences between the two sets of space-spanning political networks help explain the relative difficulty OHR Sarajevo and the entities had in definitively placing the District in a subordinate position in Bosnia despite the clear preponderance of political power they appeared to possess. It remains to be seen whether Brčko's independence—and the attendant peacebuilding progress made to date—can be sustained now that active supervision has ended, especially given deteriorating political conditions in the rest of the country. This, though, is a question for the next chapter.

CONCLUSION

Rather than rehearsing the reasons for the divergence in peacebuilding processes in Brčko and Mostar since the end of the war, I want to use the conclusion to address two broader issues raised by this research. The first concerns the promises and limitations of subnational, or local, peacebuilding projects. I anticipate that the reader may wonder just how significant the outcomes in these two towns have been for the overall peacebuilding effort in Bosnia. Why, for instance, has progress in Brčko not had a positive effect on other regions or municipalities; conversely, how much does failure in Mostar matter in the grand scheme of things? Additionally, just how sustainable are achievements in the District given problems in the rest of the country? The second issue concerns more general, policy-oriented insights that can be extracted from this analysis of localized peacebuilding processes. The final section offers three suggestions for reorienting the spatiality of peacebuilding practices and institutions in ways that will enable practitioners to better navigate the inherent challenges of peacebuilding intervention.

Promises and Limitations of Local Peacebuilding Missions

More than a decade ago Bosnia's first High Representative, Carl Bildt, re-marked, "One day, the final act in the drama of the peace process will be played out here. What happens to Brčko will determine much of the fate of Bosnia, and perhaps the fate of the Balkans."[1] Brčko today bears little resemblance to the devastated and deeply divided town that so shocked Bildt on his first visit in the aftermath of the war. Yet despite all the prog-ress achieved in the District to date, it appears to have had little effect on the rest of the country. Indeed, ever since the failed parliamentary vote on constitutional reforms in spring 2006—and the divisive nationalist campaigns that dominated the general elections later that year—Bosnia has fallen into a downward spiral of political stagnation and mount-ing nationalist rhetoric. In a speech before the United Nations in Sep-tember 2008, for instance, the Bosniak member of the tripartite Bosnian Presidency, Haris Silajdžić, called the RS a product of ethnic cleansing and genocide and questioned its right to exist.[2] In response SNSD head Milorad Dodik, the dominant political figure in the RS, has repeatedly characterized Bosnia as a failed state and threatened to hold a referen-dum on secession.

The 2010 general elections in Bosnia did little to improve the situation. It took over a year for squabbling parties to establish a government at the state level and it collapsed only months later. While Silajdžić was defeated by Bakir Izetbegović (Alija's son), a somewhat more moderate Bosniak na-tionalist from the SDA, Dodik—who was elected president of the RS—has stepped up his challenges against the authority of a number of state institu-tions created in the postwar period. Most significantly, under his direction the RS National Assembly voted in April 2011 to hold a referendum on whether the entity should recognize the legitimacy of Bosnia's state court and prosecution office.[3] The next month the EU's High Representative for Foreign Affairs and Security Policy, Catherine Ashton, made a visit to Banja Luka, during which she persuaded Dodik to drop the threatened referendum in exchange for entering a "structured dialogue" about the functioning and future of the state-level judiciary and other institutions in Bosnia.[4]

Political crisis has also engulfed the Federation. Disaffected by what they perceive as Bosniak political dominance within the entity the two main Croat nationalist parties, HDZ and HDZ 1990, convened a "Croat

National Assembly" and renewed long dormant calls for the establishment of a third, Croat-dominated entity—an action that would inevitably further destabilize the situation in Mostar.[5] The contentious collapse of the Federation's ruling coalition in May 2012 has further exacerbated Bosniak-Croat divisions and ground normal governing functions in the entity to a halt. In light of these escalating tensions Bosnians from all three communities are increasingly pessimistic, with almost 90 percent indicating that the country is moving in the wrong direction according to one recent NDI poll.[6] Additionally, both domestic and international commentators have issued warnings about the specter of renewed violent conflict in the country.[7]

Given this, was Bildt wrong? Or to put it more generally and pointedly, are local peacebuilding missions like Brčko and Mostar unhelpful distractions to comprehensive peacebuilding initiatives or countrywide statebuilding projects—as OHR Sarajevo later came to view the supervisory regime in the District? The answer in both cases is, in my view, a qualified no.

Beginning with the more general question, there is ample research that identifies conflicts in specific, subnational contexts as central drivers of violence within a country. Séverine Autesserre, for instance, highlights failures to address local conflicts over land in the Kivu provinces of eastern Congo as the "main reason that the peace-building strategy in Congo has failed."[8] Of course, not all local conflicts are equal in importance, thus it is necessary to identify key sites that may merit special attention. Crucially, ethno-nationally divided cities often present some of the most intractable obstacles to peace processes in contested states—in part due to their political and/or symbolic importance for certain communities.[9] Prominent examples outside of Bosnia include Jerusalem (Israel/Palestine), Mitrovica (Kosovo), Beirut (Lebanon), Kirkuk and Baghdad (Iraq), Belfast and Derry/Londonderry (Northern Ireland), Nicosia (Cyprus), and Osh (Kyrgyzstan).[10] As this by no means comprehensive list illustrates, Mostar and Brčko are far from the only ethno-territorially contested cities that have an outsized impact on the broader dynamics of peace and conflict. Distinct political frameworks and/or peacebuilding missions that aim to address the complex problem of creating conditions conducive to peaceful coexistence in such divided cities may be crucial for achieving lasting peace in a number of countries that have experienced violent conflict in recent years.

What effect, then, have Mostar and Brčko had on postwar peacebuilding in Bosnia? Beginning with the former, the failure to unify the city politically or ease ethnic tensions continues to negatively impact Croat-Bosniak relations throughout the country. It also plays a significant role in the continuing political dysfunctionality of the Federation—both as a periodic site of violence and the most prominent symbol of the inability of the entity's multilevel ethno-territorial consociational framework to provide a workable modus vivendi.[11] Given Mostar's central significance for Croats in Bosnia it is difficult to imagine improvements in political and social relations in the Federation as long as the city continues to fester.[12] Mostar, then, illustrates the key role that ethno-nationally divided cities often play in the perpetuation of conflict dynamics even after war has ended—and thus the importance of efforts that address these "local" conflicts in achieving broader peacebuilding goals.

In Brčko, in contrast, the question is: what impact has the relative success to date in creating functional multiethnic institutions and facilitating social reintegration had on broader peacebuilding efforts in the country? Many in Bosnia have dismissed the District's significance, in part because it appears to have had little positive spillover effect on other regions in the country. Representative is ICG's recent claim that supervision "involves only the town's internal governance; it cannot affect BiH-wide security."[13] This, though, gets things precisely backward. First, it overlooks just how volatile the political conflict surrounding Brčko was at the end of the war—and could be again in the future. Not only was control of the town the only issue which was too contentious to resolve during negotiations at Dayton, as noted in chapter 3, prior to the announcement of the First Award leaders from both the RS and Federation also threatened the resumption of violence if they did not gain control of the Brčko area. The intensity of these tensions is easy to forget given peaceful relations in the city today. But the District remains a chokepoint connecting—or dividing, depending on one's point of view—the eastern and western halves of the RS. As such it remains highly strategic territory, and its continued existence serves as a critical brake on any potential secessionist moves by the RS.

Second, Brčko serves as an exemplar of what multiethnic Bosnia could be—rather than the ethno-territorial division of the country otherwise established by the DPA. Its integrated education system, in particular, has been promoted as a model for education reforms elsewhere in the country.[14] Developments in Brčko have also served at times as a precursor of and model for positive political reforms throughout the country. For example, the early comparative advantage of the District's relatively honest border custom point and lower overall taxes, and the political battles with the entities this precipitated, played a key role in pushing forward greater economic integration in the country, including a unified customs service and the statewide ITA.

What peacebuilding progress in Brčko has not been able to do is change the basic dynamic that Bosnia remains an unsettled state. As Gerard Toal and Carl Dahlman note, "Dayton has been a poor foundation for peacebuilding because it institutionalized unresolved conflict, ethnic division, and fragmentation at the heart of the Bosnian state."[15] Moreover, in recent years it has become clear that political elites from the RS have not fully reconciled themselves with the District's status—especially with the renewal of talk about secession or the dissolution of Bosnia. In January 2009, for instance, Milorad Dodik declared, "There are no long-term solutions for Brčko, and it will share the fate of BiH."[16] Later that June OHR banned several RS private security companies from operating in Brčko after discovering that they had been conducting "hostile" intelligence activities against District officials and OHR Brčko personnel.[17] Additionally, until recently official maps in the RS continued to show the now legally extinguished IEBL, which previously divided the Brčko area into Federation and RS controlled territories.[18] Consequently a number of international officials—but especially American diplomats—in Bosnia worry that the RS still harbors ambitions to undermine and eventually re-divide the District along ethnic lines. Somewhat shockingly, opposition to the supervisory regime's continued presence in Brčko is so strong among certain countries in the EU that even recognition of the central role that the District plays in maintaining broader security in Bosnia does not deter efforts to end supervision. As one EU diplomat recently stated, "We have to close the arbitration even if it means that BiH falls apart."[19]

The result is pessimism among many political and economic elites in Brčko about the District's future viability, which is especially acute now that the supervisory regime no longer plays the role of protective patron. In 2007 one former member of the District Assembly summarized the political situation in this way: "Everyone is against the District except Americans and a few politicians in the District . . . it can only survive as long as it has a 'mentor' [the supervisor] . . . very soon it will be as in Mostar if you give this District to the European Union."[20] This view was echoed by a current District Assembly member in 2011: "We have to remind ourselves about the fact that Brčko cuts the RS in half. This issue has never been put aside in the RS in terms of their relations to this area. . . . As long as there are entities this [outside pressure] will continue to exist."[21] In addition to acknowledging OHR Brčko's historical role in defending the District, these quotes also illustrate the fragility of peacebuilding progress in Brčko. Active supervision has now come to an end, but to this day the District lacks the necessary legal and political standing in Bosnia to adequately defend itself, and there is little local authorities could do if one or both of the entities tried to destabilize the situation politically or socially in the District.

In many ways, then, Brčko illustrates the promise and limitations of subnational peacebuilding initiatives. While peacebuilding efforts have defused what was once arguably the most contentious flashpoint in all of Bosnia in the immediate postwar period—thus creating the space necessary for countrywide progress—they have not in themselves been able to alter the broader political contradictions which continue to plague Dayton Bosnia. Still, from 1997 to 2012 the supervisory regime served not just as the guarantor of peace in Brčko, it was also one of the most effective means through which the potential renewal of violent conflict in Bosnia, and in particular any secessionist movement by the RS, was kept in check. This leverage, though, was dependent on a continued international presence in the District. Paradoxically, then, the very success of localized peacebuilding in Brčko to date—which was a key factor animating the drive to end active supervision—may play a role in undermining the continued peace and security of both the District itself and Bosnia as a whole.

Reorienting the Spatiality of Peacebuilding Practices and Institutions

The Brčko District and the supervisory regime established there is a unique case of peacebuilding intervention, unlikely to be replicated in the future. Nonetheless despite—or perhaps because of—its distinctiveness it offers several insights into the ways in which peacebuilding practices and institutions can be improved in the future. Three lessons in particular are worth outlining in more detail here. The first is the need to realign peace-building activities around context rather than content. What does it mean to say that content is the orienting principle of peacebuilding? Simply put, international organizations are generally dedicated to, and organized to carry out, fairly specific programmatic mandates—for instance, privati-zation, elections, and the return of refugees. And they possess a signifi-cant degree of autonomy in the pursuit of their respective tasks. In Bosnia in the 1990s, for example, OSCE was charged with organizing elections, UNHCR with facilitating the return of refugees and internally displaced people, SFOR with demilitarization and peacekeeping, IPTF with con-ducting police reform, and the World Bank and IMF with distributing aid and pursuing economic restructuring.

This division of labor according to content can be linked to at least three problems. To begin, it fuels a tendency to pursue programmatic priori-ties regardless of local conditions. In true procrustean fashion this begins with a preconceived policy template, around which individual countries, regions or cities should be fitted. The clearest example of this in Bosnia as a whole, and Mostar in particular, was the pursuit of rapid political and eco-nomic liberalization despite a clear absence of the social, political, and in-stitutional conditions necessary for the successful implementation of such reforms. Additionally, as with NGOs, the ebb and flow of funds for projects tends to be dictated by the distant whims of organizational headquarters or donors rather than the needs of local populations.[22] As the European Stability Initiative observed about international organizations in Bosnia, "Each is answerable to a different hierarchy or constituency, with pro-gramming and funding decisions taken in isolation and at a distance."[23] In other words, the prioritization of content exacerbates the dangers of top-down peacebuilding.

A second problem with content-centric peacebuilding is that it in-creases the difficulty of effectively coordinating efforts. Recall the World Bank's decision to offer a loan for refurbishing Mostar's hydroelectric plants, thereby undermining the EUAM's attempt to condition funds on the relinquishment of nationalist parties' control over the plants to a unified city administration, or the refusal of SFOR forces in the city to sufficiently back the raids on Hercegovačka Banka in 2001. The third shortcoming is related to this last one: information about conditions on the ground tends to be fragmented into a series of vertical organizational silos. This was a recurring problem with attempts to reform police forces in the RS in 1997 as both SFOR and IPTF were often reluctant to share information about specific actors or courses of action with each other, leading to a number of mishaps, such as the failed attempt to take over the police stations in RS Brčko. As we saw in Mostar as well, the shifting and nonoverlapping areas of responsibility of international organizations— which was dictated by individual programmatic goals—also impeded policy coordination and the development and dissemination of shared knowledge of local conditions.

One potential solution to these last two issues is to designate a lead organization with the responsibility of coordinating and devising policy within a country. This was the path pursued by OHR starting with Wolfgang Petritsch and continuing through Paddy Ashdown's tenure, both of which moved forcefully to centralize authority within the organization, but also in relation to other international actors. This approach, however, tends to exacerbate the problem of top-down peacebuilding imposition and reduces the independence of locally based practitioners.

Rather than pursuing centralization at the national level, peacebuilders would be better served by reorganizing operations and priorities around specific subnational territories or sites, as happened with establishment of a supervisory regime dedicated solely to the Brčko area. The clear, place-based hierarchy established in Brčko not only improved informational awareness and the coordination of policy among different organizations, it also directed peacebuilding activities toward the particular problems and challenges faced by those who lived in the area rather than programmatic dictates. This context—rather than content—centric approach to peacebuilding stands in stark contrast to Mostar, where distant political concerns and organizational mandates fueled the drive for rapid elections and economic restructuring in spite of the fact that these were inappropriate policies to pursue given local conditions at that time.

The second, related, lesson is the need for greater political independence of locally situated international officials. As I documented in chapter 6, peacebuilding efforts in Mostar have been constantly hampered by outside interference, beginning with the EU's "traveling circus of responsibility" that undercut EUAM administrator Hans Koschnick, and extending to the negotiation and implementation of Mostar's administrative unification in recent years. The presence of weak field offices lacking the authority to devise and execute context-specific solutions has also tended to go hand-in-hand with the top-down imposition of inappropriate policies and poor coordination. Finally, a lack of independence also undercut the ability of field-based internationals in Mostar to create effective working relationships with local officials who, seeing their interlocutors routinely ignored or overruled, attempted to communicate directly with their distant superiors. Again, Brčko provides an instructive example of the benefits of independent, effectively localized international peacebuilding, as the concentration of political authority in OHR Brčko's hands afforded supervisors greater latitude to tailor their policies to the needs of people living in the Brčko area. It also facilitated the development of close and productive local-international relations, especially following the creation of the District when the supervisory regime utilized its political authority to play the role of a "patron" protecting Brčko against the entities.

This is not necessarily to advocate for political clientelism of the type that emerged in Brčko as a general model for peacebuilding. First, such a closely bound political alliance is unlikely to arise absent the unique legal and political conditions that were created by the Arbitral Tribunal's awards. Second, given the infighting that this relationship generated at times within and among international organizations in Bosnia, there is a risk that such political clientelism could prove counterproductive to overall peacebuilding goals. Though I do not believe this was the case in Brčko, it is clearly a risk. That said, one way in which international officials in field offices might build greater local support for peacebuilding reforms is to prioritize efforts to fight for the interests of the places in which they operate vis-à-vis the state and other regions. They could, for example, incorporate as a central component of their mission working as advocates for local communities in terms of political representation at the state level, gaining a fair share of public investments in infrastructure, having a voice in land use policies, or fighting for the equitable retention of revenues from natural resource exploitation, to provide just a few examples. This form of political and social patronage is often feasible given the prevalence of decentralized political frameworks in states that have experienced violent conflict.

My final observation concerns the importance of embeddedness in peacebuilding interventions. As noted in chapter 6, I use the concept of embeddedness to refer to the degree to which international officials become effectively localized in relation to the social practices, political networks, and institutions that mediate relations at the sites in which they operate. I am borrowing the idea of embeddedness from economic geographers and sociologists, who have developed the concept to analyze the ways in which economic activity by firms or individuals is shaped by the social and spatial networks in which it is embedded.[24] At a basic level embeddedness refers to the structural composition of socio-spatial networks—such as the number and forms of ties between both economic and noneconomic actors in a given territory—and the ways in which such socio-spatial relations shape economic activity.[25]

So why does embeddedness matter in the context of international peacebuilding? One of the primary insights from the literature is that "embedded ties perform unique functions and have three features: Trust, fine-grained information transfer, and joint problem-solving arrangements."[26] Embeddedness, in other words, profoundly impacts the quality of personal relationships, information awareness, and the coordination of activities between and among different actors—all crucial elements of successful peacebuilding. Put more simply, embeddedness enhances the ability of international officials to develop productive relationships with local actors and read situations on the ground correctly. Promoting the political independence of peacebuilders working in the field will do little good if they are not sufficiently embedded in their sites to effectively take advantage of such authority.

I am not the first to identify embeddedness as a critical component of peacebuilding. Anne Holohan also highlights this factor in her analysis of UN operations in two municipalities in Kosovo.[27] Holohan's argument focuses on "social embeddedness" (personal ties) and the ways in which it is shaped by (1) formal versus informal and (2) hierarchical versus networked bureaucratic practices. The conceptualization of embeddedness adopted here is broader, encompassing not just social, but also political and legal embeddedness, and a wider range of peacebuilding practices and institutions that facilitate or inhibit its development. This is not to dismiss the importance of social embeddedness. As noted in chapter 6, during research I discovered that a surprising number of international officials spent years working and developing relationships with their local counterparts in the District. Additionally, isolated from central offices in Sarajevo and the diversions of the Adriatic coast, the social activities of the international cohort assigned to this small outpost in Bosnia was often remarkably "local" and informal—visiting with friends or colleagues from the District on the weekends, putting in extra hours at the office, or hanging out at the handful of restaurants and cafés in the town. Mostar, in contrast, experienced rapid turnover in international staff as people quickly become frustrated by outside interference and a lack of progress. And those working in Mostar spent relatively less time in the city while off-duty.

There are several unique factors that have facilitated the political and legal embeddedness of international peacebuilders in Brčko through the years. Perhaps most important have been the Arbitral Tribunal awards themselves, which emphasized context over content and provided the supervisory regime with a great degree of political independence. This is especially the case with the Final Award, which offered a unique "condominium" solution tailored specifically to defuse conflict over control of the territory of the Brčko area, and which charged the OHR Brčko office with creating the conditions necessary for the emergence and sustainable development of this new political entity. In effect, the Final Award effectively localized the supervisory regime by embedding it in the District's institutional framework, giving it both the responsibility of developing Brčko's multiethnic institutions and guarding the District's political autonomy in Bosnia. To carry out this ambitious mandate international officials working in Brčko found it necessary to, in Henry Clarke's words, "meet regularly, face to face, with all the key actors" in order to negotiate, coordinate and implement reforms in the District.

As Clarke's comments suggest, another reason the supervisory regime in Brčko received broad support for its activities over the years is that local actors were consistently encouraged to take an active role in the process; as engaged participants in the development of the District, local elites tended to feel invested in its continued success. In Mostar, in contrast, the lead role played by distant international officials who periodically "parachuted" into the city for a political meeting or ceremony undermined efforts to create a sense of meaningful local participation—both among politicians and ordinary citizens—fueling apathy and disinterest in the peacebuilding process. When inadequate attention has been paid to local input in the District, such as the rushed introduction of integrated schools in 2000, setbacks have resulted. The broader point, again, is that the cultivation of good working relationships with local actors is fundamental to the success of peacebuilding operations, and such relationships can only be established through regular interaction and dialogue.

To sum up, successful peacebuilding is not just a matter of devising correct policies. Theoretically impressive laws and institutions are worthless if they are not appropriate to local conditions or properly implemented. And assuring their implementation, in turn, depends on productive and meaningful relationships between international and local actors on the ground, and the successful coordination of resources and policy efforts. To improve the chances of fulfilling peacebuilding goals in the aftermath of violent conflict, in other words, requires reorienting the spatiality of peacebuilding practices and institutions to promote embeddedness, independence, and a contextual rather than content-centric focus. These are relative attributes, a matter of degree rather than kind. Hence this prospective framework cannot be reduced to a template, applicable the same way in different environments. Instead it involves rethinking how peacebuilding is done—a shift in the habitus or culture that governs peacebuilding activities and priorities today.

NOTES

Introduction

1. The full name of the country is Bosnia and Herzegovina. However, for the sake of brevity—and following common convention in English—I will primarily use the shortened label "Bosnia" in this text. Bosniak is the current preferred label of Bosnia's Muslim population. It is often used to refer to anyone whose family is of Muslim background, though a significant number of Bosniaks are not religiously observant.

2. It is a common misconception that Mostar is divided into Bosniak and Croat sides by the Neretva River, which runs through middle the town. While this is true in the northern and southern edges of the city, in the downtown areas the line ran directly through the urban core on the west bank of the river.

3. For more on violence and boundary activations see, Tilly 2003.

4. For more on these events, see Moore 2011.

5. "Navijački rat u Mostaru," *Nezavisne Novine*, June 15, 2006; "Mostar pod opsadom huligana," *Dnevni List*, June 15, 2006. One local employee of a well-known international NGO in the city, whose apartment is located along the boulevard in East Mostar, told me that he saw armed men who were not police patrolling outside his residence the night following the clashes. Though I was not able to corroborate this account with others I talked to, one former ARBiH soldier who fought along the front line during the war did acknowledge the existence of an informal network of war veterans which could be mobilized at short notice to conduct armed patrols in the city.

6. "Ponovo 'rat' na ulicama 200 huligani tražilo sukob s 'balijama' pa napalo policije," *Dnevni List*, June 20, 2012.

7. "Na džamiju ispaljena zolja," *Oslobodjenje*, October 11, 2006.

8. Doyle and Sambanis 2006.

9. Binnendijk et al. 2006. Brčko's first supervisor, Robert Farrand, is also quite blunt about the difficulties he encountered in obtaining adequate funding for reconstruction from donors during his tenure, something that was not in short supply in Mostar. See Farrand 2011, chapter 7.

10. *Special Report No 2/96 concerning the accounts of the Administrator and the European Union Administration, Mostar (EUAM) accompanied by the replies of the Commission and the Administrator of Mostar*, paragraph 31. According to the same report, when the costs of the WEU police mission were added in the total expenditures were nearly 3,000 ECU per person.

11. Reichel 2000, 14.

12. This research also found little evidence that NGO or civil society capacity has had a significant differential impact on the peace process in these two towns. Though hard data is lacking, it is quite clear that Mostar has experienced vastly more investment in aid and personnel in this sector since the end of the war, and the city also possesses a more vigorous civil society presence— including both international and domestic organizations, such as OKC Abrašević (http://www.okcabrasevic.org/)—than in Brčko. For more on the ambivalence of civil society and peacebuilding in Brčko, see Jeffrey 2007. For more on the promises and limits of civil society and peacebuilding more generally, see Paffenholz 2010.

13. Tilly 1994, 270.

14. Paige 1999. This also corresponds with Charles Ragin's observation that "the logic of case study is fundamentally configurational." See Ragin 2000, 68.

15. Abbott 1992, 68.

16. For more on the distinction between negative and positive peace, see Galtung 1969.

17. Hampson 1996; Howard 2008;

18. Cousens 2000; Downs and Stedman 2002.

19. Fortna 2008.

20. Doyle and Sambanis 2006; Call 2008.

21. Paris 2004; Ghani et al. 2006; Roberts 2008.

22. Lederach 1997; Bloomfield et al. 2003; Daly and Sarkin 2007.

23. Justice is a polyvalent term—indeed, social justice was one of the "essentially contested concepts" originally identified by W. B. Gallie (see Gallie 1956). For overviews on the relationship between justice and peacebuilding, see Mani 2002; Lambourne 2009.

24. UNDP 1994; Cockell 2000; Richmond 2006; Newman 2011.

25. Pouligny 2006; Heathershaw 2007; Autesserre forthcoming.

26. For a comprehensive analysis of these debates, see Diehl and Druckman 2010.

27. Autesserre 2009, 276. On this point, see also Hoglund and Kovacs 2010; Belloni 2007, 10.

28. MacGinty 2006.

29. In both towns nonviolent incidents—such as verbal insults, racist graffiti and vandalism of cemeteries, homes, monuments, and religious properties—still occur. Though accurate statistics on these types of ethnic tensions are not available, it is quite clear talking with international officials and residents in both towns that they are much more prevalent in Mostar than Brčko. Moreover contention over graffiti in the former has resulted in physical violence as well. In February 2010, for instance, members of a small, multiethnic activist group called Kreaktiva were attacked by a group of hooligans from West Mostar armed with stones, bottles and Molotov cocktails while they were removing fascist graffiti along the boulevard. Fortunately police intervened before the Molotov cocktails were used. See "Napadnuti antifašistički aktivisti u Mostaru," *Dnevni Avaz,* February 14, 2010.

30. Interview with Ivo Filipović, July 10, 2011.

31. Toal and Dahlman 2011; Pickering 2007.

32. UNHCR statistics quoted in Bieber 2005, 430. See also, Toal and Dahlman 2011, 297. As Toal and Dahlman note, the reliability of return figures in the country is debatable given different counting methodologies and recording of statistics over the years and in different communities.

Another problem with estimating returns is that official statistics only indicate whether property has been reclaimed, not whether people are actually living in their former residences (many who successfully reclaimed property subsequently sold it or are still waiting to rebuild). For more on this, see Toal and Dahlman 2011, chapter 10.

33. For more on attempts to portray the rebuilding of the bridge as a symbol of social reintegration, as well as its more ambivalent meaning among residents of Mostar, see Grodach 2002; Makaš 2007, chapter 3.

34. *Key Issues and Institutions in Brčko District*, Joint OHR/OSCE Report, March 12, 2011.

35. *Report from the Supervisor of Brčko to the Peace Implementation Council Steering Board on the Progress of Implementation of the Final Award of the International Arbitral Tribunal for Brčko, 8 March 2003–8 March 2004*, OHR Brčko, March 8, 2004.

36. Interview with Ratko Stjepanović, July 11, 2011. Stjepanović, a District Assembly councilor and president of the SDS board in Brčko—and displaced person himself, who was originally from Vareš—has been one of the key figures in improving the status of displaced Serbs in Brčko, especially those living in the Ilička neighborhood where many were resettled. Political and social marginalization of those displaced from other communities is also a significant phenomenon in Mostar. For more on this, see Vetters 2007.

37. This is not a new phenomenon. Like most villages in Bosnia the villages in the Brčko area were largely monoethnic before the war. See Dahlman and O'Tuathail 2006, 656.

38. E.g., Clark 2010.

39. See, for example, Charles 2006.

40. Bergesen and Herman 1998; Davis 2006.

41. For more on the advantages of subnational comparative analysis, see Kalyvas 2008a. For an excellent example of the advantages of utilizing subnational comparative analysis to shed light on the dynamics of ethnic conflict within states, see Varshney 2003.

42. On selection bias and the importance of variation in the dependent variable in comparative research, see Geddes 1990. On subnational comparative methods and spatially uneven political processes, see Snyder 2001. For more on the strengths and weaknesses of paired comparisons, see Tarrow 2007.

43. Dahlman and O'Tuathail 2005. For more on scale as a category of analysis and practice, see Moore 2008.

44. MacGinty 2011; Richmond 2011; Autesserre forthcoming.

45. Autesserre forthcoming.

46. It is important to note that these figures are rough estimates, as there has not been a census in Bosnia since 1991. 100,000 is the estimate provided to me by local politicians and officials in OHR Brčko. The International Crisis Group, in a recent report on Brčko (ICG 2011b) provides an estimate of 40,000 residents in the District—a preposterous figure that is just one of many inaccuracies in this report. For Mostar's population estimate, see *Federacija Bosne I Herzegovine u brojkama* [Federal Office of Statistics], Federation of Bosnia and Herzegovina, Sarajevo, 2011: http://www.fzs.ba/Podaci/Federacija%20BiH%20u%20brojkama%202011.pdf. Another rough measure that suggests similar population ratios in the two towns is the number of people registered to vote in the 2008 municipal elections (80,200 in Brčko and 90,500 in Mostar). See http://www.izbori.ba/Mandati27102008/ShowMunicipality.asp?MunicipalityCode=200 and http://www.izbori.ba/Mandati27102008/ShowMunicipality.asp?MunicipalityCode=199.

47. For more on the importance of peacebuilding practices, see Autesserre forthcoming.

48. To protect sources I made the decision to cite by name in the text and endnotes only senior international officials, elected politicians, or high ranking local officials in the two cities who agreed to speak on record. Local residents and junior officials (local or international) are quoted anonymously, even if they agreed to speak for attribution.

49. Fujii 2010.

50. Pred 1990.

1. The Study of Peacebuilding

1. Paris and Sisk 2009, 1.
2. Arend Lijphart popularized the term *consociationalism*, though he now prefers to call his theory *power-sharing democracy* (see Lijphart 2002). Several edited volumes focused on this debate over political institutions have appeared in the past decade: e.g., Reynolds 2002; Roeder and Rothchild 2005; Noel 2005; Choudhry 2008; Taylor 2009.
3. Lijphart 2004.
4. Lijphart 1969.
5. Lijphart 1979, 2004; McGarry and O'Leary 2005, 2009b; O'Leary 2005b.
6. Lijphart 1985, 106–7.
7. Lijphart 1979, 2004; McGarry and O'Leary 2009b.
8. Lijphart 1979.
9. See Horowitz 2008; Reilly 2001, 2006a, 2006b.
10. Reilly 2006a.
11. Sisk 2003, 145.
12. Horowitz 2000, 602–4. For a more general critique of ethno-federalism, see Roeder 2009.
13. Horowitz 2007; Suberu 2009.
14. Horowitz 2002, 25.
15. Brass 1991.
16. Andeweg 2000, 520.
17. Gagnon 2004.
18. Horowitz 1991, 171.
19. Tsebelis 1990.
20. O'Leary 2005a.
21. Ibid.; McGarry and O'Leary 2007, 2009a. See also Lijphart 1995.
22. O'Leary 2006, xxii.
23. Colletta and Cullen 2000; Collier et al. 2003; Walter 2004.
24. Wood 2008. For a broader critique of this political economy literature, see Cramer 2002.
25. Campbell 1998.
26. Hoffman 2003; Denov and Maclure 2007.
27. Straus 2007.
28. Ferme 2001.
29. Wood 2003.
30. Reno 2003; Andreas 2004; Andreas 2008.
31. Allen 1996; Lubkemann 2008; Toal and Dahlman 2011.
32. Bellows and Miguel 2009.
33. Blattman 2009.
34. Nordstrom 1997; Wood 2000.
35. One recent exception is Gerard Toal and Carl Dahlman's multisited research on postwar returns and the legacy of ethnic cleansing in Bosnia, see Toal and Dahlman 2011.
36. Wood 2008, 556.
37. E.g., Bax 2000; Wood 2003; Straus 2006; Weinstein 2007. See also the recent special issues in the *Journal of Peace Research* (Verwimp, Justino, and Bruck 2009) and the *Journal of Conflict Resolution* (Cederman and Gleditsch 2009) for more quantitatively oriented research on disaggregation and microlevel analyses of conflict dynamics in civil wars.
38. Kalyvas 2006.
39. Kalyvas 2003, 47.
40. Fearon and Laitin 2000.
41. Gagnon 2004.

42. E.g., Posen 1993; Kaufmann 1996.
43. Kalyvas 2008b.
44. See Kalyvas 2006, chapter 11.
45. Paris 1997.
46. Doyle 1983; Levy 1988; Rummel 1997; Oneal and Russert 1997; Russert and Oneal 2001.
47. Paris 2002.
48. Boutros-Ghali 1996, 7, 9.
49. Snyder 2000.
50. Hegre et al. 2001; Cederman et al. 2010.
51. Lyons 2004; Brancati and Snyder 2011, forthcoming; Flores and Nooruddin 2012.
52. Cederman, Gleditsch, and Hug forthcoming; Hoglund 2009. For an excellent overview of the various predicaments surrounding elections following war, see Hoglund et al. 2009. On elections and subnational variations in ethnic violence in an established democracy, see Wilkinson 2004.
53. Stiglitz 2002; Chua 2003.
54. Hegre and Sambanis 2006.
55. Walton and Seddon 1994; Kaiser 1996; Pugh 2002; Bussmann et al. 2005; Bussmann and Schneider 2007; Hartzell et al. 2010.
56. Fukuyama 2004; Mansfield and Snyder 2005; Doyle and Sambanis 2006.
57. Paris 2004, 205.
58. Chesterman 2004.
59. Lyons 2002.
60. Chandler 1999; Knaus and Martin 2003; Bain 2006; Chandler 2006.
61. Donais 2009; Barnett and Zurcher 2009.
62. Paris and Sisk 2009, 3. See also Jarstad and Sisk 2008.
63. Paris and Sisk 2009, 305–9. On footprint and duration dilemmas, see Chesterman 2004; Fearon and Laitin 2004; Caplan 2005; Edelstein 2009; Suhrke 2009. On local ownership dilemmas, see Scheye and Peake 2005; Chesterman 2007; Donais 2009; Narten 2009. On coordination and coherence dilemmas, see Cooley and Ron 2002; Jones 2002; de Coning 2007; Paris 2009.
64. Paris and Sisk 2009, 311.
65. Chopra 2002; Paffenholz 2003; Chopra and Hohe 2004.
66. MacGinty 2010. See also Lederach 1997 for a detailed analysis of the interactive dynamics of the multiple "levels" of peacebuilding.
67. I.e., Chandler 2006; Richmond 2011.
68. Paris 2010, 38.
69. Howard 2008.
70. Autesserre 2010.
71. Talentino 2007; Nathan 2007; Suhrke 2009.

2. Collapse of Yugoslavia and the Balkan Wars

1. Ball et al. 2007; Toal and Dahlman 2011.
2. To be precise, Cambodia was the first instance of internationally administered statebuilding in the post–Cold War period, but the UN Transitional Authority mission established there in 1992–93 was neither as extensive nor as influential as the mission undertaken in Bosnia. For more on international territorial administration and statebuilding, see Wilde 2001; Caplan 2005.
3. Toal and Maksić 2011.
4. For an excellent discussion of the various explanations for the collapse of Yugoslavia, see Toal and Dahlman 2011, chapter 1. For earlier overviews of postwar peacebuilding efforts in Bosnia, see Chandler 1999; Bose 2002; Bieber 2005; Donais 2005; Belloni 2007.

5. To give a sense of the scale of this phenomenon, in 1981 remittances from abroad totaled more than $5 billion, which represented roughly one quarter of Yugoslavia's total foreign exchange revenues. See Grečić 1990, 202.

6. Dubravčić 1993, 263.

7. The unemployment problem was also highly variable across republics. In Kosovo and Macedonia it exceeded 20 percent during the 1980s while in Slovenia it remained well below 5 percent. See Woodward 1995b, 204.

8. For an excellent account of these economic debates between the republics, see Woodward 1995a.

9. The primary exception was the right to self-determination, which only the six republics were granted. For more on the ethno-political implications of the 1974 constitution, see Hayden 2000; Jović 2009.

10. Lampe 2000, 347.

11. For more on the SANU memorandum and the rise of Milošević, see Sell 2002, chapter 2.

12. Vladisavljević 2008.

13. The six republics and two autonomous provinces each contributed one representative to the collective State Presidency.

14. The JNA was adamantly opposed to a multiparty system and also styled itself as the primary defender of Yugoslav unity. Additionally, by this time both the leadership and ranks of the JNA was overwhelmingly Serb or Montenegrin as a result of political maneuvering by Milošević and widespread defections from other provinces. For more on the role of the JNA in the wars, see Gow 2003, chapter 3.

15. Ramet 2006, chapter 13. Territorial Defense units introduced established by the 1974 constitution. Motivated in part by the Soviet Union's invasion of Czechoslovakia in 1969, they were decentralized military forces controlled by the republics.

16. Thompson 1999; MacDonald 2003.

17. Slavonia is a fertile agricultural region located in eastern Croatia along the border with Serbia. Krajina (which means "frontier" or "borderland") is an arc of territory in Croatia stretching along the border of the northwestern corner of Bosnia.

18. In January 1992 a cease-fire was declared and United Nations Protection Force (UNPROFOR) observers deployed. This lead to a decrease in violent clashes in the two regions until the summer of 1995, when the Croatian military mounted major operations which drove Serb forces and civilians out of the territories. For more on the the war in Croatia, see Glenny 1996; Tanner 2001; Magaš and Zanić 2001; Burg and Shoup 1999.

19. Ramet 2006, 418.

20. For more on the 1990 elections, see Arnautović 1996.

21. Andjelić 2003, 189.

22. Pejanović 2004, 23.

23. For a map of the SAOs, see Toal and Dahlman 2011, 108.

24. Ibid., 104.

25. Burg and Shoup 1999, 74.

26. In the 1991 census 43 percent of the population declared themselves Muslim, 31 percent Serb, 17 percent Croat, 6 percent Yugoslav, and 2 percent marked another ethnic category.

27. Toal and Dahlman 2011, 69.

28. Sells 1996.

29. Hockenos 2003. It is worth noting that Franciscans in Bosnia are divided into Herzegovinian and Bosnian orders, and that the latter have a diametrically different vision of the country, supporting a unified and multiethnic Bosnia. See Andjelović 2007.

30. Radić 1998, 170.

31. Ramet 2006, 418.

32. For more on this, see Hoare 2004.

33. Though Abdić received the most votes he ceded the position of the head of the collective presidency to Izetbegović, for reasons that are not entirely clear.

34. For more on the conflict between the ARBiH and Abdić's supporters, see Christia 2008.

35. The anthropologist Mart Bax provides a fascinating account of one *mali rat* surrounding the Medjugorje pilgrimage site in Herzegovina in 1992. See Bax 1997.

36. For this map Sarajevo's ten districts have been combined into a single unit, which better represents the theater of conflict encompassing the city during the war. Sarajevo and these fourteen municipalities were the sites of 57 percent of the killings, with the two most affected districts (Sarajevo ~14,400, and Srebrenica ~9,400) representing nearly a quarter of the total deaths alone. See Ball et al. 2007, 37.

37. Ibid., 34.

38. Hayden 1996, 783–84.

39. Ramet 2006, 440.

40. For a personal account of these events, see Komšić 2006.

41. For more on the deleterious effects of Vance-Owens and other wartime peace plans based upon ethno-territorial logics, see Campbell 1998; Toal and Dahlman 2011, chapter 5.

42. Palairet 1977, 591.

43. Source for census numbers in Brčko and Mostar: *Ethnic composition of Bosnia-Herzegovina population, by municipalities and settlements*, Zavod za statistiku Bosne i Hercegovine, Bilten No. 234, Sarajevo 1991. Brčko was the ninth largest municipality by population in Bosnia, and Mostar the fifth.

44. See Dahlman and O'Tuathail 2006, 656.

45. Luchetta 2009, 6–7. In response to tensions with the Soviet Union in the 1950s Tito instituted a strategic policy of concentrating heavy industry and military manufacturing in Bosnia, where it would be more protected in the event of an invasion.

46. For more on the development of Medjugorje, see Bax 1995.

47. Hayden 1996, 788.

48. Bose 2002, 102.

49. Kadrić 1998, 23.

50. Ibid., 34–5.

51. The Brčko area was one of the most heavily mined parts of Bosnia during the war, which was a significant factor delaying reconstruction efforts in the early years. For more on this, see Bolton 2003. To give a sense of the scale of this problem, the commander of the first U.S. SFOR troops in the Brčko area following the war, Colonel Gregory Fontenot, notes that his brigade encountered "some 1,800 minefields along and outside 200 kilometers of trenches and field fortifications" in the first twelve months of operations. See Fontenot 2007, 53.

52. One resident of Brčko who fought in the ARBiH described to me the concerted attempts to ethnicize and Islamize the armed forces, stating: "At the beginning of the war we all knew we were fighting for Bosnia, our homeland. But as the war went on these *hodže* (Islamic religious leaders) started to show up at the frontlines and tell us that we were fighting for Islam."

53. Bjelakovic and Strazzari 1999, 78.

54. Hoare 2004, 66. At the time neither the ARBiH nor the local TO forces were effectively organized in the Mostar region, so many Bosniaks joined HOS or other paramilitary units such as the "Convicts' Brigade" (see chapter 4).

55. For more on the concept of urbacide as the destruction of urban heterogeneity in Mostar, see Coward 2002.

56. Prior to the war more than thirty thousand Bosniaks lived on the western side of Mostar, while nearly six thousand Croats resided in eastern neighborhoods and villages. See Bose 2002, 99–100.

57. In September 1991 the UN imposed an arms embargo on Yugoslavia and its successor states. This disproportionately affected Muslim forces who could only receive arms that were transported through Croat lines, which were blocked during the Croat-Bosniak war. Following the Washington Agreement the U.S. encouraged covert arms shipments from Iran through Croatia to better arm the ARBiH. For more on this, see Wiebes 2003, chapter 4.

58. Strategic planning for the operation was conducted by Military Professional Resources Inc. (MPRI), a private security firm composed primarily of former high-ranking officers in the U.S. armed forces. MPRI was also charged with professionalizing Federation armed forces after the war in Bosnia. For more on this, see Avant 2005.

59. Holbrooke 1999, 101.

60. USDOS 1997, 247–49.

61. Bose 2002, 216; Belloni 2004, 336. For the full text of the DPA, see http://www.ohr.int/dpa/default.asp?content_id=380.

62. The ten Federation cantons are Posavina, West Herzegovina and Canton 10 (Croat majority); Una-Sana, Zenica-Doboj, Sarajevo, Bosnia-Podrinje and Tuzla (Bosniak majority); and Herzegovina-Neretva and Central Bosnia (ethnically mixed).

63. Hayden 2000, 126.

64. It was at the U.S.'s insistence that military peacekeepers' activities were limited to this narrow set of activities, due primarily to the Pentagon's fear of "mission creep." See Holbrooke 1999, 215–26.

65. DPA, Annex 10, Article 2.

66. Neville-Jones 1996, 50.

67. As the case of Mostar suggests, peacebuilding dynamics in Mostar and Brčko have been influenced by broader developments in the country, but they also had their own rhythm and trajectories.

68. *PIC Bonn Conclusions*, Peace Implementation Council, December 10, 1997. http://www.ohr.int/pic/default.asp?content_id=5182.

69. Toal and Dahlman 2011, 11.

70. Prior to OHR's decision on common license plates, vehicles could clearly be identified as coming from Serb, Croat, or Bosniak controlled territories. Widespread harassment targeting occupants of vehicles that strayed outside of "their" ethnic territories inhibited freedom of movement across entity lines.

71. Wolfgang Petritsch, *The future of Bosnia and Herzegovina in an integrative Europe*, September 7, 2000, http://www.ohr.int/ohr-dept/presso/presssp/default.asp?content_id=3246.

72. E.g., Chandler 1999; Pugh 2001; Knaus and Martin 2003.

73. Silajdžić defeated SDA leader Sulejman Tihić in the election for the Bosniak member of the State Presidency, while Dodik's party, SNSD, swept to power in the RS, ending the longtime dominance of SDS.

74. Azinović et al. 2011.

75. ICG 2012.

76. Joseph 2009, 9.

3. Institutions

1. *Memorandum of Understanding on the European Administration of Mostar*, Article 2. July 5, 1994.

2. ICG 2000, 8.

3. *Annex to the Dayton Agreement on Implementing the Federation of Bosnia and Herzegovina: Agreed Principles for the Interim Statute of the City of Mostar*, November 10, 1995.

4. Indeed, even in areas supposed under control of the shared city administration—such as urban planning decisions—each city-municipality established its own independing urban planning institutions. See Makaš 2011.

5. ICG 2000, 8. For an excellent account of the history of the central zone under the Interim Statute, see Makaš 2011.

6. Bollens 2007, chapter 6.

7. The majority of Mostar's urban core was located in the central zone, and the Stari Grad and Southwest municipalities, while the other four municipalities covered the city's more sparsely populated suburbs and outlying villages.

8. The Interim Statute originally called for a forty-seven-person city council, with a similar composition, but this was reduced to thirty prior to the 1997 municipal elections.

9. The one exception being the Southeast municipality in East Mostar: see *Interim Statute of the City of Mostar*, February 7, 1996, Article 56.

10. *Commission for Reforming the City of Mostar: Recommendations of the Commission Report of the Chairman*, OHR: http://www.ohr.int/archive/report-mostar/pdf/Reforming%20Mostar-Report%20(EN).pdf.

11. Ibid., 54.

12. Bieber 2005, 424.

13. ESI 2000, 18.

14. *Decision Adding the Fundamental Interest Clause and the Position of Deputy Head of Municipality to the Mostar City Municipalities Statutes*, OHR Sarajevo, July 6, 1999: http://www.ohr.int/decisions/mo-hncantdec/default.asp?content_id=109.

15. Mile Puljić, president of the HDZ board in Mostar, quoted in, ICG 2000, 16.

16. ESI 2000, 18.

17. Of these only the Franciscan church and tower were ultimately completed. The cathedral and theater, which were both located in the central zone, were eventually stopped due to opposition from international officials and Bosniaks in the city. For more on these actions, see Makaš 2011.

18. Makaš 2007, chapter 4; Bollens 2007, chapter 6; Grodach 2002; Wimmen 2004.

19. Interview with OHR regional official, November 2, 2007.

20. *Decision Establishing the Commission for Reforming the City of Mostar*, OHR Sarajevo, September 17, 2003: http://www.ohr.int/decisions/mo-hncantdec/default.asp?content_id=30823.

21. *Decision Enacting the Statute of the City of Mostar*, OHR Sarajevo, January 28, 2004: http://www.ohr.int/decisions/mo-hncantdec/default.asp?content_id=31707.

22. The former central zone has also been merged into the territories of the former Mostar Southwest and Old Town municipalities for administrative purposes. See Makaš 2011, 9, 14.

23. *Statute of the City of Mostar*, Article 7. For the full text of Mostar's current statute see Ashdown's *Decision Enacting the Statute of the City of Mostar*, in the preceding footnote.

24. For official statistics on the 2008 municipal election in Mostar see http://www.izbori.ba/Mandati27102008/ShowMunicipality.asp?MunicipalityCode=199.

25. ICG 2009, 4. See pp. 11–13 of the same report for several examples of continued parallelism in public services.

26. Interview with OSCE regional official, July 28, 2011; interview with OHR regional official, July 18, 2012.

27. Interview with Aner Žuljević, SDP Mostar, December 6, 2007.

28. Interview with Rolf van Uye, director of the Mostar office of the OSCE, March 24, 2007. The existence of protection rackets was confirmed in subsequent conversations with businessmen in Stari Grad. International officials I talked with speculated that this situation is the product of an informal agreement in which Croats will not challenge Bosniak control over, and tourist revenues from, Stari Grad in exchange for Bosniaks not questioning the apparent undercontribution of taxes to the federal budget from Croat-controlled Medjugorje, a nearby devotional center to the Virgin Mary, which is the largest tourist attraction in the country.

29. See "Okončani 441. tradicionalni viteški skokovi sa Starog mosta," *Oslobodjenje*, July 30, 2007; "Možemo naplatiti skakanje!" *Dnevni Avaz*, July 28, 2007; http://forum.bljesak.info/viewtopic.php?f=3&t=12291&start=0&sid=be8cf3058d997002f2e50e904468db47.

30. ICG 2009, 3.

31. Ibid. This was confirmed to me by international officials in the city.

32. *Decision Extending the Temporary Financing of the City of Mostar for the Period from 1 April 2009 to 30 September 2009*, OHR Sarajevo, September 29, 2009.

33. *Decision Enacting Amendment to the Statute of the City of Mostar*, OHR Sarajevo, December 14, 2009.

34. For more on this see, Kesic et al. 2012.

35. See "Anarhija u Mostaru Inzko blokirao Gradsko Vijeće," *Dnevni List*, November 22, 2012; "Mostar u pat-poziciji!" *Dnevni List*, November 23, 2012.

36. "Bošnjaci bojkotirali otvaranje vijećnice," *Dnevni List*, March 27, 2012.

37. Interview with OHR regional official, July 18, 2012.

38. *Ispitivanje javnog mnijenje*, Prism Research, April 2008.

39. "Public opinion poll in Mostar," Ipsos Public Affairs, April 27, 2012.

40. The section laying out the procedures for international arbitration of Brčko is located in Article V of Annex 2 of the DPA.

41. ICG 1997, 4; BBC 1996.

42. *Award of the Arbitral Tribunal for the Dispute over the Inter-Entity Boundary in the Brčko Area*, February 14, 1997.

43. Baros 1998. One likely reason for this oversight is that at the time the RS was represented by a Serb American lawyer from Milwaukee. Though presumably loyal to his ethnic compatriots the lawyer clearly lacked the training or competence to properly represent the entity in the arbitration process. His submissions to the Tribunal are riddled with spelling errors, non-sequiturs and specious legal arguments.

44. Parish 2009, 69–72.

45. Bildt 1998, 330.

46. *Award of the Arbitral Tribunal for the Dispute over the Inter-Entity Boundary in the Brčko Area*, February 14, 1997, Paragraph 98.

47. Ibid., Paragraph 104. To provide some context about the extent of the powers the supervisor possessed, at the time of the First Award the High Representative of OHR had the authority only to "coordinate," "monitor," and "facilitate" civilian implementation of DPA (Annex 10). The distinctiveness and importance of these powers is discussed in depth in chapters 6 and 7.

48. *Order on Multi-ethnic Administration in the RS Municipality of Brčko*, OHR Brčko, October 10, 1997: http://www.ohr.int/ohr-offices/brcko/bc-so/default.asp?content_id=5337; *Order on Judiciary in the RS Municipality of Brčko*, OHR Brčko, October 10, 1997: http://www.ohr.int/ohr-offices/brcko/bc-so/default.asp?content_id=5336; *Order on Multi-Ethnic Police in the RS Municipality of Brčko*, October 13, 1997: http://www.ohr.int/ohr-offices/brcko/bc-so/default.asp?content_id=5338.

49. *Supplemental Award of the Brčko Arbitral Tribunal for Dispute over the Inter-Entity Boundary in Brčko Area*, March 15, 1998, Paragraph 21: http://www.ohr.int/ohr-offices/brcko/arbitration/default.asp?content_id=5345.

50. Ibid., Paragraph 27.

51. *Final Award of the Arbitral Tribunal for Dispute Over Inter-Entity Boundary in Brčko Area*, March 5, 1999, Paragraph 9: http://www.ohr.int/ohr-offices/brcko/default.asp?content_id=5358.

52. Ibid., Paragraph 11.

53. Ibid., Paragraphs 6 and 7.

54. Holbrooke 1999, 249; USDOS 1997, 201.

55. *Final Award of the Arbitral Tribunal for Dispute Over Inter-Entity Boundary in Brčko Area*, March 5, 1999, Paragraph 36: http://www.ohr.int/ohr-offices/brcko/default.asp?content_id=5358.

56. In practice there was no clear territorial boundary between Brčko Rahić and Ravne Brčko (contra the map in Dahlman and O'Tuathail 2006, 658), as Bosniak and Croat villages were interspersed in the southern parts of the District.

57. All four secondary schools in the District, and four of the five primary schools in Brčko town have a multiethnic composition of students. In contrast, in the rural villages of the District only two of the ten primary schools have a significantly multiethnic student population. In all schools, however, the structure of teachers is multiethnic. Interview with Peter Appleby, OHR Brčko deputy supervisor, July 29, 2012.

58. This informal 4-4-2 approach was devised by Brčko's first supervisor, Robert Farrand, prior to the establishment of the District.

59. The IEBL was legally abolished in the District by supervisory order in 2006. See *Supervisory Order Abolishing Entity Legislation Within Brčko District And Declaring the Inter-entity Boundary Line to Be of No Further Legal Significance in the District*, OHR Brčko, August 4, 2006: http://www.ohr.int/ohr-offices/brcko/bc-so/default.asp?content_id=37764.

60. *Highlights of Recent Public Opinion Research: Brčko District*, National Democratic Institute, Brčko District Office, December 16, 2003, 3.

61. *Public Opinion Survey Results: Brčko District*, EUFOR, November 2009.

62. *Lessons from Education Reform in Brčko*, OSCE Mission to BiH Education Department, October 2007, 9.

63. *Highlights of Public Opinion Survey on Education in BiH: Citizen Opinion in December 2006*, Organization for Security and Co-operation in Europe, n.d.

64. *Tailoring Catchment Areas: School Catchment Areas in Bosnia and Herzegovina, a Status Report*, Organization for Security and Cooperation in Europe, September 2007.

65. See also Jones 2012.

66. Hromadžić 2008, 542. See also Hromadžić 2011.

67. Ten months earlier the BiH Election Commission ruled that Pajić had violated conflict of interest laws and should resign. In May the entire Bosniak bloc of District councilors—along with a handful of Croat and Serb colleagues—voted to remove him from office, prompting most Serb and Croat councilors to walk out it protest. This vote was annulled by the Brčko Court of Appeals the following month, precipitating a political crisis requiring OHR Brčko's behind-the-scenes mediation, which resulted in Pajić resigning and being replaced as mayor by another SNSD councilor, Miroslav Gavrić.

68. The intent is not, as it has been explained to me, necessarily to win a positive judgment in court for the full amount of claimed damages. Instead, an out of court settlement, which prevents the investigation of procedural irregularities while providing firms and officials with a reduced payment, is the most likely outcome of these lawsuits.

69. ICG 2011b, 1. The primary aim of this remarkably shoddy report was to provide ammunition for those who have been calling for the end of supervision in the District in recent years. As one senior international official in Brčko told me, off the record, "They came with an agenda and slanted the information we gave them to suit their story."

70. Divjak and Pugh 2008.

71. ICG 2003b, 2.

72. *Štela* is an informal BCS term meaning, roughly, "pull" or "connections." It is similar to the Russian concept of "blat" or the Chinese term "guanxi." For an example of what I am referring to see, ICG 2009, 11.

73. *Supervisory Order Amending the Statute of Brčko District, Enacting the Election Law of Brčko District, Enacting the Rules of Procedure of the Assembly of Brčko District and Amendments to Respective Regulations of Brčko District*, OHR Brčko, May 6, 2008: http://www.ohr.int/ohr-offices/brcko/bc-so/default.asp?content_id=41660; *Supervisor Gregorian Amends the Statute of the Brčko District, and Enacts District Election Law and Rules of Procedure for the District Assembly*, OHR Brčko Press Release, May 6, 2008: http://www.ohr.int/ohr-dept/presso/pressr/default.asp?content_id=41664.

74. Reilly 2006.

75. This was especially the case following the 2004 election which saw a handful of politicians switch parties or buck party leadership during their votes on the composition of the District government due to lucrative promises and, in the case of two SDA councilors, substantial cash payments from a prominent SDP supporter, who boasted about his actions in an interview with me in 2007.

76. *Supervisor Calls for Concentration Government in Brčko District*, OHR Brčko, January 13, 2009: http://www.ohr.int/ohr-dept/presso/pressr/default.asp?content_id=42915.

77. Rumors that Domić might emerge as an acceptable mayoral candidate among parties that were looking to freeze SDP out of government swirled throughout the summer and fall in the District. Unlike in 2008 (see chapter 7) OHR did not intervene to prevent this from happening.

78. For more on ethnocracy as a political regime type see, Yiftachel and Yacobi 2003; Yiftachel and Ghanem 2004; Yiftachel 2006; Howard 2012.

79. McMahon and Western 2009.

80. Mujkić 2007; Touquet 2011.

81. Pugh 2002.

82. Mujkić 2007, 113.

83. Lijphart 1979.

84. *Opinion on the Constitutional Situation in Bosnia and Herzegovina and the Powers of the High Representative*, Council of Europe's European Commission for Democracy through Law (Venice Commission), March 11, 2005: http://www.venice.coe.int/docs/2005/CDL-AD(2005)004-e.asp; *Case of Sejdić and Finci v. Bosnia and Herzegovina*, European Court of Human Rights. December 22, 2009: http://hudoc.echr.coe.int/sites/eng/pages/search.aspx?i=001-96491.

4. Wartime Legacies

1. As should be clear from the overview of the war in Mostar and Brčko provided in chapter 2, these are not the only differences in wartime processes or legacies in the two towns, but rather the most consequential.

2. In all, SK-SDP, Ante Marković's Alliance of Reform Forces of Yugoslavia (SRSJ), and the Green Party took thirty-one out of ninety seats in the Municipal Assembly. Interview with Hamed Jerković, former president of the Brčko office of the Muslim Bosniak Association (MBO) party, November 9, 2006.

3. Kadrić 1998, 23.

4. Ibid., 69.

5. "Izbori 2004-konačni rezultati Brčko Distrikt BiH," *Central Election Commission, BiH*: http://www.izbori.ba/Documents/Documents/Rezultati%20izbora%2096-2002/Rezultati2004/Kratki/Skupstina%20Brcko%20Distrikta%20Bosne%20i%20Hercegovine.pdf. SDP is still officially multiethnic, though it draws the majority of its electoral support in Brčko from those of a Bosniak background. Further evidence of SDA's political problems in the District is the fact that in the 2008 election the party also received barely half the support of SBiH, the Bosniak nationalist party led by Haris Silajdžić.

6. "Lokalni izbori 2012: Potvr eni rezultati," *Central Election Commission, BiH*: http://www.izbori.ba/Rezultati/RezultatiPotvrdjeni/files/Glavni_report_trka_9_opstina_200.html.

7. E.g., "Šušak je predao Posavinu," *Nacional,* January 30, 2007; "Dvaput su me spriječili da presiječem srpski koridor," *Nacional,* April 10, 2007.

8. *Pregled nacionalne strukture pripadnika HVO*. June 9, 1993, http://www.slobodanpraljak.com/SUKOB_ABiH_i_HVO_LIPANJ_93.html. Bosniaks in Brčko I have talked with who fought in HVO units during the war claim that the actual percentage was even higher.

9. Interview with Ivo Filipović, commander of HVO's 108th Posavina brigade at the time, July 10, 2011.

10. Interview with Ivan Krndelj, January 27, 2007.

11. The *War Presidency* was a civilian successor to prewar municipal governments. This institution was utilized by all three sides during the war. Excerpt from *Brčko War Presidency Situation Report*, May 1992, ICTY Exhibit P1120.1.

12. Arkan was a notorious criminal in former Yugoslavia who established the Tigers under the patronage of Serbia's security services. The militia members were largely recruited from the Belgrade underworld and fans of the football club Belgrade Red Star. For more on this, see Foer 2004; Mills 2009.

13. For more on this see, *Case Information Sheet (IT-03–69) Stanišić & Simatović*, ICTY: http://www.icty.org/x/cases/stanisic_simatovic/cis/en/cis_stanisic_simatovic_en.pdf.

14. "The Coup in Banja Luka," *Vreme*, September 13, 1993. See http://www.scc.rutgers.edu/serbian_digest/.

15. "The Banja Luka Rebellion: A State without Bread," *Vreme*, September 20, 1993. See http://www.scc.rutgers.edu/serbian_digest/.

16. For a more detailed analysis of political and social tensions within the wartime RS, see Caspersen 2010.

17. This was not unusual. In other towns in the Republika Srpska that were home to significant numbers of displaced Serbs, such as Doboj, SDS also relied on this population as a key political base. See Toal and Dahlman 2011, 275.

18. According to Hugh Griffiths, who was the OSCE Human Rights Officer in Brčko from October 1997 till March 1998, both OHR and OSCE identified Savić as responsible for the greatest number of human rights abuses in Brčko prior to his removal from the office in February 1998. Interview with Hugh Griffiths, March 16, 2007. For more on Savić's role in intimidating refugees and IDPs to follow the SDS line, see ICG 1998, 10; Griffiths 1999.

19. Farrand 2011, 123.

20. In addition to Anić and Krndelj—the two most powerful Croat political figures in Brčko at the time—the municipal council president (Mato Jurišić), and the majority of the municipal assembly councilors, also joined NHI.

21. Interview with Mijo Anić, July 8, 2012.

22. For more on the Arizona Market, see Farrand 2011, chapter 7.

23. Ibid., 135–36; *Supervisory Order*, OHR Brčko, July 13, 1998: http://www.ohr.int/ohr-offices/brcko/bc-so/default.asp?content_id=5346; *Order on Ravne Brčko*, OHR Brčko, November 11, 1998: http://www.ohr.int/ohr-offices/brcko/bc-so/default.asp?content_id=5350; *Order Suspending Councilor from the Ravne-Brčko Municipal Council*, OHR Brčko, December 3, 1998: http://www.ohr.int/ohr-offices/brcko/bc-so/default.asp?content_id=5352.

24. Farrand 2011, 120.

25. All residents who lived in the RS-controlled portion of Brčko prior to the war were eligible to vote in this election, thereby ensuring that the results would produce a multiethnic municipal council. Because of the boycott, ethnic Croat parties received only 6 percent of the votes in the election, less than half the estimated Croat population in the Brčko area.

26. ICG 1997, 5.

27. Interview with Žarko Čošić, October 27, 2006; interview with Djordje Ristanić, November 1, 2006.

28. Mauzer was consulted on the composition of the newly formed multiethnic police in Brčko, presumably to help international officials identify those who supported Plavšić and those who were loyal to SDS. See Griffiths 1998, 133.

29. Krajišnik was the other RS vice president during the war and was, along with his close associate Momčilo Mandić, one of the most frequent targets of war profiteering charges among SDS's leadership.

30. Baumann et al. 2004, 151–158; Farrand 2011, 174–8.

31. Interview with Žarko Čošić, October 16, 2006.

32. For more on this, see Griffiths 1998; Jeffrey 2006.

33. *Supervisory Order*, OHR Brčko, September, 19, 1997: http://www.ohr.int/ohr-offices/brcko/bc-so/default.asp?content_id=5334.

34. *Report from the Brcko Supervisor to Presiding Arbitrator Roberts Owen*, OHR North, August 16–September 30, 1997, 4.

35. Eric Shinseki, SFOR's commanding general at the time made this very point to Farrand a month after the incident, which helped to convince him to move forward with reforms despite the violence. See Farrand 2011, 179.

36. Farrand 2011, 93–101.

37. Kisić was mayor from April 1999 to November 2003. He had also been appointed minister of the economy in the original multiethnic administration established in RS Brčko in 1997.

38. *Report from the Supervisor of Brčko to Presiding Arbitrator Roberts Owen July 15–August 31, 1998*, OHR (N), n.d.

39. Interview with Siniša Kisić, July 10, 2011.

40. In November 2003 interim supervisor Gerhard Sontheim revoked Kisić's appointment as mayor following an indictment against him for abuse of office. Following his acquittal he was appointed Brčko District's coordinator for cooperation with the BiH Council of Ministers. *Supervisory Order on the Revocation of the Appointment of Sinisa Kisic to the Position of Mayor of the Brcko District of BiH, and Ismet Dedeic to the Position of Head of Department of Urbanism, Real Estate Affairs and Economic Development*, OHR Brčko, November 12, 2003: http://www.ohr.int/ohr-offices/brcko/bc-so/default.asp?content_id=31160.

41. Bjelakovic and Strazzari 1999, 97.

42. For more on this, see Hadžiosmanović 2006.

43. Bjelakovic and Strazzari 1999, 84.

44. Several people I talked with in Mostar suggested that Oručević's relative Teufik Velagić was instrumental in securing Izetbegović's eventual support. Hadžiosmanović also hints that Velagić played a role in his ouster (see Hadžiosmanović 2006, 139). Velagić was a Mladi Muslimani compatriot of Izetbegović who lived in Vienna and was a longtime leader of Bosniak public relations efforts in the West. Indeed, he played an instrumental role in publicizing Izetbegović's book, *Islamic Declaration*, outside of Yugoslavia in the early 1980s.

45. *Sporazum*, January 8, 1993: http://www.slobodanpraljak.com/SUKOB_ABiH_I_HVO_SIJECANJ_93.html.

46. ICG 2000, 10–11.

47. Portions of this and another interview with the journal *Dani* were translated by the Bosnia Institute and posted on its website. See "Mostar Coalitions and the SDA," *Bosnia Report*, March–June 2000: http://www.bosnia.org.uk/bosrep/report_format.cfm?articleid=2866&reportid=129.

48. Grandits 2007; Hockenos 2003.

49. Burg and Shoup 1999, 377.

50. Dulic 2005, 85.

51. *Proglas*, Ratni Stožer HOS-a, Ljubuški, May 9, 1992.

52. Hoare 2004, 83.

53. Bjelakovic and Strazzari 1999, 85.

54. For an excellent analysis of the military-mafia-political nexus in Herzegovina, see Bojicic-Dzelilovic 2006.

55. *The EU Administration of Mostar—a Balance after One Year*, Hans Koschnick, August 1995.

56. "Croats Riot against Mostar Peace Plan," *The Independent*, February 8, 1996; "Croatian exercise in grassroots democracy," *Oslobodjenje*, February 15, 1996: http://www.ex-yupress.com/oslob/oslob10.html.

57. Yarwood 1999, 13.

58. ICG 1996, 2. Musa, the prewar director of Mostar's massive aluminum manufacturing firm, Aluminij (see chapter 5), had assembled a multiethnic list of eleven Bosniaks, three Serbs, and seven Croats—including Mostar's sole elected prewar mayor, Milivoj Gagro.

59. *OHR Bulletin 9—July 5 1996,* OHR Sarajevo: http://www.ohr.int/ohr-dept/presso/chronology/bulletins/default.asp?content_id=4934#2.

60. *Evictions List (22/10–12/12/96),* UNHCR (quoted in ICG 2000).

61. *Human Rights and Security Situation: 1 January–15 February 1997,* UN IPTF, n.d.

62. *Report in Pursuance of the Decisions on Mostar of 12 February 1997,* United Nations: Special Investigation Group Mission Headquarters.

63. *Transcript of the Press Conference held on 21 February 1997,* SFOR: http://www.nato.int/sfor/trans/1997/t970221a.htm.

64. HRW 1998. West Mostar's police chief at that time, Marko Radić, was eventually found guilty of war crimes committed at detention camp near Mostar over which he was the commanding military officer.

65. "War-bred Underworld Threatens Bosnian Peace," *New York Times,* May 1, 1996.

66. ICG 2000, 3.

67. Bose 2002, 110. One of Garrod's deputies at the time stated to me that his primary reasons for leaving Mostar were health problems and because he was "deeply disappointed with the lack of support or even interest from OHR [Sarajevo]." Email communication with Gerhard Sontheim, November 27, 2012.

68. Both had fled to Croatia prior to their indictment where they were protectively held under the pretense of domestic criminal charges. Martinović was eventually handed over August 1999 while Tuta managed to avoid extradition until March 2000.

69. The generals, led by Ante Gotovina, had published an open letter accusing Mesić of betraying those who had fought in the "homeland war." See "Nova generalska prijetna Mesiću," *Nacional,* no. 255, October 5, 2000: http://web.archive.org/web/20001017205004/www.nacional.hr/htm/255003.hr.htm.

70. Bojicic-Dzelilovic 2006.

71. Bieber 2001.

72. Makaš 2007, 291.

73. *OHR BiH Media Round-up, 06/02/2001:* http://www.ohr.int/ohr-dept/presso/bh-media-rep/round-ups/default.asp?content_id=431.

74. Quote from an untitled petition distributed by the *mjesna zajednica* "Rondo" in West Mostar, April 2003. For more on this, see Makaš 2007, 291.

75. "Može li Liska harem ostati harem?" *Mostar Islamic Community,* February 23, 2007: http://www.miz-mostar.com/miz/index.php?option=com_content&task=view&id=68&Itemid=2.

76. Interview with Rolf van Ueye, director of the Mostar office of the OSCE: March 24, 2007; Interview with OHR regional officer: December 20, 2007; Interview with OSCE regional officer: July 28, 2011.

77. ICG 2009; Kesic et al 2012; "Bosniaks request new municipalities in Mostar" *b92,* October 26, 2012:http://www.b92.net/eng/news/region-article.php?yyyy=2012&mm=10&dd=26&nav_id=82855

78. ICG 2009.

79. Ibid.

80. *Subject: Bosnia—High Rep puts temporary lid on bubbling Mostar cauldron,* Confidential U.S. diplomatic cable from Embassy Sarajevo, July 31, 2009: http://wikileaks.org/cable/2009/07/09SARAJEVO934.html.

5. Sequencing

1. Yarwood 1999, 24.

2. *Agreement on Mostar,* February 18, 1996.

3. *Annex to the Dayton Agreement on Implementing the Federation of Bosnia and Herzegovina: Agreed Principles for the Interim Statute of the City of Mostar,* November 10, 1995, Article 12.

4. ICG 1996.

5. Interview with Radmilo Andrić, August 1, 2007.

6. Bollens 2007, chapter 6. One of these new towns built near Čapljina was even officially named Bobanovo Selo (Boban's village), and another Šuškovo selo (Šušak's village), after Gojko Šušak.

7. *OHR Bulletin 9—July 5 1996*: http://www.ohr.int/ohr-dept/presso/chronology/bulletins/default.asp?content_id=4934#2.

8. ICG 1996. As I detail in chapter 3, HDZ would quickly learn to also take advantage of this electoral quota system, especially within the three city-municipalities in which they constituted a majority.

9. Bildt 1998, 266–67.

10. ICG 1996, 3.

11. *96/442/CFSP: Joint Action of 15 July 1996 adopted by the Council on the basis of Article J.3 of the Treaty on European Union, on the nomination of a Special Envoy of the European Union in the city of Mostar*: http://eur-lex.europa.eu/LexUriServ/LexUriServ.do?uri=CELEX:31996E0442:EN:HTML.

12. Interview with Rolf van Ueye, director of the Mostar office of the OSCE, March 24, 2007; Interview with OHR regional officer, December 20, 2007.

13. World Bank 1997, 47.

14. Donais 2005.

15. Donais 2002, 5–6.

16. ICG 2001c, 16.

17. ICG 2001a, 19.

18. Amnesty International 2006, Section 4a.

19. Ibid.

20. ICG 2000, 55–56.

21. Ibid.

22. Pugh 2005, 451.

23. "The suspicious privatization of Aluminij," *Nacional*, September 6, 2001: http://web.archive.org/web/20011024112111/www.nacional.hr/htm/303052.en.htm.

24. *Supervisory Order*, OHR Brčko, June 11, 1997.

25. *Supplemental Award of the Brčko Arbitral Tribunal for Dispute over the Inter-Entity Boundary in Brčko Area*, March 15, 1998, Paragraph 25: http://www.ohr.int/ohr-offices/brcko/arbitration/default.asp?content_id=5345.

26. Interview with Robert Farrand, February 7, 2008. See also Farrand 2011, chapter 7.

27. *Supplementary Supervisory Order on Privatization*, OHR Brčko, June 26, 1999: http://www.ohr.int/ohr-offices/brcko/bc-so/default.asp?content_id=5361.

28. *Consolidating Supervisory Order on Privatization in the Brčko District of Bosnia and Herzegovina*, OHR Brčko, August 14, 2001: http://www.ohr.int/ohr-offices/brcko/bc-so/default.asp?content_id=6062.

29. *Supervisory Order On The Conduct Of Privatization Of The State Capital Of Enterprises in the Brčko District Of BiH*, OHR Brčko, September 19, 2001: http://www.ohr.int/ohr-offices/brcko/bc-so/default.asp?content_id=5973.

30. See http://www.sco-group.com/index.php?option=com_content&view=article&id=89&Itemid=55&lang=en.

31. Clarke 2004b, 14–15.

32. Interview with Peter Appleby, OHR Brčko deputy supervisor, July 14, 2011.

33. ICG 2011b.

34. Pickering 2006.

35. Clarke 2004b, 16.

36. Chandler 1999, 86.

37. *Case No. ME-113*, Election Appeals Subcommission, July 21, 1997.

38. Griffiths 1998, 78.

39. See ICG 1998 and Griffiths 1998 for further details of this episode, the outlines of which were confirmed to me in a November 27, 2007, interview with Finn Lynghem, the Norwegian judge who issued the initial EASC ruling.

40. In all RS-based parties won a total of thirty seats in the municipal assembly while Federation based parties took twenty-six.

41. *Addendum to the Order*, OHR Brčko, November 15, 1997; Farrand 2011, 128–31.

42. For a detailed account of this, see Farrand 2011, 131–51.

43. Sommers 2002.

44. *Brčko Weekly Report #41*, OHR Brčko, March 18–24, 2001.

6. Peacebuilding Practices and Institutions

1. *Award of the Arbitral Tribunal for the Dispute over the Inter-Entity Boundary in the Brčko Area*, February 14, 1997, Paragraph 104.

2. Parish 2009, 107.

3. Clarke 2004a, 2.

4. Farrand 2011, chapter 2.

5. ESI 2000, 22.

6. Pred 1990.

7. Farrand 2011, 28.

8. OSCE continued to use this phrase to describe its Brčko office for several years. E.g., *Survey of OSCE Field Operations*, OSCE, October 1, 2008, 12: http://web.archive.org/web/20100528094310/ http://www.osce.org/documents/cpc/2008/10/3242_en.pdf.

9. Interview with Robert Farrand, February 7, 2007.

10. Farrand 2011, 92. Needless to say these actions, which went beyond SFOR's limited mandate, would likely not have been authorized if requested through formal channels.

11. Clarke 2004a, 2.

12. Joseph 2007.

13. *Chairman's Final Report*, Brčko Law Review Commission, December 31, 2001: http://www.esiweb.org/pdf/bridges/bosnia/BLRC_ChairmansRep.pdf.

14. Sommers 2002. Originally the DMT was scheduled to work in the District for only six months, a ridiculously—but typically—short contract which was extended several times. The independent auditor which examined DMT's operations assessed—accurately it turns out—that even this amount of time would be inadequate. See Rosenbaum 2001.

15. Interview with Osman Osmanović, July 21, 2011.

16. Interview with Siniša Kisić, July 10, 2011.

17. On the importance of local-international consultation and cultivating local elites as partners in the peacebuilding process, see Barnett 2006.

18. Matthews did not inform District officials of his intentions until the middle of July, with provisions for only a single meeting with parents prior to the beginning of the school year: *Actions to Be Taken by the Start of the Next School Year*, OHR Brčko, July 14, 2000.

19. Karnavas 2003, 125.

20. One indication of the success of Clarke's approach after the initial conflicts over integration is a 2006 poll conducted for OSCE which found that 63 percent of District residents supported the involvement of international officials in education reform: *Highlights of Public Opinion Survey on Education in BiH: Citizen Opinion in December 2006*, Organization for Security and Cooperation in Europe, n.d., 10–11.

21. The importance of embeddedness in peacebuilding missions is outlined in greater detail in the conclusion.

22. Though before my period of fieldwork, this dynamic was clear when going through the OHR Brčko archives, which are replete with memos or emails whose timestamps indicate they were drafted or sent during weekends or late in the evening.

23. Farrand 2011, 28. Weekly interagency meetings were also hosted by OHR in Mostar during this time, but as I describe below these were much less successful in improving policy coordination than they were in Brčko.

24. These were, in chronological order, Hans Koschnick (1994–96), Ricardo Perez Casado (1996), Martin Garrod (1996–98), Richard Ellerkmann (1998–99), Finn Lynghjem (2000–2001), Colin Munro (2001), Jean-Pierre Bercot (2001–3), Jacques Andrieu (2003–4), and Anatoly Viktorov (2004–10).

25. These have been, in chronological order, Robert Farrand (1997–2000), Gary Matthews (2000–2001), Henry Clarke (2001–3), Susan Johnson (2004–6), Raffi Gregorian (2006–10), and Roderick Moore (2010–present).

26. Farrand 2011, 237.

27. Gilbert 2008, 278–80.

28. Coles 2002.

29. Sommers 2002, 9.

30. The bulk of these letters occurred early in the period I examined, tapering off significantly by the beginning of 2007, which suggests improvement in local governance. Complaints about reconstruction assistance in particular declined significantly within a year of the 2004 elections and subsequent appointment of a new, more competent and responsive, head of the District Department of DPs, Refugees, and Housing Issues. Having read through all of these letters, what is perhaps most interesting about their content is the absence of an ethnic element to the complaints, which almost never attribute problems to the ethnic identity of officials or petitioners.

31. *Supervisory Order on urban planning annulling certain decisions made by the Appellate Commission and reinforcing certain urban approvals and dismissing certain officials from the District Government and mandating changes to District urban planning rules and imposing certain legislative amendments relating to the operation of the Appellate Commission*, OHR Brčko, March 23, 2007.

32. *Special Report No 2/96 concerning the accounts of the Administrator and the European Union Administration, Mostar (EUAM) accompanied by the replies of the Commission and the Administrator of Mostar*, Court of Auditors, September 30, 1996, Paragraph 46.

33. Ibid., Paragraph 50.

34. Ibid., Paragraphs 62–67.

35. *Report on Special Report No 2/96 of the Court of Auditors concerning the accounts of the Administrator and the European Administration, Mostar*, European Parliament, November 21, 1996, Paragraph 18.

36. Ibid., Paragraph 19.

37. Ibid.

38. Bildt 1998, 193.

39. http://www.hri.org/news/balkans/bosnet/1996/96-03-12_2.bos.html.

40. *Resolution on Special Report No 2/96 of the Court of Auditors concerning the accounts of the Administrator and the European Union Administration, Mostar (EUAM), accompanied by the replies of the Commission and the Administrator of Mostar*, European Parliament, January 20, 1997.

41. Interview with Gerhard Sontheim, former deputy head of OHR Mostar (prior to his appointment as deputy supervisor in Brčko), September 23, 2006. Sontheim notes that during his tenure at OHR Mostar he met personally with Carlos Westendorp—the High Representative at the time—only once.

42. Interview with Finn Lynghjem, November 27, 2007.

43. Interview with OHR regional officer, July 18, 2011. Echoing Sontheim's comments, this official notes that Lájcak met with staff in the office only once during his time as High Representative.

44. Ashdown 2007, 271.

45. *Decision on the Implementation of the Reorganization of the City of Mostar*, OHR Sarajevo, January 28, 2004: http://www.ohr.int/decisions/mo-hncantdec/default.asp?content_id=31725.

46. Interview with OHR regional officer, November 2, 2007.

47. Interview with OSCE regional officer, September 18, 2007. Ashdown wanted to be the last High Representative in Bosnia, thus he was pushing for all loose ends, such as the implementation of Mostar's new statute, to be tied up as soon as possible, regardless of the situation on the ground. As I describe in the following chapter, this goal also generated serious tensions with OHR Brčko.

48. ICG 2000, 54; ESI 2000, 45.

49. *Report on Special Report No 2/96 of the Court of Auditors concerning the accounts of the Administrator and the European Administration, Mostar*, European Parliament, November 21, 1996, Paragraph 14.

50. Ibid., Paragraph 7.

51. *Weekly Report*, WEU Police Mostar, n.d.

52. Interview with Gerhard Sontheim, September 23, 2006.

53. Reichel 2000, 15.

54. Neville-Jones 1996, 50.

55. Holbrooke 1999, 215–26.

56. Generally French officials in Bosnia were perceived to be skeptical about the broader "Dayton agenda," which shaped their opposition to assertive peacebuilding measures. See, ICG 2001b.

57. Bojicic-Dzelilovic 2006.

58. Recounting the incident, Lynghjem observed, "This was again this problem with the French, it's always been a problem." Later in the same interview he stated: "We had more use of the American Embassy branch [in Mostar] and the EU than we ever had with SFOR. I can't remember a thing where we had any use with SFOR—for any purpose." Interview with Finn Lynghjem, November 27, 2007.

59. ICG 2001b, 4–5.

60. Siegel 1998, 128–9.

61. *RC Mostar Weekly Report: 19–25 June 1999*, OSCE Regional Center Mostar, June 1999.

62. Interview with Finn Lynghjem, November 27, 2007.

63. Interview with Ljubo Golemac, November 18, 2007.

64. Farrand 2011, 237 (italics in the original). See also Autesserre 2010, 264.

65. *Special Report No 2/96 concerning the accounts of the Administrator and the European Union Administration, Mostar (EUAM) accompanied by the replies of the Commission and the Administrator of Mostar*, Court of Auditors, September 30, 1996.

66. One official who worked at OHR Mostar at the time suggested that Andrieu's appointment was pushed by Berçot as a way of getting back at Ashdown for interfering with his management of administrative unification efforts in the city. Andrieu's cv can be seen here: http://www.ohr.int/ohr-offices/mostar/history/default.asp?content_id=30904.

67. "New Mostar Administrator Unburdened by History," *Radio Free Europe/Radio Liberty*, no. 61, part II, March 26, 1996.

7. Patron-Clientelism in the Brčko District

1. Lemarchand and Legg 1972.

2. Scott 1972. While Scott's definition of patron-clientelism focuses on personal relations, I follow Lemarchand and Legg in recognizing that clientelism can also take more political and institutional forms.

3. *Final Award of the Arbitral Tribunal for Dispute over Inter-Entity Boundary in Brčko Area*, March 5, 1999, Paragraph 10: http://www.ohr.int/ohr-offices/brcko/default.asp?content_id=5358.

4. O'Connell 1969, 78.

5. Parish 2009, 116.

6. *Award of the Arbitral Tribunal for the Dispute over the Inter-Entity Boundary in the Brčko Area*, February 14, 1997, Paragraph 93.

7. *Annex to the Final Award of the Arbitral Tribunal for the Dispute over the Inter-Entity Boundary in the Brčko Area*, August 18, 1999: http://www.ohr.int/ohr-offices/brcko/arbitration/default.asp?content_id=5362.

8. *Final Award of the Arbitral Tribunal for Dispute over Inter-Entity Boundary in Brčko Area*, March 5, 1999, Paragraph 67: http://www.ohr.int/ohr-offices/brcko/default.asp?content_id=5358.

9. Copeland 1999, 3100.

10. Interview with Asim Mujkić, Federation negotiating team member, September 25, 2006.

11. ICG 1999.

12. Interview with Roderick Moore, OHR Brčko supervisor, July 18, 2011.

13. Interview with Robert Farrand, June 18, 2008. Farrand claims that by the end of his time in office in 2000 he was spending more time and energy battling with cohorts in Sarajevo than working with local authorities in Brčko.

14. *Memo: Comments on Annex to Brčko Award*, OHR Sarajevo Legal Department, June 11, 1999, 1–2.

15. *Chairman's Conclusions*, Peace Implementation Council, March 7, 1997: http://www.ohr.int/pic/default.asp?content_id=5863; *PIC Luxembourg Declaration*, Peace Implementation Council, June 9, 1998: http://www.ohr.int/pic/default.asp?content_id=5188.

16. *Memo: Supervisor's authority*, OHR Brčko Legal Department, June 19, 1999, 1–2.

17. For more on this dispute, see Farrand 2011, 50–54.

18. *Memo: Comments on Annex to Brčko Award*, OHR Sarajevo Legal Department, June 11, 1999, 1.

19. Ibid., 1.

20. ICG 2003a, 12.

21. *Final Award of the Arbitral Tribunal for Dispute over Inter-Entity Boundary in Brčko Area*, March 5 1999, Paragraphs 9, 61: http://www.ohr.int/ohr-offices/brcko/default.asp?content_id=5358.

22. Letter from Johan Van Lamoen to Roberts Owen, December 6, 1999; letter from Roberts Owen to Johan Van Lamoen, December 8, 1999.

23. *Questions RWF Would Like to Have Answered by OHR-Sarajevo (Legal)*, OHR Brčko, January 25, 2000.

24. *Chairman's Final Report*, Brčko Law Review Commission, December 31, 2001: http://www.esiweb.org/pdf/bridges/bosnia/BLRC_ChairmansRep.pdf.

25. Petritsch was aggressively pursuing the centralization of power both within OHR and vis-à-vis other international organizations. During this time his closest staffers in Sarajevo—most of whom were relatively young and from Austria or Germany—were sarcastically referred to as the "Hitlerjugend" (Hitler Youth) in the three main field offices of Mostar, Brčko and Banja Luka.

26. *Chairman's Final Report*, Brčko Law Review Commission, December 31, 2001, 8–9: http://www.esiweb.org/pdf/bridges/bosnia/BLRC_ChairmansRep.pdf.

27. E.g., Karnavas 2003, 131.

28. This widely circulated story was confirmed to me, off the record, by an OHR official who was at the meeting.

29. Interview with OHR Brčko legal officer Matthew Parish, September 2006.

30. Farrand 2001, 546.

31. ICG 1999.

32. *Supervisory Order on the Financial System of the Brčko District of Bosnia and Herzegovina*, OHR Brčko, April 14, 2000: http://www.ohr.int/ohr-offices/brcko/bc-so/default.asp?content_id=5281.

33. Interview with Robert Farrand, February 7, 2008. Looking back on these disputes he observes: "One of great mistakes, one of the great lessons to have been learned is that the supervisor should not have been brought under the Office of the High Representative. That really became a problem over time."

34. *Addendum to the Supervisory Order on the Financial System of the Brčko District of Bosnia and Herzegovina*, OHR Brčko, June 22, 2000: http://www.ohr.int/ohr-offices/brcko/bc-so/default.asp?content_id=5289.

35. ICG 2003a, 14.

36. ICG 2001a, 1.

37. Arizona emerged as a giant black market in the Brčko area immediately following the war. It was eventually cleaned up by local and international police and turned into a privately run market managed by Italproject, thus becoming a significant source of revenues for the District. For more on the Arizona Market see Farrand 2011, 222–33.

38. *Brčko Weekly Report #13*, OHR Brčko, August 28–September 3, 2000.

39. *Agreement on the Implementation of Entity Obligations Set Forth by the Final Arbitral Award for Brčko*, October 24, 2000: http://www.ohr.int/ohr-offices/brcko/arbitration/default.asp?content_id=5307.

40. Over two years later the entities still had more than 10 million KM (2 KM = 1 Euro) in outstanding obligations to the District from this period: *Report from the Supervisor of Brčko to the Peace Implementation Council Steering Board on the Progress of Implementation of the Final Award of the International Arbitral Tribunal for Brčko (8 March 2002–8 March 2003)*, OHR Brčko, March 8, 2003.

41. *Brčko Report #31*, OHR Brčko, January 8–14, 2001.

42. ICG 2003a.

43. Interview with Osman Osmanović, July 21, 2011.

44. Interview with William Quayle, former OHR Brčko returns officer, and subsequently senior political advisor for Johnson, April 25, 2007.

45. *Brčko Weekly Overview #59*, OHR Brčko, July 22–28, 2001.

46. *Memo: End of Inter-Entity Trade in Petroleum Products: RS Establishes Monopolies, Police Harass Brčko Truck Drivers*, OHR Brčko, November 26, 2001.

47. *Weekly Report #3*, OHR-N/Brčko, January 21–February 2, 2002.

48. *Report from the Supervisor of Brčko to the Peace Implementation Council Steering Board on the Progress of Implementation of the Final Award of the International Arbitral Tribunal for Brčko (8 March 2002–8 March 2003)*, OHR Brčko, March 8, 2003.

49. *Agreement on Coordination and Cooperation between the Council of Ministers of Bosnia and Herzegovina and the Brčko District of Bosnia and Herzegovina*, October 24, 2002. A District office in the CoM was finally established in 2006. However this office has no decision-making authority and thus provides Brčko with no more than a pro forma voice in the CoM: *High Representative and Brčko Supervisor Welcome Establishing of District Office within CoM BiH*, April 13, 2006: http://www.ohr.int/ohr-dept/presso/pressr/default.asp?content_id=37002.

50. U.S. support for the Brčko District had flagged significantly by 2003. The wars in Afghanistan and Iraq were consuming the bulk of economic resources, political capital, and military personnel (American SFOR troops departed the country in 2004) to the detriment of state-building and diplomatic efforts in countries like Bosnia. See ICG 2003a, 31.

51. *Memo: Ending the Brčko Supervisory Mandate: Our April 16 Meeting*, OHR Brčko, April 7, 2003.

52. E-mail correspondence with Susan Johnson, September 30, 2008.

53. On Ashdown's comments, see *High Representative's Open Letter to the Citizens of BiH*, OHR Sarajevo, November 26, 2004: http://www.ohr.int/ohr-dept/presso/pressa/default.asp?content_id=33585.

54. *Consolidating the Self-Governing Status of the Brčko District of Bosnia and Herzegovina: A Legal and Political Brief*, Paragraph 20, OHR Sarajevo, March 17, 2005.

55. *Initial Comments on the 17 March Brief OHR Sarajevo*, OHR Brčko, April 21, 2005.

56. Clarke 2005.

57. *Report from the Supervisor of Brčko to the Peace Implementation Council Steering Board on the Progress of Implementation of the Final Award of the International Arbitral Tribunal for Brčko (8 March 2004–8 March 2005)*, OHR Brčko, March 8, 2005.

58. Letter from Paddy Ashdown to Roberts Owen, May 4, 2005.

59. Parish 2009, 179.

60. *Memorandum to the Representatives of the State of Bosnia ("BiH"); the Federation of Bosnia and Herzegovina ("the Federation"); Republika Srpska ("the RS"); the Brčko District of Bosnia and Herzegovina ("the District"); the Office of the High Representative ("OHR")*, Arbitral Tribunal for the Dispute over Inter-Entity Boundary in Brčko Area, January 12, 2006.

61. Interview with Mirsad Djapo, July 11, 2011.

62. Interview with William Quayle, April 25, 2007. Before being appointed to the position of High Representative Ashdown was the leader of the Liberal Democrat party in England. Quayle, who worked in the Brčko area for nearly a decade, notes that Johnson also encountered sexism from the predominately male political authorities in the Brčko District, which presented challenges not faced by her predecessors.

63. According to one State Department official I talked with, while serving as supervisor Gregorian held a Schedule C appointment. Schedule C positions are noncareer, limited-term appointments that can be rescinded without recourse. Therefore unlike the previous supervisors who had been career foreign service officers—and thus possessed a degree of independence—his continued employment could be tied to support for the prevailing political desires of the State Department and OHR Sarajevo.

64. Parish 2009, 187.

65. E-mail correspondence with Susan Johnson, September 20, 2008. In August 2011 I conducted a series of e-mail question and answer exchanges with Gregorian concerning his time as supervisor. He insisted that all his comments be treated as off-the-record, therefore no direct quotes or citations are included in the following paragraphs. It is quite clear, however, that balancing the contrasting interests of OHR Sarajevo and the Brčko District was a constant challenge during his tenure.

66. *Bosnia—Temporary Agreement Reached on Single Account*, unclassified U.S. diplomatic cable from Embassy Sarajevo, April 28, 2006: http://wikileaks.org/cable/2006/04/06SARAJEVO946.html; *Subject: Bosnia: Brčko's ITA battle prompts return to the Tribunal*, confidential U.S. diplomatic cable from Embassy Sarajevo, August 4, 2006: http://wikileaks.org/cable/2006/08/06SARAJEVO1772.html.

67. Parish 2009, 187–88.

68. Schwarz-Schilling had been effectively fired by the PIC in January 2007 after a year of disastrous inaction as High Representative. But he did not officially step down until June (see ICG 2007). In the interim Gregorian, as the PDHR, was one of the primary drivers of OHR policy decisions. The two decisions fixed the District's allocated share of the revenues at 3.55 percent for 2007 and stipulated that irrespective of the allocated share the District should receive no less than 124 million KM for the years 2007–11. See *Decision Enacting the Law on Amendments to the Law on the Indirect Taxation System in Bosnia and Herzegovina*, OHR Sarajevo, May 4, 2007: http://www.ohr.int/decisions/econdec/default.asp?content_id=39687; *Decision Enacting the Law*

on Amendments to the Law on Payments into the Single Account and Distribution of Revenues, OHR Sarajevo, May 4, 2007: http://www.ohr.int/decisions/econdec/default.asp?content_id=39689.

69. *Fact Sheet*, OHR, May 4, 2007.

70. *Memorandum to the Representatives of the State of Bosnia and Herzegovina ("BiH"); the Federation of Bosnia and Herzegovina ("the Federation"); Republika Srpska ("the RS"); the Brčko District of Bosnia and Herzegovina ("the District"); the Office of the High Representative ("OHR")*, Arbitral Tribunal for the Dispute over Inter-Entity Boundary in Brčko Area, May 22, 2007.

71. Draft letter from Proskauer Rose LLP to Roberts Owen, June 2007, 2 (copy on file with author).

72. Interview with Mirsad Djapo, July 11, 2011. See also Parish 2009, 193n31.

73. E-mail correspondence with Roberts Owen, September 30, 2008.

74. *Addendum to the Final Award*. Arbitral Tribunal for the Dispute over Inter-Entity Boundary in Brčko Area, Paragraph 5, June 25, 2007. That Owen gave little credence to the received account of the process can be clearly inferred from the language of the third paragraph of the Addendum, which casts a skeptical eye on Gregorian's claims: "The High Representative . . . *evidently* conducted discussions and negotiations involving the three [OHR, the entities and the District] and on 4 May, 2007, he issued three documents . . . with the District's *apparent* consent . . ." and, "the High Representative's documents of 4 May, 2007 *represent* that the Brčko District has consented to—indeed is 'in favor of'—the new allocation arrangements as ordered by the High Representative" (italics mine).

75. *Subject: Bosnia—it is time to put Brčko back on the political agenda*, Unclassified U.S. diplomatic cable from Embassy Sarajevo, July 23, 2007: http://wikileaks.org/cable/2007/07/07SARAJEVO1577.html.

76. Ibid.

77. Parish 2009, 194.

78. *Subject: Bosnia: PIC meets amid brewing political crises in Bosnia and fundamental challenges to Dayton*, Confidential U.S. diplomatic cable from Embassy Sarajevo, February 21, 2008: http://wikileaks.org/cable/2008/02/08SARAJEVO348.html; *Declaration of the Steering Board of the Peace Implementation Council*, Peace Implementation Council, February 27, 2008: http://www.ohr.int/pic/default.asp?content_id=41352.

79. Actually negotiations on a state law that would regulate the District's relations with the state had been under negotiation since 2006, but due to concerns about the constitutionality of this approach a constitutional amendment was settled on instead.

80. *Raffi Gregorian Attends Final Public Debate on Brčko Constitutional Amendment*, OHR Press Release, March 17, 2009: http://www.ohr.int/ohr-dept/presso/pressr/default.asp?content_id=43210.

81. *Subject: Bosnia—BiH Constitutional Court decisions send shock waves*, Confidential U.S. diplomatic cable from Embassy Sarajevo, October 21, 2008: http://wikileaks.org/cable/2008/10/08SARAJEVO1628.html.

82. According to the U.S. Embassy in Sarajevo Dodik was withholding support in part due to antagonistic personal relations with Gregorian. See *Subject: Bosnia—backsliding on Brčko*, Confidential U.S. diplomatic cable from Embassy Sarajevo, October 24, 2008: http://wikileaks.org/cable/2008/10/08SARAJEVO1655.html. For the full text of the amendment see http://www.ccbh.ba/eng/article.php?pid=1527&kat=518&pkat=500.

83. *Subject: Bosnia—Time to seize an opportunity in Brčko*, Confidential U.S. diplomatic cable from Embassy Sarajevo, February 2, 2009: http://wikileaks.org/cable/2009/02/09SARAJEVO134.html.

84. Henry Clarke in particular focused on economic development, arguing that "the rest of the [reform] effort would fail without it." See ICG 2003a, 18.

85. Brčko's economic elites have unusually close interethnic relations, due both to prewar connections and shared economic interests created by the District. Indeed, shortly after its establishment in 2000 a multiethnic Brčko Chamber of Commerce was established to represent business interests in the District.

86. Interview with Ismet Dedeić, December 12, 2006. As Dedeić, a prominent business figure in his own right, and advisor to the Mayor of Brčko at the time, put it to me: "All the people who have decided to invest here, in their mind was always the presence of the international community and active support of OHR to help them." See also Clarke 2005, 26.

87. Interview with Mirsad Djapo, July 11, 2011. Djapo was far from alone in expressing reservations about this decision, though several officials I spoke with were still uncomfortable speaking about the issue on the record in 2011 and 2012.

88. Interview with Ratko Stjepanović, District Assembly councilor, July 11, 2011.

89. Interview with Dragan Pajić, July 14, 2011. Former mayor and then-Brčko District co-ordinator Siniša Kisić also notes that the concentration government was formed "under pressure from OHR [Brčko]." Interview with Siniša Kisić, July 10, 2011.

90. Following Dodik's election as prime minister of the RS in 2006 Pajić's firm was given a lucrative contract to import pharmaceuticals into the RS from abroad. While Pajić is by all accounts an excellent doctor, during interviews and conversations in Brčko in 2006 I heard tales—usually unprompted—by hospital staff and former Serb refugees in RS Brčko concerning bribes for services or employment, personal appropriation and sales of donated equipment and medical supplies, and dodgy pharmaceutical distribution schemes.

91. As one high-ranking District official quipped to me in 2011, "We knew he would try to steal, we just didn't think it would be this much."

92. The respected Bosnian political journal *Dani* also posted a lengthy story on this alleged quid pro quo. See http://www.bosnia.org.uk/news/news_body.cfm?newsid=2609.

93. *Supervisory Order Ordering the District Assembly to Amend Its Code of Conduct and Fining Mr Semso Sakovic Councilor in the Assembly of Brcko District*, OHR Brčko, May 8, 2007: http://www.ohr.int/ohr-offices/brcko/bc-so/default.asp?content_id=39708.

94. *Supervisory Order on Temporary Suspension on Payments of Salaries and All Remunerations to the Members of Brcko District Government and Councilors of the Assembly of Brcko District*, OHR Brčko, December 4, 2007: http://www.ohr.int/ohr-offices/brcko/bc-so/default.asp?content_id=40944.

95. *Supervisory Order on Fining Members of the Brcko District Government and Directing Measures to Be Taken by the Brcko District Assembly to Facilitate Adoption of a Budget for Fiscal Year 2009*, OHR Brčko, October 8, 2008: http://www.ohr.int/ohr-offices/brcko/bc-so/default.asp?content_id=42385.

96. Interview with Šemso Saković, District Assembly councilor, July 14, 2011.

97. *Highlights of Recent Public Opinion Research: Brčko District*, National Democratic Institute for International Affairs (NDI), December 16, 2003.

98. *Public Opinion Poll, Bosnia and Herzegovina (BiH)*, National Democratic Institute for International Affairs (NDI), August 2010.

99. *Termination of the Supervisory Regime in Brčko: Action Plan for Closure of "the Brčko Final Award Office" (BFAO). Target Date: June 2007*, OHR Brčko, June 6, 2006.

100. Interview with OHR Brčko deputy supervisor Peter Appleby, July 14, 2011. Appleby noted that the entire annual budget for the OHR Brčko office at the time was less than $1 million.

101. Interview with Anto Domić, July 23, 2011.

102. *Brčko Supervisor Roderick Moore Suspends Functions*, OHR press release, August 31, 2012: http://www.ohr.int/ohr-dept/presso/pressr/default.asp?content_id=47427.

103. Scott 1972, 97.

Conclusion

1. Bildt 1998, 6.
2. For a full transcript of the speech, see http://www.un.org/en/ga/63/generaldebate/pdf/bosniaherzegovina_en.pdf.
3. For a detailed analysis of the politics of referendum in Bosnia, see Toal and Maksić 2011.
4. ICG 2011a.
5. Eldin Hadzovic, "Bosnian Parties Split over New Croat Assembly," *Balkan Insight*, April 21, 2011: http://www.balkaninsight.com/en/article/reactions-to-croatian-assembly.
6. *Public Opinion Poll, Bosnia and Herzegovina (BiH)*, National Democratic Institute for International Affairs (NDI), August 2010.
7. E.g., Azinović et al. 2011; Paddy Ashdown, "We Must Stop Bosnia from Becoming Another Libya." *The Times*, April 12, 2011; "Hoće li biti rata!" *Dnevni Avaz*, October 17, 2009.
8. Autesserre 2008, 95.
9. Anderson 2008, 2010.
10. E.g., Bollens 2000; Fumagalli 2007; Calame and Charlesworth 2009; Goddard 2010.
11. For more on ongoing political problems in the Federation, see ICG 2010.
12. ICG 2009.
13. ICG 2011b, 1.
14. *Lessons from Education Reform in Brčko*, OSCE Mission to BiH Education Department. October 2007.
15. Toal and Dahlman 2011, 310.
16. Interview with Peter Appleby, OHR Brčko deputy supervisor, July 29, 2012.
17. *Supervisory Order Preventing Certain Private Security Agencies from Operating in the Brčko District of Bosnia and Herzegovina*, OHR Brčko, June 8, 2009: http://www.ohr.int/ohr-offices/brcko/bc-so/default.asp?content_id=43584.
18. Interview with Roderick Moore, OHR Brčko supervisor, July 18, 2011.
19. Quoted in, ICG 2011b, 12.
20. Interview with Djordje Ristanić, November 1, 2006.
21. Interview with Esad Kadrić, SDA councilor, July 13, 2011.
22. Belloni 2001; Gagnon 2002.
23. ESI 2000, 22.
24. Granovetter 1985; Hess 2004.
25. Zukin and DiMaggio 1990; Dicken and Thrift 1992.
26. Uzzi 1996, 677.
27. Holohan 2005.

References

Abbott, Andrew. 1992. "What Do Cases Do? Some Notes on Activity in Sociological Analysis." In *What Is a Case?* ed. Charles Ragin, 53–82. Cambridge: Cambridge University Press.

Allen, Tim, ed. 1996. *In Search of Cool Ground: War, Flight, and Homecoming in Northeast Africa*. Geneva: UNRISD.

Amnesty International. 2006. *Bosnia and Herzegovina—Behind Closed Gates: Ethnic Discrimination in Employment*. January 26. http://www.amnesty.org/en/library/asset/EUR63/001/2006/en/3ffdf870-d46f-11dd-8743-d305bea2b2c7/eur630012006en.pdf.

Andjelović, Petar. 2007. *Fratar I njegova Bosna*. Sarajevo: Rabic.

Anderson, James. 2008. "From Empires to Ethno-National Conflicts: A Framework for Studying 'Divided Cities' in 'Contested States' (Part I)." Divided Cities/Contested States Working Paper No. 1. http://www.conflictincities.org/PDFs/WorkingPaper1_5.8.08.pdf.

———. 2010. "Democracy, Territoriality, and Ethno-National Conflict: A Framework for Studying Ethno-Nationally Divided Cities (Part II)." Divided Cities/Contested States Working Paper No. 18. http://www.conflictincities.org/PDFs/Working%20Paper18_2010.pdf.

Andeweg, Rudy B. 2000. "Consociational Democracy." *Annual Review of Political Science* 3: 509–36.

Andjelić, Neven. 2003. *Bosnia-Herzegovina: The End of a Legacy*. New York: Routledge.

Andreas, Peter. 2004. "The Clandestine Political Economy of War and Peace in Bosnia." *International Studies Quarterly* 48, no. 1: 29–52.

———. 2008. *Blue Helmets and Black Markets: The Business of Survival in the Siege of Sarajevo*. Ithaca: Cornell University Press.

Arnautović, Suad. 1996. *Izbori u Bosni i Hercegovini '90*. Sarajevo: Promocult.

Ashdown, Paddy. 2007. *Swords and Ploughshares: Bringing Peace to the 21st Century*. Ann Arbor: University of Michigan.

Autesserre, Séverine. 2008. "The trouble with the Congo: How Local Disputes Fuel Regional Conflict." *Foreign Affairs* 87, no. 3: 94–110.

———. 2009. "Hobbes and the Congo: Frames, Local Violence, and International Intervention." *International Organization* 63, no. 2: 249–80.

———. 2010. *The Trouble with the Congo: Local Violence and the Failure of International Peacebuilding*. Cambridge: Cambridge University Press.

———. Forthcoming. *Peaceland: An Ethnography of International Intervention*.

Avant, Deborah D. 2005. *The Market for Force: The Consequences of Privatizing Security*. Cambridge: Cambridge University Press.

Azinović, Vlado, Kurt Bassuener, and Bodo Weber. 2011. *Assessing the Potential for Renewed Ethnic Violence in Bosnia and Herzegovina: A Security Risk Analysis*. Atlantic Initiative, Democratization Policy Council. October. http://www.atlanticinitiative. org/images/stories/ai/pdf/ai-dpc%20bih%20security%20study%20final%2010–9-11. pdf.

Bain, William. 2006. "In Praise of Folly: International Administration and the Corruption of Humanity." *International Affairs* 82, no. 3: 525–38.

Ball, Patrick, Ewa Tabeau, and Philip Verwimp. 2007. *The Bosnian Book of the Dead: Assessment of the Database (Full Report)*. Institute of Development Studies, University of Sussex. http://www.hicn.org/research_design/rdn5.pdf.

Barnett, Michael. 2006. "Building a Republican Peace: Stablizing States after War." *International Security* 30, no. 4: 87–112.

Barnett, Michael, and Christoph Zurcher. 2009. "The Peacebuilder's Contract: How External Statebuilding Reinforces Weak Statehood." In *The Dilemmas of Statebuilding: Confronting the Contradictions of Postwar Peace Operations*, ed. Roland Paris and Timothy D. Sisk, 23–52. New York: Routledge.

Baros, Miroslav. 1998. "The Arbitral Tribunal's Award for the Dispute over the Inter-Entity Boundary in the Brčko area: A Devastating Blow to the Principle of Consensuality or an Ephemeral Adjuticative Episode?" *Journal of Armed Conflict Law* 3, no. 2: 233–69.

Baumann, Robert F., George W. Gawrych, and Walter E. Kretchik. 2004. *Armed Peacekeepers in Bosnia*. Fort Leavenworth, KS: Combat Studies Institute Press.

Bax, Mart. 1995. *Medjugorje: Religion, Politics, and Violence in Rural Bosnia*. Amsterdam: Amsterdam University Press.

———. 1997. "Mass Graves, Stagnating Identification, and Violence: A Case Study in the Local Sources of 'the War' in Bosnia Herzegovina." *Anthropological Quarterly* 70, no. 1: 11–19.

———. 2000. "Warlords, Priests and the Politics of Ethnic Cleansing: A Case Study from Rural Bosnia Hercegovina." *Ethnic and Racial Studies* 23, no. 1: 16–36.

Belloni, Roberto. 2001. "Civil Society and Peacebuilding in Bosnia and Herzegovina." *Journal of Peace Research* 38, no. 2: 163–80.

———. 2004. "Peacebuilding and Consociational Electoral Engineering in Bosnia and Herzegovina." *International Peacekeeping* 11, no. 2: 334–53.

———. 2007. *Statebuilding and International Intervention in Bosnia*. New York: Routledge.

Bellows, John, and Edward Miguel. 2009. "War and Local Collective Action in Sierra Leone." *Journal of Public Economics* 93, nos. 11–12: 1144–57.

Bergesen, Albert, and Max Herman. 1998. "Immigration, Race and Riot: The 1992 Los Angeles Uprising." *American Sociological Review* 63, no. 1: 39–54.

Bieber, Florian. 2001. "Croat Self-Government in Bosnia—A Challenge for Dayton?" *European Center for Minority Issues, Brief #5* May. http://www.ecmi.de/download/brief_5.pdf.

———. 2005. "Local Institutional Engineering: A Tale of Two Cities, Mostar and Brčko." *International Peacekeeping* 12, no. 3: 420–33.

———. 2006. *Post-War Bosnia: Ethnicity, Inequality, and Public Sector Governance*. Basingstoke, UK: Palgrave.

Bildt, Carl. 1998. *Peace Journey: The Struggle for Peace in Bosnia*. London: Weidenfeld and Nicolson.

Binnendijk, Hans, Charles Barry, Gina Cordero, Laura Peterson Nussbaum, and Melissa Sinclair. 2006. *Solutions for Northern Kosovo: Lessons Learned in Mostar, Eastern Slavonia, and Brčko*. Washington, DC: National Defense University.

Bjelakovic, Nebojsa, and Francesco Strazzari. 1999. "The Sack of Mostar 1992–1994: The Politico-Military Connection." *European Security* 8, no. 2: 73–102.

Blattman, Christopher. 2009. "From Violence to Voting: War and Political Participation in Uganda." *American Political Science Review* 103, no. 2: 231–47.

Bloomfield, David, Teresa Barnes, and Luc Huyse, eds. 2003. *Reconciliation after Conflict: A Handbook*. Stockholm: International Idea.

Bojicic-Dzelilovic, Vesna. 2006. "Peace on Whose Terms? War Veterans' Associations in Bosnia and Herzegovina." In *Challenges to Peacebuilding: Managing Spoilers during Conflict Resolution*, ed. Edward Newman and Oliver Richmond, 200–218. Tokyo: United Nations University Press.

Bollens, Scott. 2000. *On Narrow Ground: Urban Policy and Ethnic Conflict in Jerusalem and Belfast*. Albany: SUNY Press.

———. 2007. *Cities, Nationalism, and Democratization*. London: Routledge.

Bolton, Mathew. 2003. "Mine Action in Bosnia's Special District: A Case Study." *Journal of Mine Action* 7, no. 2. http://maic.jmu.edu/journal/7.2/focus/bolton/bolton.htm.

Bose, Sumantra. 2002. *Bosnia after Dayton: Nationalist Partition and International Intervention*. London: Hurst and Company.

Boutros-Ghali, Boutros. 1996. *An Agenda for Democratization*. New York: United Nations.

Brancati, Dawn, and Jack Snyder. 2011. "Rushing to the Polls: The Causes of Premature Postconflict Elections." *Journal of Conflict Resolution* 55, no. 3: 469–92.

———. Forthcoming. "Time to Kill: The Impact of Election Timing on Post-conflict Stability." *Journal of Conflict Resolution*.

Brass, Paul. 1991. *Ethnicity and Nationalism: Theory and Comparison*. London: Sage.

British Broadcasting Corporation (BBC). 1996. "President Says Federation Will Defend Its Right to Brčko." *BBC Summary of World Broadcasts*, December 20.

Burg, Steven L., and Paul S. Shoup. 1999. *The War in Bosnia and Herzegovina: Ethnic Conflict and International Intervention.* Armonk, NY: M. E. Sharpe.

Bussmann, Margit, and Gerald Schneider. 2007. "When Globalization Discontent Turns Violent: Foreign Economic Liberalization and Internal War." *International Studies Quarterly* 51, no. 1: 79–97.

Bussmann, Margit, Gerald Schneider, and Nina Wiesehomeier. 2005. "Foreign Economic Liberalization and Peace: The Case of Sub-Saharan Africa." *European Journal of International Relations* 11, no. 4: 551–79.

Calame, Jon, and Esther Charlesworth. 2009. *Divided Cities: Belfast, Beirut, Jerusalem, Mostar, and Nicosia.* Philadelphia: University of Pennsylvania Press.

Call, Charles T. 2008. "Knowing Peace When You See It: Setting Standards for Peacebuilding Success." *Civil Wars* 10, no. 2: 173–94.

Campbell, David. 1998. *National Deconstruction: Violence, Identity, and Justice in Bosnia.* Minneapolis: University of Minnesota Press.

Caplan, Richard. 2005. *International Governance of War-Torn Territories: Rule and Reconstruction.* Oxford: Oxford University Press.

Caspersen, Nina. 2010. *Contested Nationalism: Serb Elite Rivalry in Croatia and Bosnia in the 1990s.* Oxford: Berghan Books.

Cederman, Lars-Erik, and Kristian S. Gleditsch. 2009. "Introduction to Special Issue on 'Disaggregating Civil War.'" *Journal of Conflict Resolution* 53, no. 4: 487–95.

Cederman, Lars-Erik, Simon Hug, and Lutz F. Krebs. 2010. "Democratization and Civil War: Empirical Evidence." *Journal of Peace Research* 47, no. 4: 377–94.

Cederman, Lars-Erik, Kristian S. Gleditsch, and Simon Hug. Forthcoming. "Elections and Ethnic Civil War." *Comparative Political Studies.*

Chandler, David. 1999. *Bosnia: Faking Democracy after Dayton.* London: Pluto.

———. 2006. *Empire in Denial: The Politics of State-Building.* London: Pluto.

Charles, Camille Z. 2006. *Won't You Be My Neighbor? Race, Class, and Residence in Los Angeles.* New York: Russell Sage Foundation.

Chesterman, Simon. 2004. *You, the People: The United Nations, Transitional Administration, and State-Building.* Oxford: Oxford University Press.

———. 2007. "Ownership in Theory and Practice: Transfer of Authority in UN Statebuilding Operations." *Journal of Intervention and Statebuilding* 1, no. 1: 3–26.

Chopra, Jarat. 2002. "Building State Failure in East Timor." *Development and Change* 33, no. 5: 979–1000.

Chopra, Jarat, and Tanja Hohe. 2004. "Participatory Intervention." *Global Governance* 10, no. 3: 289–305.

Choudhry, Sujit, ed. 2008. *Constitutional Design for Divided Societies: Integration or Accommodation?* New York: Oxford University Press.

Christia, Fotini. 2008. "Following the Money: Muslim versus Muslim in Bosnia's Civil War." *Comparative Politics* 40, no. 4: 461–80.

Chua, Amy. 2003. *World on Fire: How Exporting Free Market Democracy Breeds Ethnic Hatred and Global Instability.* New York: Doubleday.

Clark, Janine N. 2010. "Bosnia's Success Story? Brčko District and the 'View from Below.'" *International Peacekeeping* 17, no. 1: 67–79.

Clarke, Henry. 2004a. *Brčko District: An Example of Progress in Basic Reforms in Bosnia and Herzegovina*. Presentation to the Woodrow Wilson Center for Scholars, Washington, DC. October 25. http://www.wilsoncenter.org/topics/pubs/MR293Clarke. doc.

———. 2004b. *Privatization in Brčko District: Why It Is Different and Why It Works*. East European Studies at the Woodrow Wilson Center. Occasional Paper #72.

———. 2005. *Number 74: Changes in the Constitutional Structure of Bosnia and Herzegovina*. Woodrow Wilson Center Occasional Papers Series. http://www.wilsoncenter. org/publication/74-changes-the-constitutional-structure-bosnia-and-herzegovina.

Cockell, John G. 2000. "Conceptualizing Peacebuilding: Human Security and Sustainable Peace." In *Regeneration of War-Torn Societies*, ed. Michael Pugh, 15–34. London: MacMillan.

Coles, Kimberley A. 2002. "Ambivalent Builders: Europeanization, the Production of Difference, and Internationals in Bosnia-Herzegovina." *PoLAR: Political and Legal Anthropology Review* 25, no. 1: 1–18.

Colletta, Nat J., and Michael L. Cullen. 2000. *Violent Conflict and the Transformation of Social Capital: Lessons from Cambodia, Rwanda, Guatemala, and Somalia*. Washington, DC: World Bank.

Collier, Paul, V. L. Elliott, Havard Hegre, Anke Hoeffler, Marta Reynol-Querol, and Nicholas Sambanis. 2003. *Breaking the Conflict Trap: Civil War and Development Policy*. Washington, DC: World Bank.

Cooley, Alexander, and James Ron. 2002. "The NGO Scramble: Organizational Insecurity and the Political Economy of Transnational Action." *International Security* 27, no. 1: 5–39.

Copeland, Carla S. 1999. "The Use of Arbitration to Settle Territorial Issues." *Fordham Law Review* 67, no. 6: 3073–108.

Cousens, Elizabeth M. 2000. Introduction to *Peacebuilding as Politics: Cultivating Peace in Fragile Societies*, ed. Elizabeth M. Cousens, Chetan Kumar, and Karin Wermester. Boulder, CO: Lynne Rienner.

Coward, Martin. 2002. "Community as Heterogeneous Ensemble: Mostar and Multiculturalism." *Alternatives: Global, Local, Political* 27, no. 1: 29–66.

Cramer, C. 2002. "Homo Economicus Goes to War: Methodological Individualism, Rational Choice and the Political Economy of War." *World Development* 30, no. 11: 1845–64.

Dahlman, Carl, and Gearoid O'Tuathail. 2005. "Broken Bosnia: The Localized Geopolitics of Displacement and Return in Two Bosnian Places." *Annals of the Association of American Geographers* 95, no. 3: 644–62.

Dahlman, Carl, and Gearoid O'Tuathail. 2006. "Bosnia's Third Space? Nationalist Separatism and International Supervision in Bosnia's Brčko District." *Geopolitics* 11, no. 4: 651–75.

Daly, Erin, and Jeremy Sarkin. 2007. *Reconciliation in Divided Societies: Finding Common Ground*. Philadelphia: University of Pennsylvania Press.

Davis, Mike. 2006. *City of Quartz: Excavating the Future in Los Angeles*. New York: Verso.

de Coning, Cedric. 2007. "Coherence and Coordination in United Nations Peace-building and Integrated Missions—A Norwegian Perspective." Norwegian Institute of International Affairs, Security in Practice No. 5. http://kms1.isn.ethz.ch/serviceengine/Files/ISN/46185/ipublicationdocument_singledocument/F2522BDB-1A00–4197-AD32-BA7B692C60DE/en/2007_Coherence_Coordination_UN_Peacebuilding.pdf.

Diehl, Paul F., and Daniel Druckman. 2010. *Evaluating Peace Operations.* Boulder, CO: Lynne Rienner.

Denov, Myriam, and Richard Maclure. 2007. "Turnings and Epiphanies: Militarization, Life Histories, and the Making and Unmaking of Two Child Soldiers in Sierra Leone." *Journal of Youth Studies* 10, no. 2: 243–61.

Dicken, Peter, and Nigel Thrift. 1992. "The Organization of Production and the Production of Organization: Why Business Enterprises Matter in the Study of Geographical Industrialization." *Transactions of the British Institute of Geographers* 17, no. 3: 279–91.

Divjak, Boris, and Michael Pugh. 2008. "The Political Economy of Corruption in Bosnia and Herzegovina." *International Peacekeeping* 15, no. 3: 373–86.

Donais, Timothy. 2002. "The Politics of Privatization in Post-Dayton Bosnia." *Southeast European Politics* 3, no. 1: 3–19.

———. 2005. *The Political Economy of Peacebuilding in Post-Dayton Bosnia.* New York: Routledge.

———. 2009. "Empowerment or Imposition? Dilemmas of Local Ownership in Post-conflict Peacebuilding Processes." *Peace and Change* 34, no. 1: 3–26.

Downs, George, and Stephen J. Stedman. 2002. "Evaluation Issues in Peace Implementation." In *Ending Civil Wars: The Implementation of Peace Agreements*, ed. Stephen J. Stedman, Donald Rothchild, and Elizabeth M. Cousens, 43–69. Boulder, CO: Lynne Rienner.

Doyle, Michael W. 1983. "Kant, Liberal Legacies, and Foreign Affairs (Parts 1 and 2)." *Philosophy and Public Affairs* 12, no. 3: 205–54; and no. 4: 323–53.

Doyle, Michael W., and Nicholas Sambanis. 2006. *Making War and Building Peace: United Nations Peace Operations.* Princeton: Princeton University Press.

Dubravčić, Dinko. 1993. "Economic Causes and Political Context of the Dissolution of a Multinational Federal State: The case of Yugoslavia." *Post-Communist Economies* 5, no. 3: 259–72.

Dulić, Tomislav. 2005. "Utopias of Nation: Local Mass Killing in Bosnia and Herzegovina, 1941–42." Ph.D. diss., Uppsala University.

Edelstein, David M. 2009. "Foreign Militaries, Sustainable Institutions and Postwar Statebuilding." In *The Dilemmas of Statebuilding: Confronting the Contradictions of Postwar Peace Operations*, ed. Roland Paris and Timothy D. Sisk, 81–103. New York: Routledge.

European Stability Initiative (ESI). 2000. *Reshaping International Priorities in Bosnia and Herzegovina. Part 2: International Power in Bosnia.* European Stability Initiative. March 30.

Farrand, Peter. 2001. "Lessons from Brčko: Necessary Components for Future Internationally Supervised Territories." *Emory International Law Review* 15, no. 2: 529–91.

Farrand, Robert. 2011. *Reconstruction and Peacebuilding in the Balkans: The Brčko Experience*. Lanham, MD: Rowman and Littlefield.

Fearon, James D., and David D. Laitin. 2000. "Violence and the Social Construction of Ethnic Identity." *International Organization* 54, no. 4: 845–77.

———. 2004. "Neotrusteeship and the Problem of Weak States." *International Security* 28, no. 4: 5–43.

Ferme, Mariane C. 2001. *The Underneath of Things: Violence, History, and the Everyday in Sierra Leone*. Berkeley: University of California Press.

Flores, Thomas E., and Irfan Nooruddin. 2012. "The Effect of Elections on Postconflict Peace and Reconstruction." *Journal of Politics* 74, no. 2: 558–70.

Foer, Franklin. 2004. *How Soccer Explains the World: An Unlikely Theory of Globalization*. New York: Harper Collins.

Fontenot, Gregory. 2007. "Peace in the Posavina, or Deal with Us!" *Military Review* 87, no. 4: 45–59.

Fortna, Virginia P. 2008. *Does Peacekeeping Work? Shaping Belligerents' Choices after Civil War*. Princeton: Princeton University Press.

Fortna, Virginia P., and Lise M. Howard. 2008. "Pitfalls and Prospects in the Peacekeeping Literature." *Annual Review of Political Science* 11: 283–301.

Fujii, Lee A. 2010. "Shades of Truth and Lies: Interpreting Testimonies of War and Violence." *Journal of Peace Research* 47, no. 2: 231–41.

Fukuyama, Francis. 2004. *Statebuilding: Governance and World Order in the 21st Century*. Ithaca: Cornell University Press.

Fumagalli, Matteo. 2007. "Informal Ethnopolitics and Local Authority Figures in Osh, Kyrgyzstan." *Ethnopolitics* 6, no. 2: 211–33.

Gagnon, V. P. 2002. "International NGOs in Bosnia: Attempting to Build Civil Society." In *The Power and Limits of NGOs*, ed. Sarah E. Mendelson and John K. Glenn, 207–31. New York: Columbia University Press.

———. 2004. *The Myth of Ethnic War: Serbia and Croatia in the 1990s*. Ithaca: Cornell University Press.

Gallie, W. B. 1956. "Essentially Contested Concepts." *Proceedings of the Aristotelian Society* 56: 167–98.

Galtung, John. 1969. "Violence, Peace, and Peace Research." *Journal of Peace Research* 6, no. 3: 167–91.

Geddes, Barbara. 1990. "How the Cases You Choose Affect the Answers You Get: Selection Bias in Comparative Politics." *Political Analysis* 2, no. 1: 131–50.

Ghani, Ashraf, Clare Lockhart, and Michael Carnahan. 2006. "An Agenda for State-Building in the Twenty-First Century." *Fletcher Forum of World Affairs* 30, no. 1: 101–23.

Gilbert, Andrew. 2008. *Foreign Authority and the Politics of Impartiality in Postwar Bosnia-Herzegovina*. Ph.D. diss., University of Chicago.

Glenny, Misha. 1996. *The Fall of Yugoslavia: The Third Balkan War*. New York: Penguin.

Goddard, Stacie E. 2010. *Indivisible Territory and the Politics of Legitimacy: Jerusalem and Northern Ireland*. Cambridge: Cambridge University Press.

Gow, James. 2003. *The Serbian Project and Its Adversaries: A Strategy of War Crimes*. Quebec: McGill-Queen's University Press.

Grandits, Hannes. 2007. "The Power of 'Armchair Politicians': Ethnic Loyalty and Political Factionalism among Herzegovinian Croats." In *The New Bosnian Mosaic: Identities, Memories and Moral Claims in a Post-war Society*, ed. Xavier Bougarel, Elissa Helms, and Ger Duijzings, 101–22. Hampton, UK: Ashgate.

Granovetter, Mark. 1985. "Economic Action and Social Structure: The Problem of Embeddedness." *American Journal of Sociology* 91, no. 3: 481–510.

Grečić, V. 1990. "The Importance of Migrant Workers' and Emigrants' Remittances for the Yugoslav Economy." *International Migration* 28, no. 2: 201–13.

Griffiths, Hugh. 1998. *The Dynamics of Multi-national Intervention: Brčko under International Supervision*. M.Phil thesis, University of Amsterdam.

———. 1999. "A Political Economy of Ethnic Conflict, Ethno-nationalism, and Organized Crime." *Civil Wars* 2, no. 2: 56–73.

Grodach, Carl. 2002. "Reconstituting Identity and History in Post-war Mostar, Bosnia-Herzegovina." *City* 6, no. 1: 61–82.

Hadžiosmanović, Ismet. 2006. *Bošnjačko-Hrvatski politički obračun*. Mostar.

Hampson, Fen O. 1996. *Nurturing Peace: Why Peace Settlements Succeed or Fail*. Washington, DC: USIP Press.

Hartzell, Caroline A., Matthew Hoddie, and Molly Bauer. 2010. "Economic Liberalization via IMF Structural Adjustment: Sowing the Seeds of Civil War?" *International Organization* 64, no. 2: 339–56.

Hayden, Robert. 1996. "Imagined Communities and Real Victims: Self-Determination and Ethnic Cleansing in Yugoslavia." *American Ethnologist* 23, no. 4: 783–801.

———. 2000. *Blueprints for a House Divided: The Constitutional Logic of the Yugoslav Conflicts*. Ann Arbor: University of Michigan Press.

Heathershaw, John. 2007. "Peacebuilding as Practice: Discourses from Post-conflict Tajikistan." *International Peacekeeping* 14, no. 2: 219–36.

Hegre, Håvard, Tanja Ellingsen, Scott Gates, and Nils Petter Gleditsch. 2001. "Toward a Democratic Civil Peace? Democracy, Political Change, and Civil War, 1816–1992." *American Political Science Review* 95, no. 1: 33–48.

Hegre, Håvard, and Nicholas Sambanis. 2006. "Sensitivity Analysis of Empirical Results on Civil War Onset." *Journal of Conflict Resolution* 50, no. 4: 508–35.

Hess, Martin. 2004. "'Spatial' Relationships? Towards a Reconceptualization of Embeddedness." *Progress in Human Geography* 28, no. 2: 165–86.

Hoare, Marko A. 2004. *How Bosnia Armed*. London: Saqi Books.

Hockenos, Paul. 2003. *Homeland Calling: Exile Patriotism and the Balkan Wars*. Ithaca: Cornell University Press.

Hoffman, Danny. 2003. "Like Beasts in the Bush: Synonyms of Childhood and Youth in Sierra Leone." *Postcolonial Studies* 6, no. 3: 295–308.

Hoglund, Kristine. 2009. "Electoral Violence in Conflict-Ridden Societies: Concepts, Causes, and Consequences." *Terrorism and Political Violence* 21, no. 3: 412–27.

Hoglund, Kristine, Anna K. Jarstad, and Mimmi S. Kovacs. 2009. "The Predicament of Elections in War-Torn Societies." *Democratization* 16, no. 3: 530–57.

Hoglund, Kristine, and Mimmi S. Kovacs. 2010. "Beyond the Absence of War: The Diversity of Peace in Post-settlement Societies." *Review of International Studies* 36, no. 2: 367–90.

Holbrooke, Richard. 1999. *To End a War.* New York: Modern Library.

Holohan, Anne. 2005. *Networks of Democracy: Lessons from Kosovo for Afghanistan, Iraq and Beyond.* Stanford, CA: Stanford University Press.

Horowitz, Donald L. 1985. *Ethnic Groups in Conflict.* Berkeley: University of California Press.

———. 1991. *Democratic South Africa? Constitutional Engineering in a Divided Society.* Berkeley: University of California Press.

———. 2000. *Ethnic Groups in Conflict.* 2nd ed. Berkeley: University of California Press.

———. 2002. "Constitutional Design: Proposals versus Processes." In *The Architecture of Democracy: Constitutional Design, Conflict Management, and Democracy,* ed. Andrew Reynolds, 15–36. Oxford: Oxford University Press.

———. 2007. "The Many Uses of Federalism." *Drake Law Review* 55, no. 4: 953–66.

———. 2008. "Conciliatory Institutions and Constitutional Processes in Post-conflict States." *William and Mary Law Review* 49: 1213–48.

Howard, Lise M. 2008. *UN Peacekeeping in Civil Wars.* Cambridge: Cambridge University Press.

———. 2012. "The Ethnocracy Trap." *Journal of Democracy* 23, no. 4: 155–69.

Hromadžić, Azra. 2008. "Discourses of Integration and Practices of Reunification at the Mostar Gymnasium, Bosnia and Herzegovina." *Comparative Education Review* 52, no. 4: 541–63.

———. 2011. "Bathroom Mixing: Youth Negotiate Democratization in Postconflict Bosnia and Herzegovina." *Political and Legal Anthropology Review* 34, no. 2: 268–89.

Human Rights Watch (HRW). 1998. *Bosnia and Herzegovina beyond Restraint: Politics and the Policing Agenda of the United Nations International Police Task Force.* Volume 10, no. 5 (July). http://www.hrw.org/reports98/bosnia/.

International Crisis Group (ICG). 1996. *Lessons from Mostar.* July 13.

———. 1998. *Brčko: What Bosnia Could Be.* ICG Bosnia Project-Report no. 31. February 10.

———. 1999. *Brčko: A Comprehensive Solution.* ICG Balkans Report no. 55. February 2.

———. 2000. *Reunifying Mostar: Opportunities for Progress.* ICG Balkans Report no. 90. April 19.

———. 2001a. *Bosnia's Precarious Economy: Still Not Open for Business.* ICG Balkans Report no. 115. August 7.

———. 2001b. *No Early Exit: NATO's Continuing Challenge in Bosnia.* ICG Balkans Report no. 110. May 22.

———. 2001c. *The Wages of Sin: Confronting Bosnia's Republika Srpska.* Balkans Report no. 118. October 8.

———. 2003a. *Bosnia's Brčko: Getting In, Getting On, and Getting Out.* Balkans Report no. 144. June 2.

———. 2003b. *Building Bridges in Mostar.* Europe Report no. 150. November 20.

———. 2007. *Ensuring Bosnia's Future: A New International Engagement Strategy.* Europe Report no. 180. February 15.

———. 2009. *Bosnia: A Test of Political Maturity in Mostar.* Europe Briefing no. 54. July 29.

———. 2010. *Federation of Bosnia and Herzegovina—A Parallel Crisis.* Europe Report no. 209. September 28.

———. 2011a. *Bosnia: What Does Republika Srpska Want?* Europe Report no. 214. October 6.

———. 2011b. *Brčko Unsupervised.* Europe Briefing no. 66. December 8.

———. 2012. *Bosnia's Gordian Knot: Constitutional Reform.* Europe Briefing no. 68. July 12.

Jarstad, Anna K., and Timothy D. Sisk. 2008. *From War to Democracy: Dilemmas of Peacebuilding.* Cambridge: Cambridge University Press.

Jeffrey, Alex. 2006. "Building State Capacity in Post-conflict Bosnia and Herzegovina: The Case of Brčko District." *Political Geography* 25, no. 2: 203–27.

———. 2007. "The Geopolitical Framing of Localized Struggles: NGOs in Bosnia and Herzegovina." *Development and Change* 38, no. 2: 251–74.

Jones, Briony. 2012. "Exploring the Politics of Reconciliation through Education Reform: The Case of Brčko District, Bosnia and Herzegovina." *International Journal of Transitional Justice* 6, no. 1: 126–48.

Jones, Bruce D. 2002. "The Challenges of Strategic Coordination." In *Ending Civil Wars: The Implementation of Peace Agreements,* ed. Donald Rothchild, Stephen J. Stedman, and Elizabeth M. Cousens, 89–115. Boulder, CO: Lynne Rienner.

Joseph, Edward. 2007. "Ownership Is Over-rated." *SAIS Review* 27, no. 2: 109–23.

———. 2009. "What to Do about Bosnia and Herzegovina? The Case for Accelerated NATO Membership and OSCE Coordination of Constitutional Reform." *USIP Peace Briefing.* May. http://www.usip.org/files/resources/Bosnia%20and%20Herzegovina.pdf.

Jović, Dejan. 2009. *Yugoslavia: A State that Withered Away.* West Lafayette, IN: Purdue University Press.

Kadrić, Jusuf. 1998. *Brčko: Genocid i svjedočenja.* Sarajevo: Institut za Istrašivanje Zločina Protiv čovječnosti i Međunarodnog Prava.

Kaiser, Paul J. 1996. "Structural Adjustment and the Fragile Nation: The Demise of Social Unity in Tanzania." *Journal of Modern African Studies* 34, no. 2: 227–37.

Kalyvas, Stathis. 2003. "The Ontology of 'Political Violence': Action and Identity in Civil Wars." *Perspectives on Politics* 1, no. 3: 475–94.

———. 2006. *The Logic of Violence in Civil War.* Cambridge: Cambridge University Press.

———. 2008a. "Ethnic Defection in Civil War." *Comparative Political Studies* 41, no. 8: 1043–68.

———. 2008b. "Promises and Pitfalls of an Emerging Research Program: The Microdynamics of Civil War." In *Order, Conflict, and Violence,* ed. Stathis Kalyvas, Ian Shapiro, and Tarek Masoud, 397–421. Cambridge: Cambridge University Press.

Karnavas, Michael. 2003. "Creating the Legal Framework of the Brcko District of Bosnia and Herzegovina: A Model for the Region and Other Postconflict Countries." *The American Journal of International Law* 97, no. 1: 111–31.

Kaufmann, Chaim. 1996. "Possible and Impossible Solutions to Ethnic Civil Wars." *International Security* 20, no. 4: 136–75.

Kesic, Obrad, Steven Meyer, and Drina Vlastelic-Rajic. 2012. "The Battle for Mostar." *Transconflict.* June 12. http://www.transconflict.com/2012/06/the-battle-for-mostar-066/.

Knaus, Gerald, and Felix Martin. 2003. "Travails of the European Raj." *Journal of Democracy* 14, no. 3: 60–74.

Komšić, Ivan. 2006. *Preživljena zemlja: Tko je, kada and gdje dijelo BiH.* Zagreb: Prometej.

Lambourne, Wendy 2009. "Transitional Justice and Peacebuilding after Mass Violence." *International Journal of Transitional Justice* 3, no. 1: 28–48.

Lampe, John. 2000. *Yugoslavia as History: Twice There Was a Country.* Cambridge: Cambridge University Press.

Lederach, John P. 1997. *Building Peace: Sustainable Reconciliation in Divided Societies.* Washington, DC: United States Institute of Peace.

Lemarchand, Rene, and Keith Legg. 1972. "Political Clientelism and Development: A Preliminary Analysis." *Comparative Politics* 4, no. 2: 149–78.

Levy, Jack S. 1988. "Domestic Politics and War." *Journal of Interdisciplinary History* 18, no. 4: 653–73.

Lijphart, Arend. 1969. "Consociational Democracy." *World Politics* 21, no. 2: 207–25.

———. 1977. *Democracy in Plural Societies.* New Haven: Yale University Press.

———. 1979. "Consociation and Federation: Conceptual and Empirical Links." *Canadian Journal of Political Science* 12, no. 3: 499–515.

———. 1985. *Power-Sharing in South Africa.* Berkeley, CA: Institute of International Studies.

———. 1995. "Self-Determination Versus Pre-Determination of Ethnic Minorities in Power-Sharing Systems." In *The Rights of Minority Cultures*, ed. Will Kimlycka, 275–87. Oxford: Oxford University Press.

———. 2002. "The Wave of Power-Sharing Democracy." In *The Architecture of Democracy: Constitutional Design, Conflict Management, and Democracy*, ed. Andrew Reynolds, 37–54. Oxford: Oxford University Press.

———. 2004. "Constitutional Design for Divided Societies." *Journal of Democracy* 15, no. 2: 96–109.

Lubkemann, Stephen C. 2008. *Culture in Chaos: An Anthropology of the Social Condition in War.* Chicago: University of Chicago Press.

Luchetta, Andrea. 2009. *Mostar and the Loss of Its (Partial) Uniqueness: A History, 1990–2009.* Geneva: Graduate Institute of International and Development Studies.

Lyons, Terrence. 2002. "The Role of Post-settlement Elections." In *Ending Civil Wars: The Implementation of Peace Agreements*, ed. Donald Rothchild, Stephen J. Stedman, and Elizabeth M. Cousens, 215–35. Boulder, CO: Lynne Rienner.

———. 2004. "Post-conflict Elections and the Process of Demilitarizing Politics: The Role of Electoral Administration." *Democratization* 11, no. 3: 36–62.

MacDonald, David B. 2003. *Balkan Holocausts? Serbian and Croatian Victim-Centered Propaganda and the War in Yugoslavia.* Manchester: Manchester University Press.

MacGinty, Roger. 2006. *No War, No Peace: The Rejuvenation of Stalled Peace Processes and Peace Accords.* Basingstoke, UK: Palgrave.

———. 2010. "Hybrid Peace: The Interaction between Top-Down and Bottom-Up Peace." *Security Dialogue* 41, no. 4: 391–412.

———. 2011. *International Peacebuilding and Local Resistance: Hybrid Forms of Peace.* London: Palgrave.

Magaš, Branka, and Ivo Žanić. 2001. *The War in Croatia and Bosnia-Herzegovina— 1991–1995.* New York: Frank Cass.

Makaš, Emily. 2007. "Representing Competing Identities: Building and Rebuilding in Postwar Mostar, Bosnia and Herzegovina." Ph.D. diss., Cornell University.

------. 2011. "Mostar's Central Zone: Battles over Shared Space in a Divided City." *Urban Conflicts: Ethno-Nationalist Divisions, States and Cities Conference*, Queen's University, Belfast. http://www.academia.edu/2211340/Mostars_Central_Zone_Battles_over_Shared_Space_in_a_Divided_City_Queens_U_Belfast_2011_.

Mani, Rama. 2002. *Beyond Retribution: Seeking Justice in the Shadows of War.* Oxford: Polity.

Mansfield, Edward D., and Jack Snyder. 2005. *Electing to Fight: Why Emerging Democracies Go to War.* Cambridge, MA: MIT Press.

McGarry, John, and Brendan O'Leary. 2005. "Federation as a Method of Ethnic Conflict Regulation." In *From Power Sharing to Democracy: Post-conflict Institutions in Ethnically Divided Societies,* ed. Sid Noel, 263–96. Montreal: McGill-Queen's Press.

------. 2007. "Iraq's Constitution of 2005: Liberal Consociation as Political Prescription." *International Journal of Constitutional Law* 5, no. 4: 670–98.

------. 2009a. "Power Shared after the Deaths of Thousands." In *Consociational Theory: McGarry and O'Leary and the Northern Ireland Conflict*, ed. Rupert Taylor, 15–85. New York: Routledge, 2009.

------. 2009b. "Must Plurinational Federations Fail?" *Ethnopolitics* 8, no. 1: 5–25.

McMahon, Patrice C., and Jon Western. 2009. "The Death of Dayton: How to Stop Bosnia from Falling Apart." *Foreign Affairs* 88, no. 5: 69–83.

Mills, Richard. 2009. " 'It All Ended in an Unsporting Way': Serbian Football and the Disintegration of Yugoslavia, 1989–2006." *International Journal of the History of Sport* 26, no. 9: 1187–217.

Moore, Adam. 2008. "Rethinking Scale as a Geographical Category: From Analysis to Practice." *Progress in Human Geography* 32, no. 2: 203–25.

------. 2011. "The Eventfulness of Social Reproduction." *Sociological Theory* 29, no. 4: 294–314.

Mujkić, Asim. 2007. "We, the Citizens of Ethnopolis." *Constellations* 14, no. 1: 112–28.

Narten, Jens. 2009. "Dilemmas of Promoting Local Ownership: The Case of Postwar Kosovo." In *The Dilemmas of Statebuilding: Confronting the Contradictions of Postwar Peace Operations*, ed. Roland Paris and Timothy D. Sisk, 252–84. New York: Routledge.

Nathan, Laurie. 2007. *No Ownership, No Commitment: A Guide to Local Ownership of Security Sector Reform.* Technical report. Birmingham, UK: University of Birmingham.

Neville-Jones, Pauline. 1996. "Dayton, IFOR and Alliance Relations in Bosnia." *Survival* 38, no. 4: 45–65.

Newman, Edward. 2011. "A Human Security Peace-Building Agenda." *Human Rights Quarterly* 32, no. 10: 1737–56.

Noel, Sid, ed. 2005. *From Power Sharing to Democracy: Post-conflict Institutions in Ethnically Divided Societies.* Montreal: McGill-Queen's Press.

Nordstrom, Carolyn. 1997. *A Different Kind of War Story.* Philadelphia: University of Pennsylvania Press.

O'Connell, D. P. 1969. "The Condominium of the New Hebrides." *British Yearbook of International Law* 43: 71–145.

O'Leary, Brendan. 2005a. "Debating Consociational Politics: Normative and Explanatory Arguments." In *From Power Sharing to Democracy: Post-conflict Institutions in Ethnically Divided Societies*, ed. Sid Noel, 3–43. Montreal: McGill-Queen's Press.

——. 2005b. "Power-Sharing, Pluralist Federation, and Federacy." In *The Future of Kurdistan in Iraq*, eds. Brendan O'Leary, John McGarry, and Khaled Salih, 47–91. Philadelphia: University of Pennsylvania Press.

——. 2006. "Forward: The Realism of Power-Sharing." In *Imposing Power-Sharing: Conflict and Coexistence in Northern Ireland and Lebanon*, ed. Michael Kerr, xxvii–xxxv. Dublin: Irish Academic Press.

Oneal, John R., and Bruce M. Russett. 1997. "The Classical Liberals Were Right: Democracy, Interdependence, and Conflict, 1950–1985." *International Studies Quarterly* 41, no. 2: 267–94.

O'Tuathail, Gearoid. 2010. "Localizing Geopolitics: Disaggregating Violence and Return in Conflict Regions." *Political Geography* 29, no. 5: 256–65.

Paffenholz, Thania. 2003. *Community Based Bottom-Up Peacebuilding. The Development of the Life and Peace Institute's Approach to Peacebuilding and Lessons Learned from the Somolia Experience*. Uppsala: Life and Peace Institute.

——, ed. 2010. *Civil Society and Peacebuilding: A Critical Assessment*. Boulder, CO: Lynne Rienner.

Paige, Jeffery M. 1999. "Conjuncture, Comparison, and Conditional Theory in Macrosocial Inquiry." *American Journal of Sociology* 105, no. 3: 781–800.

Palairet, Michael. 1977. "Merchant Enterprise and the Development of the Plum Based Trades in Serbia, 1847–1911." *Economic History Review* 30, no. 4: 582–601.

Paris, Roland. 1997. "Peacebuilding and the Limits of Liberal Internationalism." *International Security* 22, no. 2: 54–89.

——. 2002. "International Peacebuilding and the 'Mission Civilisatrice.'" *Review of International Studies* 28, no. 4: 637–56.

——. 2004. *At Wars End: Building Peace after Civil Conflict*. Cambridge: Cambridge University Press.

——. 2009. "Understanding the 'Coordination Problem' in Postwar Statebuilding." In *The Dilemmas of Statebuilding: Confronting the Contradictions of Postwar Peace Operations*, ed. Roland Paris and Timothy D. Sisk, 53–78. New York: Routledge.

——. 2010. "Saving Liberal Peacebuilding." *Review of International Studies* 36, no. 2: 337–65.

Paris, Roland, and Timothy D. Sisk, eds. 2009. *The Dilemmas of Statebuilding: Confronting the Contradictions of Postwar Peace Operations*. New York: Routledge.

Parish, Matthew. 2009. *A Free City in the Balkans: Reconstructing a Divided Society in Bosnia*. London: I. B. Tauris.

Pejanović, Mirko. 2004. *Through Bosnian Eyes: The Political Memoir of a Bosnian Serb*. West Lafayette, IN: Purdue University Press.

Pickering, Paula. 2006. "Generating Social Capital for Bridging Ethnic Divisions in the Balkans: Case Studies of Two Bosniak Cities." *Ethnic and Racial Studies* 29, no. 1: 79–103.

———. 2007. *Peacebuilding in the Balkans: The View from the Ground Floor.* Ithaca: Cornell University Press.

Posen, Barry. 1993. "The Security Dilemma and Ethnic Conflict." *Survival* 35, no. 1: 27–47.

Pouligny, Beatrice. 2006. *Peace Operations Seen from Below: UN Missions and Local People.* Bloomfield, CT: Kumarian Press.

Pred, Allen. 1990. *Making Histories and Constructing Human Geographies.* Oxford: Westview Press.

Pugh, Michael. 2001. "Elections and 'Protectorate Democracy' in South-East Europe." In *The United Nations and Human Security*, ed. Edward Newman and Oliver P. Richmond, 190–207. Basingstoke, UK: Palgrave.

———. 2002. "Postwar Political Economy in Bosnia and Herzegovina: The Spoils of Peace." *Global Governance* 8, no. 4: 467–82.

———. 2005. "Transformation in the Political Economy of Bosnia since Dayton." *International Peacekeeping* 12, no. 3: 448–62.

Radić, Radmila. 1998. "Serbian Orthodox Church and the War in Bosnia and Herzegovina." In *Religion and the War in Bosnia*, ed. Paul Mojzes, 160–92. Atlanta: Scholars Press.

Ragin, Charles. 2000. *Fuzzy-Set Social Science.* Chicago: University of Chicago Press.

Ramet, Sabrina P. 2006. *The Three Yugoslavias: State Building and Legitimation, 1918–2005.* Bloomington: Indiana University Press.

Reichel, Sarah. 2000. *Transitional Administrations in Former Yugoslavia: A Repetition of Failures or a Necessary Learning Process towards a Universal Peace-Building Tool after Ethno-political War?* Wissenschaftszentrum Berlin fur Sozialforschung. March. http://bibliothek.wz-berlin.de/pdf/2000/p00–305.pdf.

Reilly, Benjamin. 2001. *Democracy in Divided Societies: Electoral Engineering for Conflict Management.* Cambridge: Cambridge University Press.

———. 2006a. *Democracy and Diversity: Political Engineering in the Asia-Pacific.* Oxford: Oxford University Press.

———. 2006b. "Political Engineering and Party Politics in Conflict-Prone Societies." *Democratization* 13, no. 5: 811–27.

Reno, William. 2003. "Political Networks in a Failing State: The Roots and Future of Violent Conflict in Sierra Leone." *International Politics and Society* 2: 29–43.

Reynolds, Andrew, ed. 2002. *The Architecture of Democracy: Constitutional Design, Conflict Management and Democracy.* Oxford: Oxford University Press.

Richmond, Oliver P. 2006. "Emancipatory Forms of Human Security and Liberal Peacebuilding." *International Journal* 62, no. 3: 459–77.

———. 2011. *A Post-liberal Peace.* London: Routledge.

Roberts, David. 2008. "Post-conflict Statebuilding and State Legitimacy: From Negative to Positive Peace?" *Development and Change* 39, no. 4: 537–55.

Roeder, Philip. G. 2009. "Ethnofederalism and the Mismanagement of Conflicting Nationalisms." *Regional & Federal Studies* 19, no. 2: 203–19.

Roeder, Philip G., and Donald Rothchild, eds. 2005. *Sustainable Peace: Power and Democracy after Civil Wars.* Ithaca: Cornell University Press.

Rosenbaum, Allan. 2001. *Building Equitable and Effective Local Governance in a Complex Ethnic Environment: The Case of the Brčko District Government*. http://unpan1. un.org/intradoc/groups/public/documents/nispacee/unpan004528.pdf.

Rummel, R. J. 1997. *Power Kills: Democracy as a Method of Nonviolence*. New Brunswick, NJ: Transaction.

Russett, Bruce, and John R. Oneal. 2001. *Triangulating Peace: Democracy, Interdependence, and International Organizations*. New York: W. W. Norton.

Scheye, Eric, and Gordon Peake. 2005. "Unknotting Local Ownership." In *After Intervention: Public Security in Post-conflict Societies—From Intervention to Sustainable Ownership*, ed. Anja H. Ebnother and Philipp H. Fluri, 235–60. Vienna: National Defense Academy.

Scott, James. 1972. "Patron-Client Politics and Political Change in Southeast Asia." *American Political Science Review* 66, no. 1: 91–113.

Sell, Louis. 2002. *Slobodan Milosevic and the Destruction of Yugoslavia*. Durham, NC: Duke University Press.

Sells, Michael A. 1996. *The Bridge Betrayed: Religion and Genocide in Bosnia*. Berkeley: University of California Press.

Siegel, Pascale C. 1998. *Target Bosnia: Integrating Information Activities in Peace Operations*. Washington, DC: Office of the Assistant Secretary of Defense, Command, and Control Research Program.

Sisk, Timothy D. 2003. "Power-Sharing after Civil Wars: Matching Problems to Solutions." In *Contemporary Peacemaking: Conflict, Violence, and Peace Processes*, ed. John Darby and Roger MacGinty, 139–150. New York: Palgrave Macmillan.

Snyder, Jack. 2000. *From Voting to Violence: Democratization and Nationalist Conflict*. New York: W. W. Norton.

Snyder, Richard. 2001. "Scaling Down: The Subnational Comparative Method." *Studies in Comparative International Development* 36, no. 1: 93–110.

Sommers, William. 2002. *Brčko District: Experiment to Experience*. 10th NISPAcee Annual Conference: Delivering Public Services in CEE Countries: Trends and Developments. April 25–27. http://unpan1.un.org/intradoc/groups/public/documents/ nispacee/unpan003596.pdf.

Stiglitz, Joseph E. 2002. *Globalization and Its Discontents*. New York: W. W. Norton.

Straus, Scott. 2006. *The Order of Genocide: Race, Power, and War in Rwanda*. Ithaca: Cornell University Press.

———. 2007. "Origins and Aftermaths: The Dynamics of Genocide in Rwanda and Their Post-genocide Implications." In *After Mass Crime: Rebuilding States and Communities*, ed. Beatrice Pouligny, Simon Chesterman, and Albrecht Schnabel, 122–41. Tokyo: United Nations University Press.

Suberu, Rotimi. 2009. "Federalism in Africa: The Nigerian Experience in Comparative Perspective." *Ethnopolitics* 8, no. 1: 67–86.

Suhrke, Astri. 2009. "The Dangers of a Tight Embrace: Externally Assisted Statebuilding in Afghanistan." In *The Dilemmas of Statebuilding: Confronting the Contradictions of Postwar Peace Operations*, ed. Roland Paris and Timothy D. Sisk, 227–51. New York: Routledge.

Talentino, Andrea K. 2007. "Perceptions of Peacebuilding: The Dynamic of Imposer and Imposed Upon." *International Studies Perspectives* 8, no. 2: 152–71.

Tanner, Marcus. 2001. *Croatia: A Nation Forged in War.* New Haven: Yale University Press.

Tarrow, Sidney. 2007. "The Strategy of Paired Comparison: Toward a Theory of Practice." *Comparative Political Studies* 43, no. 2: 230–59.

Taylor, Rupert, ed. 2009. *Consociational Theory: McGarry and O'Leary and the Northern Ireland Conflict.* New York: Routledge.

Thompson, Mark. 1999. *Forging War: The Media in Serbia, Croatia, Bosnia, and Herzegovina.* Luton: University of Luton Press.

Tilly, Charles. 1994. "The Time of States." *Social Research* 61, no. 2: 269–95.

———. 2003. *The Politics of Collective Violence.* New York: Cambridge University Press.

Toal, Gerard, and Carl Dahlman. 2011. *Bosnia Remade: Ethnic Cleansing and Its Reversal.* Oxford: Oxford University Press.

Toal, Gerard, and Adis Maksić. 2011. "Is Bosnia-Herzegovina Unsustainable? Implications for the Balkans and European Union." *Eurasian Geography and Economics* 52, no. 2: 279–93.

Touquet, Heleen. 2011. "Multi-Ethnic Parties in Bosnia and Herzegovina: Naša Stranka and the Paradoxes of Postethnic Politics." *Studies in Ethnicity and Nationalism* 11, no. 3: 451–67.

Tsebelis, George. 1990. "Elite Interaction and Constitution Building in Consociational Democracies." *Journal of Theoretical Politics* 2, no. 1: 5–29.

United Nations Development Program (UNDP). 1994. *Human Development Report 1994.* Oxford: Oxford University Press.

U.S. Department of State (USDOS). 1997. *The Road to Dayton: U.S. Diplomacy and the Bosnia Peace Process, May–December 1995.* Washington, DC: U.S. Department of State, Dayton History Project. http://www.gwu.edu/-nsarchiv/NSAEBB/NSAEBB171/index.htm#study

Uzzi, Brian. 1996. "The Sources and Consequences of Embeddedness for the Economic Performance of Organizations: The Network Effect." *American Sociological Review* 61, no. 4: 674–98.

Varshney, Ashutosh. 2003. *Ethnic Conflict and Civic Life: Hindus and Muslims in India.* New Haven: Yale University Press.

Verwimp, Philip, Patricia Justino, and Tilman Bruck. 2009. "The Analysis of Conflict: A Micro-level Perspective." *Journal of Peace Research* 46, no. 3: 307–14.

Vetters, Larissa. 2007. "The Power of Administrative Categories: Emerging Notions of Citizenship in the Divided City of Mostar." *Ethnopolitics* 6, no. 2: 187–209.

Vladisavljević, Nebojša. 2008. *Serbia's Anti-bureaucratic Revolution: Milošević, the Fall of Communism, and Nationalist Mobilization.* New York: Palgrave MacMillan.

Walter, Barbara F. 2004. "Does Conflict Beget Conflict? Explaining Recurring Civil War." *Journal of Peace Research* 41, no. 3: 371–88.

Walton, John K., and David Seddon. 1994. *Free Markets and Food Riots: The Politics of Global Adjustment.* Cambridge, MA: Blackwell.

Weinstein, Jeremy M. 2007. *Inside Rebellion: The Politics of Insurgent Violence.* Cambridge: Cambridge University Press.

Wiebes, Cees. 2003. *Intelligence and the War in Bosnia: 1992–1995.* Munster: Lit Verlag.

Wilde, Ralph. 2001. "From Danzig to East Timor and Beyond: The Role of International Territorial Administration." *American Journal of International Law* 95, no. 3: 583–606.

Wilkinson, Steven. 2004. *Votes and Violence: Electoral Competition and Ethnic Riots in India.* Cambridge: Cambridge University Press.

Wimmen, Heiko. 2004. "Territory, Nation and the Power of Language: Implications of Education Reform in the Herzegovinan Town of Mostar." *GSC Quarterly* 11: 1–21.

Wood, Elisabeth J. 2000. *Forging Democracy from Below: Insurgent Transitions in South Africa and El Salvador.* New York: Cambridge University Press.

———. 2003. *Insurgent Collective Action and Civil War in El Salvador.* Cambridge: Cambridge University Press.

———. 2008. "The Social Processes of Civil War: The Wartime Transformation of Social Networks." *Annual Review of Political Science* 11: 539–61.

Woodward, Susan. 1995a. *Balkan Tragedy: Chaos and Dissolution after the Cold War.* Washington, DC: Brookings Institution.

———. 1995b. *Socialist Unemployment: The Political Economy of Yugoslavia, 1945–1990.* Princeton: Princeton University Press.

World Bank. 1997. *Bosnia and Herzegovina: From Recovery to Sustainable Growth.* Washington, DC: World Bank.

Yarwood, John R. 1999. *Rebuilding Mostar: Reconstruction in a War Zone.* Liverpool: Liverpool University Press.

Yiftachel, Oren. 2006. *Ethnocracy: Land and Identity Politics in Israel/Palestine.* Philadelphia: University of Pennsylvania Press.

Yiftachel, Oren, and As'ad Ghanem. 2004. "Understanding 'Ethnocratic Regimes': The Politics of Seizing Contested Territories." *Political Geography* 23, no. 6: 647–76.

Yiftachel, Oren, and Haim Yacobi. 2003. "Urban Ethnocracy: Ethnicization and the Production of Space in an Israeli 'Mixed City.'" *Environment and Planning D: Society and Space* 21, no. 6: 673–93.

Zaum, Dominik. 2007. *The Sovereignty Paradox: The Norms and Politics of International Statebuilding.* Oxford: Oxford University Press.

Zukin, Sharon, and Paul DiMaggio. 1990. *Structures of Capital: The Social Organization of the Economy.* Cambridge: Cambridge University Press.

Index